CAMBRIDGE

English for Spanish Speakers

Interactive

Student's Book 4

Helen Hadkins, Samantha Lewis and Joanna Budden

CAMBRIDGE UNIVERSITY PRESS

Contents

Unit	Grammar	Vocabulary	Interaction, Speaking and Pronunciation	Listening, Reading and Portfolio
7 Self-image	Passive review *have/get* something done	Describing clothes and materials Body idioms	*Interaction 7*: Comparing two photos *Speak*: Items for a time capsule *Pronunciation*: Intrusive /j/, /r/ and /w/	*Read*: What your taste says about you *Listen*: A body art exhibition *Portfolio 7*: A magazine article Culture World: Jamaica
8 Something for nothing	Third conditional review Expressions of purpose, reason and result	Phrasal verbs and expressions with *give* Numbers and symbols	*Interaction 8*: Talking about money *Speak*: An interview with Mark Boyle *Pronunciation*: Large numbers	*Read*: The money-less man *Listen*: Things to do in London for free *Portfolio 8*: Writing about survey results Graphic Novel
Get it right! 7 and 8			*Review 7 and 8: Grammar, Vocabulary*	
9 Keep your cool	*should, ought to* and *had better* Expressing wishes and regrets	Adjectives of character Expressions for arguments	*Interaction 9*: Negotiating and responding *Speak*: A serious problem? *Pronunciation*: Unstressed vowel sounds /ə/ and /ɪ/	*Read*: House Rules *Listen*: How to argue *Portfolio 9*: Asking for and giving advice Song: The Anthem
10 Creating a buzz	Reporting verbs Participle clauses	Advertising Phrasal verbs with *come*	*Interaction 10*: Giving a presentation *Speak*: Opinions about advertising *Pronunciation*: Pitch in signalling words	*Read*: How to create buzz *Listen*: Privacy and the internet *Portfolio 10*: A product review Culture UK: Bristol
Get it right! 9 and 10			*Review 9 and 10: Grammar, Vocabulary*	
11 Just the job	Modal verbs of deduction and possibility review Question tag review	Compound adjectives Job collocations	*Interaction 11*: A job interview *Speak*: Opinions on jobs *Pronunciation*: Intonation in question tags	*Read*: A day in the life of a teen detective *Listen*: The best jobs in the world? *Portfolio 11*: A job application Culture World: The Great Barrier Reef
12 Changing times	Reported speech review Relative clause review	Expressions with *time* Loan words in English	*Interaction 12*: Keeping a conversation going *Speak*: Fad information swap *Pronunciation*: Pronouncing loan words in English	*Read*: Which English do you speak? *Listen*: Fads and trends *Portfolio 12*: Correcting your own mistakes Graphic Novel
Get it right! 11 and 12			*Review 11 and 12: Grammar, Vocabulary*	

Skills4Real: Units 1–4 *Skills4Real: Units 5–8* *Skills4Real: Units 9–12* *Interactive Art Unit 4*
Interactive Maths Unit 8 *Interactive Science Unit 12* *Interaction: Pronunciation practice*
Speaking activities *Interaction: Student A* *Interaction: Student B* *Interaction: Student C; Units 7 and 10*
Grammar reference *Wordlist* *Irregular verbs* *Phonemic chart*

1 Connected

Simple and continuous tense review
Perfect tense review
Vocabulary: Online communication; phrasal verbs with *up*
Interaction: Meeting face-to-face

1 Read and listen

a Read the text quickly. What is danah boyd's job? Does she think it is a good idea for teenagers to hang out online?

Social networks and social life

wall
info
photos
events
friends
links

164 people like this

Write a comment

danah boyd* is one of the world's leading experts in social media. She is a senior researcher at Microsoft Research and has studied the role that social network sites play in the lives of teenagers. For her PhD, she travelled around the USA for two years talking to young people about how they use social network sites. But what did she discover?

danah found out that when you decide to use social networks, you have to create your own online presence. This is your 'digital body'. People accessorise their digital body in an attempt to define themselves and often spend a lot of time making sure their online profiles reflect their real personalities.

The comments section or 'wall' is a key feature of social network sites, as this is where public conversations take place. Interaction on the wall can be vital in establishing and maintaining friendships. If someone writes 'Hi, what's up?' on your wall what they are actually saying is 'I'm thinking of you and I want you to publicly say that we are friends'. If the response is positive, the writer is confirming to the world: 'Yes, we are still friends and I'm thinking of you too.'

danah's research shows that young people usually use the online environment to interact with friends they already have. She considers hanging out online to be a valuable activity and a place to learn life skills. Most teenagers told her that they would prefer to spend time with their friends in real situations, but there are several reasons why online socialising is so popular. Many students have such busy schedules with school and organised activities that they have very little free time to spend with their friends. Sometimes their parents don't allow them to hang out with their friends in the evenings or at weekends as they worry about their safety. A third factor is that many people live too far away from their friends to be able to physically meet up frequently. Socialising online is one way to get around all of these problems.

danah is also studying people's visibility on the web and what their digital footprints look like. She asked teenagers questions about their privacy settings on social network sites and how they felt about being tagged in other people's photos. danah discovered that many were becoming aware of their online visibility. One girl talked about a situation where her mother became her friend on a social network and discovered that her daughter hadn't been doing her homework at her friend's house the previous Saturday as she thought. She had been at a party instead, and the photos were there for the world to see!

When teenagers get older and their groups of friends change, will their online habits change as well? Only time will tell, and if danah continues her research in this field she will surely be one of the first to find out.

*danah boyd's name is legally lower case. She does not use capital letters in her name.

Which is right? Don't look at the text!
Their parents don't allow them ***hang out/ hanging out/to hang out*** *with their friends.*

b 1.2 Read the text again and listen. Are the sentences *right* (✓), *wrong* (✗) or *doesn't say* (–)?

1 danah did a lot of her research face-to-face.
2 Most people try to reflect their personalities online.
3 Teenagers mainly use social networks to make new friends.
4 Many teachers believe social network sites are dangerous.
5 Most teenagers prefer communicating online to real situations.
6 Many parents in the USA don't allow their children to hang out with their friends in real life.

c Work with a partner. Ask and answer the questions.

1 Do you spend more time hanging out with friends in real life or online?
2 How big do you think your digital footprint is?
3 How do you think the way we use social networks is going to change in the future?

2 Grammar

Simple and continuous tense review

a Look at the examples and match them with the tenses.

present simple   present continuous   past simple   past continuous

1 *She **travelled** around the USA for two years.*
2 *danah **is** also **studying** people's visibility on the web.*
3 *She **is** a senior researcher at Microsoft Research.*
4 *danah discovered that many teenagers **were becoming** aware of their online visibility.*

b Match the uses with the examples in Exercise 2a.

A A fact or something that is always true
B An action happening now
C An action completed in the past
D An action that was in progress in the past

Grammar reference: page 134

c Complete the text with the correct form of the verb in brackets.

Now Clay Shirky [1] … (be) a writer, consultant and teacher on the social and economic effects of the internet. Before this, he [2] … (run) a theatre company in New York for several years. While he [3] … (work) there, he [4] … (become) interested in technology.
At the moment he [5] … (research) the effect of social networking on friendships. He is particularly interested in the difference between weak and strong 'ties' in his studies. Strong ties [6] … (refer) to your relationships with your best friends, and weak ties refer to people you [7] … (not know) so well. He [8] … (believe) that hundreds of weak ties in your social networks [9] … (affect) the quality of your strong ties, and your relationships with these people [10] … (not be) as good.

Get it right!

A *relation* is a member of your family; a *relationship* is the way people feel or behave towards each other.

✓ *He has a very good relationship with his sister.*
✗ *He has a very good ~~relation~~ with his sister.*

d Work with a partner. Tell your partner about …

1 … when you last used a social network site.
2 … what you were doing at ten o'clock last night.
3 … what you are doing in class at the moment.
4 … how you keep in touch with your friends.

3 Vocabulary

Online communication

a 1.3 Match the words with the definitions. Then listen and check.

1 digital footprint **2** friend/defriend **3** friend request **4** go viral **5** link **6** privacy settings **7** spam **8** tag (a photo)

A to ask to be someone's friend on a social networking site
B to label a photo with a name
C to accept / get rid of as a friend
D unwanted email, often advertising
E controls that decide how much of your online profile people can see
F information that spreads around the internet in an uncontrolled way
G a record of your online activity
H a connection between pages on the internet

b Complete the sentences with a word from Exercise 3a. Put the words in the correct form.

1 He sent me the … to his blog so I could find it easily.
2 She was really annoyed that he … a terrible photo of her.
3 You should check your … to keep your social network site secure.
4 He checked his … to know what information about him was visible online.
5 If you fall out with someone in real life, should you … them online?
6 I don't like receiving … in my inbox.

c Do you know any other words about online communication? Write them in your Workbook (page 114 Exercise 1).

d Work in a group. Ask each other questions to find out who…

1 … spends the most time online.
2 … watches the most viral videos.
3 … has the largest digital footprint.
4 … has been tagged in the most photos on social networking sites.

4 Listen

a Do you watch videos online? What do you watch? Do you think you can become famous by uploading videos on to the internet? Why? / Why not?

b 1.4 Listen and write the things you hear Jordan and Katelyn talk about.

cooking	doing make-up
hairdressing	skateboarding
unicycling	painting

c 1.4 Listen again and complete the sentences.

1 Jordan's friend wants to be a … .
2 Katelyn thought Ben's video on YouTube was … .
3 Lauren Luke used to work in a … before she was discovered on YouTube.
4 Lauren's videos have had more than … views.
5 Sam Haber gets … from other unicyclists who watch his videos.
6 Jordan heard that in the future … of data on the internet will be video.

d Complete the sentences so they are true for you. Then compare your sentences with a partner.

1 I think most online videos are … .
2 I think that in twenty years' time, the internet will be … .
3 The best video clip I've ever seen is … .
4 Before the internet was invented people probably … .

5 Vocabulary

Phrasal verbs with *up*

a 1.5 Look at the examples and match the phrasal verbs with *up* with the definitions. Then listen and check.

1 B

1 **Turn** it **up** a bit, I can't hear him!
2 She **set up** a YouTube account.
3 She's **built up** a huge following.
4 She tried to become an actress, but then she **gave up**.
5 Did you **make** that **up**? It can't be true!
6 He's **come up with** a really original idea for his website.
7 If you don't know the word, **look** it **up** in a dictionary.
8 Don't forget to **charge up** your camera before your trip.

A to invent
B to increase the volume
C to start or establish
D to develop
E to plug into an electricity system
F to stop doing something
G to search for
H to think of

b Complete the sentences with the correct form of the verbs from Exercise 6a.

charge look give set build make

1 He decided to … up a blog last month and now posts on it every day.
2 I forgot to … up my phone and the battery ran out.
3 He had to … up playing basketball when he broke his leg because he couldn't run any more.
4 You can use Twitter and Facebook to … up a network of followers.
5 He says he's had over a million views on his blog. I think he's … it up.
6 Nowadays most people … up information online rather than in books.

c Do you know any more phrasal verbs with *up*? Write them in your Workbook (page 114 Exercise 5).

d Work with a partner. Write a mini-dialogue and use as many phrasal verbs with *up* as you can.

6 Grammar

Perfect tense review

a Look at the examples and match them with the tenses below.

1 *He's **been filming** himself cooking.*
2 *How many views **has** he **had**?*
3 *She **had been working** at night in a taxi office for years.*
4 *She **had** always **loved** doing make-up.*

A present perfect
B present perfect continuous
C past perfect
D past perfect continuous

Grammar reference: pages 132 and 133

b Complete the sentences with the correct form of the verb from Exercise 6a.

1 … you … (follow) the Championship cup on TV over the last few weeks?
2 They … (watch) hundreds of online videos before they decided to make their own.
3 … your computer ever … (crash)?
4 Kevin and Sean had an argument last week. They … never … (fall out) before.
5 I … (learn) how to build websites for the last few months.
6 He … (play) tennis for two years before he won his first tournament.

c Read the email and choose the correct answer: A, B or C.

To: clara@pmail.org
From: mel@happybook.com

Hi Clara,

Sorry I [1] … written to you for a while, I've [2] … really busy. Last month I started an online video editing course. It's great, but I've been [3] … all my time on it. I [4] … been wanting to do a course for ages, and I've already [5] … some cool videos. I'll send you the links, if you like. Anyway, what have you been up to? Last time we were in touch you'd just [6] … the news about your exam results. How's your course going?

Write soon! Love Mel.

1	**A** hadn't	**B** haven't	**C** have
2	**A** be	**B** got	**C** been
3	**A** spent	**B** spending	**C** spend
4	**A** had	**B** have	**C** would
5	**A** making	**B** made	**C** been making
6	**A** get	**B** getting	**C** got

Get it right!

***Always*, *never*, *ever* and *already* come between the auxiliary verb and the main verb.**

✓ *I have always wanted to make a video.*
✗ *I ~~have wanted always~~ to make a video.*
✗ *I ~~always have wanted~~ to make a video.*

d Put the words in the correct order.

1 learning / have / new / recently / been / anything / you?
2 online / you / had / a / ever / bad / socialising / experience / have?
3 had / how much / you studied / you started / before / this / course / English?

e Work with a partner. Ask and answer the questions in Exercise 6d.

Check it out!

- *For* and *since* are often used with perfect tenses. We use *for* with a period of time and *since* with a specific point in time.
  I've been waiting for you **since** half past eight.
  I've been waiting for you **for** an hour.

7 Speak

a Work in pairs. Look at the pictures and discuss the advantages and disadvantages of each form of communication.

b Which three forms of communication do you and your partner think are the most important?

c Work with a new partner. Tell each other your answers for Exercise 7b and why. Do you agree or disagree with each other?

8 Pronunciation DVD

/ʃ/, /dʒ/ and /tʃ/

a 1.6 Listen to the /ʃ/, /dʒ/ and /tʃ/ sounds in these words.

/ʃ/ social /dʒ/ danger /tʃ/ future

b 1.7 Copy the table. Listen and write the words in the correct column.

fashion kitchen enjoy virtual nation Russia digital ocean question nature object teacher

/ʃ/	/dʒ/	/tʃ/
fashion		

c 1.8 Listen, check your answers and repeat.

d Follow the /ʃ/ sound to find a way through the puzzle. You can move up or down ⇕ and left or right ⇔. Work with a partner and say the words.

washing	injury	kitchen	virtual	adventure	butcher
machine	demonstration	delicious	mushrooms	research	picture
manager	question	damaged	fashionable	imagination	digital
watching	passenger	nature	nationality	patience	passion

e 1.9 Listen and check your answers.

Culture Vulture

Mark Zuckerberg co-created the Facebook site when he was studying at Harvard University. Nowadays it has over 1 billion users worldwide and is valued at over $100 billion. Is Facebook popular in your country? Are there other social network sites that are more popular?

Interaction 1 DVD Meeting face-to-face

a 1.10 Listen to Becky and Marta as they meet face-to-face for the first time. How do they know each other?

b 1.10 Listen again. Who says each phrase, *B* (Becky) or *M* (Marta)?

1 It's great to finally meet you!
2 You look different to how I'd imagined.
3 I feel like I know you already.
4 Are you still in touch with Sarah?
5 We've got so much in common.
6 What else are you into?
7 Do you know Joe? He's a good friend of Sarah's.

c 1.11 Turn to page 124. Listen to the sentences and repeat them. Practise sounding enthusiastic by using a higher pitch, stressing key words and making your intonation rise at the end of the sentence.

d Work with a partner.

Student A: Turn to page 126.

Student B: Turn to page 128.

Portfolio 1

An email to a friend

a Read the email that Jordi has received from his friend Paolo. Where do they usually spend time together?

http://interactive.cambridge.org

My Mail

COMPOSE

Inbox
Sent Mail
Drafts
Spam (12)
Trash

Artwork at last!

From: paolo02@speedymail.com
To: jordibarca@gmail.com

Hi Jordi!

I'm writing you an email for a change! ☺ It was good to chat last week, it's funny that we've got so much in common and we're both fans of the best game in the world! ;)

Sorry I haven't sent you a message before now, but I was waiting until I could scan in the painting and get it up on the blog. In the end I did it yesterday, so here's the link! What do you think of my artwork? The first painting is the dragon from the game and the second one is your character. Do you like it? Do you reckon I'll be a famous artist one day?

I was hoping to see you online last night, but you weren't there. Were you busy? What were you doing? You're almost always online on Tuesday evenings! Anyway, I haven't heard from Akira lately. Have you? He used to be online all the time. Last time he wrote he said that he'd been having a pretty hard time at school. He'd had loads of exams and I think he was pretty stressed out. I know the feeling … I've been studying loads recently and haven't had much time to play either. Do you think he's OK? Maybe we should get in touch and see if he wants to meet up for a game one day soon.

Write back if you have time. If not, see you soon at the usual place!

Paolo

Click here to *Reply* or *Forward*

Get it right!

***News* is always plural. Don't say *a new*, say *some news* or *a piece of news*.**

✓ *I have some good news to tell you.*
✗ *I have ~~a good new~~ to tell you.*

b Read the email again and list examples of the following tenses:

A present simple
B present continuous
C past simple
D past continuous
E present perfect
F present perfect continuous
G past perfect
H past perfect continuous

c Imagine you are Jordi. Reply to Paolo's email. Make sure you include:

- an opening and closing to the email
- at least six different tenses from Exercise b
- some news about yourself
- answers to Paolo's questions and three more questions

d Swap your email with a partner. How many different tenses did they use in their reply?

Love Online

1 Song

a How can you show people you care about or love them? Put the ideas in order from the most to the least romantic. Can you think of any other ideas?

- making someone a cup of coffee
- giving someone a present
- sending someone a message on a social networking site
- sending someone a Valentine's card
- giving someone a hug
- spending time with someone
- paying someone a compliment
- writing someone a song or poem

b 1.12 Listen to the introduction to the song. How is the singer feeling?

c Match the words (1–9) with the definitions (A–I).

1 cyber
2 connecting
3 technology
4 shut down
5 virus
6 download
7 information
8 online
9 crashing

A the practical use of scientific discoveries
B a harmful program which stops a computer working normally
C related to computers, especially the internet
D facts about something
E on the internet
F breaking or not working
G to move programs into a computer's memory
H joining or being joined
I switch off or stop working

d 1.13 Listen to the song and complete the lines with the words in Exercise 1c.

You say, you don't have to be there when I call
You don't want to tell me
Little things I long for after all

Chorus

I'm dialling up all my time
Your …'s on my mind
Everything would be just fine
If love could only live …
Sending … outlines who you are

Still we're not …
The superhighway only goes so far

Chorus

I wanna know how you …
Is there a … hanging around,
… without a sound?
…, images of Paris just for me
Though we'll never go there
We travel through the … circuitry

e 1.13 Listen to the song again, then ask and answer the questions.

1 Who is the song about? What does the singer of the song want? What is her biggest problem?
2 Do you think friendships can 'only live online'?
3 Do you think people will spend more or less time online in the future?
4 Why do you think 'love' is such a popular topic for songs?

2 Sound check

a 1.14 Songs often have lyrics that rhyme or have the same vowel sound so they sound good when sung together. Listen to the lines of the song.

Rhyming words

You say, you don't have to be there when I <u>call</u> ...
Little things I long for after <u>all</u>

Same vowel sounds

I'm dialling up all my <u>time</u> ...
Everything would be just <u>fine</u>

b Copy the table. Read the words in the box aloud, then write the word pairs in the table.

are circuitry online down mind far around me

Rhyming words	Word pairs with the same vowel sounds
call/all	time/fine

3 Musical notes

a 1.15 Listen to the chorus of a love song sung in four different styles. Number the styles in the order you hear them. Then match the styles with the photos.

Blues Folk
Reggae Alternative Rock

b Work in a group. Ask and answer the questions.

1 Which do you think is the best type of music for a love song? Which is the worst?
2 Do you like listening to songs about love? If not, why not?
3 What's your favourite love song? Why do you like it?

Get it right!

which
We spell *which* with 'wh'.
✓ *Which type of music do you like best?*
✗ ~~*wich*~~

Love songs

People have been writing love songs for thousands of years. There is evidence that love songs were sung in ancient Egypt as early as 1500 BC. The love song has never gone out of fashion, although songs about love were banned in the Middle Ages in some parts of the world. The theme of love in music has appeared in all styles and it is the most common theme in music past and present.

2 Well played!

Infinitive and +*-ing* review
***remember*, *stop* and *try* with *-ing* and the infinitive**
Vocabulary: Sports equipment; Sports collocations
Interaction 2: Making and responding to excuses

A
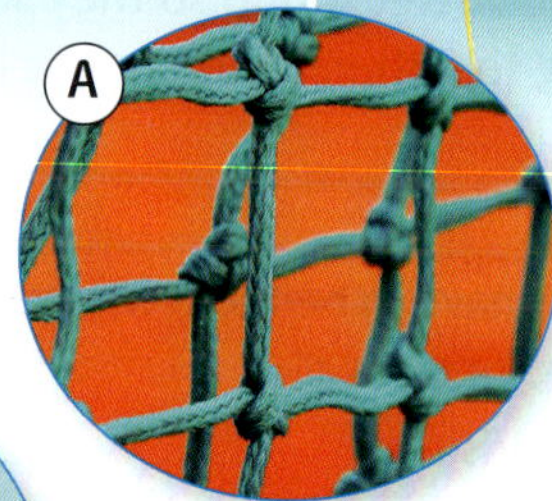
B
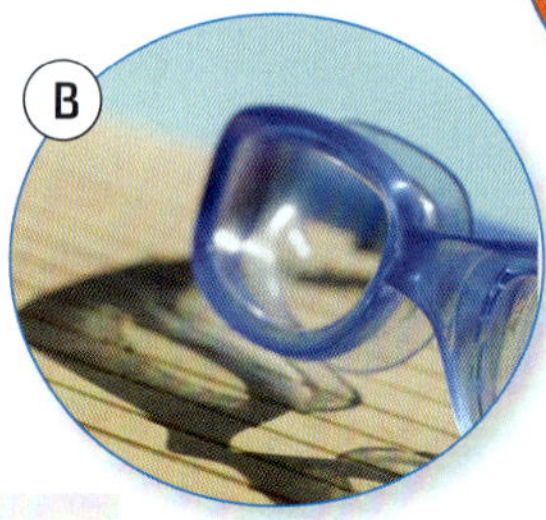
C

D

E

1 Vocabulary

Sports equipment

a 1.16 Match the words with the pictures. Then listen and check.

1 board **2** goggles **3** helmet **4** net
5 oar **6** pads **7** racket **8** skates **9** stick

F

G
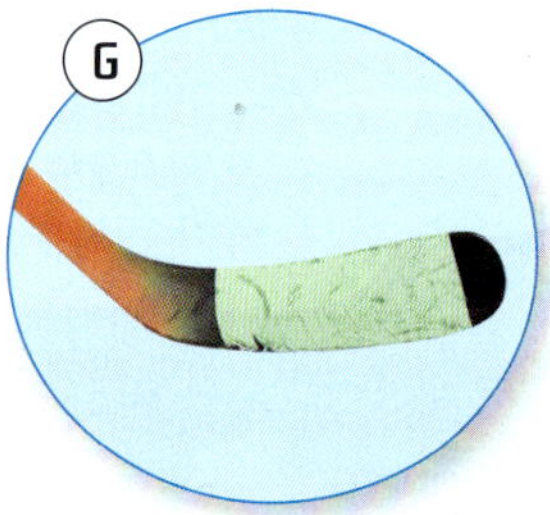
H
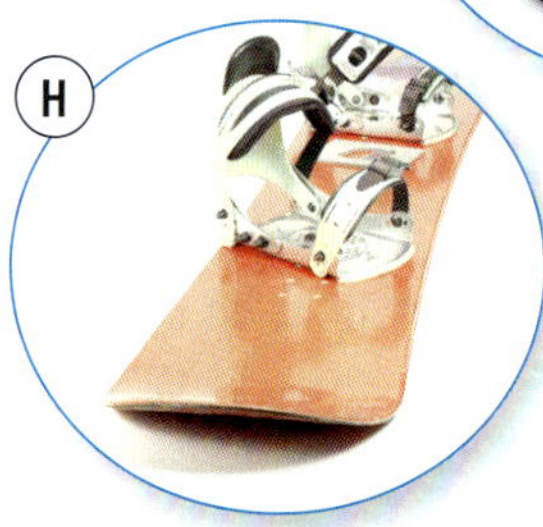
I
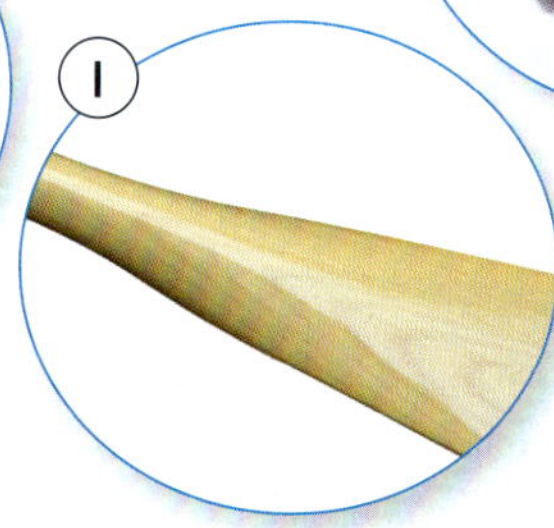

b Make word webs with the names of sports for the equipment in Exercise 1a.

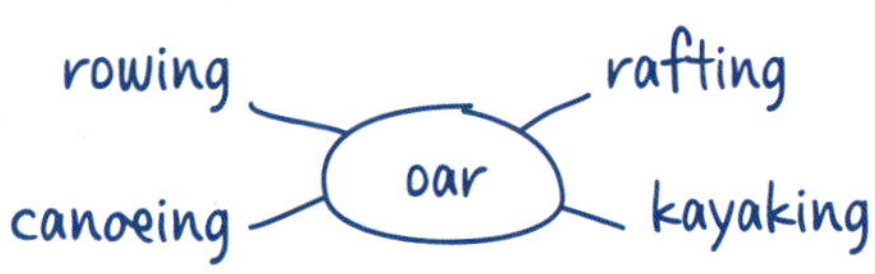

Check it out!

- We use *bat*, *club* or *stick* for different sports.
  cricket **bat** golf **club** hockey **stick**

c 1.17 Copy the table. Match the sports with the places. Then listen and check.

1 basketball **2** diving **3** football **4** ice hockey **5** skiing

A pitch	B court	C rink	D piste	E pool

d Can you add more sports to the places in Exercise 1c? Do this in your Workbook (page 115 Exercise 1).

e Work with a partner. Describe a sport, but don't say the name. Say where it is played and the equipment used. Can your partner guess the sport?

A: *You play it with a ball on a field.*
B: *Rugby?*
A: *No, there are 11 players on each team …*

2 Pronunciation DVD

Homophones

a 1.18 Homophones are words with different spellings but the same pronunciation. Listen to these words.

/bɔːd/ board bored /kɔːt/ court caught

b 1.19 Listen and write the two homophones in each group.

	A	B	C
1	there	their	they
2	on	one	won
3	hear	her	here
4	hour	our	oar
5	mail	male	meal
6	no	now	know
7	say	sea	see
8	wait	went	weight

c 1.20 Listen, check your answers and repeat.

d Work with a partner. Take turns to say a letter and number from Exercise 2b. Your partner says the word with the correct pronunciation.

1B
their

3 Read and listen

a What is unusual about the sports in the pictures? Read the texts quickly and check your ideas.

Football crazy?

Everybody knows that football, or soccer, is the most popular sport on the planet. However, there are many strange variations of the game we know and love. Which would you like to try?

Bossaball (Luis, Brazil)

If you want to try something completely different, how about playing bossaball? The word *bossa* comes from *bossa nova*, a type of Brazilian music. This team sport combines volleyball, football, gymnastics and music. Music is a major feature of a bossaball match and the 'samba referee' controls the match with the help of a whistle, a microphone, percussion instruments and a DJ set! It's a spectacular game played on an inflatable court with a trampoline on each side of the net. It's fun to play and exciting to watch. Players can touch the ball with any part of their body and try to hit the ground with the ball on the other side of the net.

Rollersoccer (Max, Holland)

Rollersoccer is football on skates. It's quite a new game which is played like normal football, but it's faster and more exciting. Imagine kicking a football while you are wearing skates! It sounds like a crazy idea to many people, but players say that although it is difficult to become an expert, it's actually easy to learn. I also think it's safer than other sports as there are no sticks and players can wear protective pads. I play in a rollersoccer league and would love to play in the World Cup one day. I think that the reason I'm good at playing rollersoccer is because I'm also good at football and hockey.

Swamp soccer (Matilda, Finland)

If you like getting dirty, swamp soccer could be the game for you. Cross-country skiers from my country started playing the sport while they were training in muddy swamps during the summer. Finland held its first tournament in 1997 and now it has become a massive soccer competition with annual tournaments around the world. The rules are similar to regular soccer, but the six players on each team can be male or female. Teams wear the same colour tops or even sometimes choose to wear fancy dress, but everyone can expect to get covered in mud.

Foot fireball (Kade, Indonesia)

Both men and women play a variation of football where I'm from in Indonesia, called foot fireball. It's like normal football except that the ball is on fire and the players don't wear boots! Spectators watch in amazement as players kick the burning ball around the field. The ball is made of coconut skin which is soaked in petrol for several hours before a match so that it keeps burning throughout the game. There is a goal, but no goalkeeper because it is too dangerous to pick up the ball. We celebrate special days by playing the game and it has also become a popular tourist attraction. However, I just recommend watching the game the first time you see it.

Which is right? Don't look at the text!
I'm good ***in/at/on*** *playing rollersoccer because I'm also good* ***in/on/at*** *playing hockey.*

b 1.21 Read the texts again and listen. Write *B* (Bossaball), *S* (Swamp soccer), *R* (Rollersoccer) or *F* (Foot fireball).

1 The ball is prepared before the game. F
2 Players can use their hands to touch the ball. B
3 It was invented by people while they were doing something else. S
4 Players sometimes use special protection. R
5 Both men and women play on the same team. F
6 Players hear something special during a match. B
7 It is played in different countries. S
8 It is linked to traditional celebrations. F

c Work with a partner. Ask and answer the questions.

1 Which variations of football would you like to play or watch? Which are the strangest? Why?
2 Which other strange sports or free time activities do you know?

Culture Vulture

Did you know that the football World Cup is usually held every four years and that Brazil has won it five times? Has your country ever played football in the World Cup? What international sports competitions are held in your country?

4 Grammar

Infinitive and *-ing* review

a Look at the examples and choose the correct words to complete the rules.

*I'm **good at playing** rollersoccer.*
*If you **want to try** something different, how about playing bossaball?*
*It is **difficult to become** an expert.*
*I just **recommend watching** the game.*

- After the verbs *enjoy, like, hate, recommend* etc., we use **infinitive** / ***-ing***.
- After the verbs *hope, want, choose, decide, would like* etc., we use **infinitive** / ***-ing***.
- After prepositions (*at, by, about, for* etc., we use **infinitive** / ***-ing***.
- After some adjectives (*easy, difficult, lucky* etc.), we use **infinitive** / ***-ing***.

Grammar reference: page 134

b Find examples of these words in the text on page 13. Are they followed by *-ing* or the infinitive?

want exciting like choose expect
imagine easy keeps dangerous by

c Complete the text with the correct form of the verbs.

Usain Bolt is always exciting [1] … watch). In 2009 he broke the 100m world record in 9.58 seconds. After this, he decided [2] … (try) to reduce his race time again to 9.4 seconds. He has other ambitions too. When he retires from athletics he is interested in [3] … (become) a professional footballer. He'd love [4] … (play) for his favourite team, Manchester United. In 2010 he trained with the German club Bayern Munich as he wanted [5] … (improve) his game. He enjoyed [6] … (learn) from other players and hopes [7] … (join) a club in the future. Who knows? If he keeps [8] … (practise) perhaps we'll see him at the next World Cup!

Check it out!

- When the second verb is *negative*, the form is *verb + not + infinitive*.
  They **decided not to go** to the match.
  NOT ~~They decided **don't go to** the match.~~

d Complete the sentences with information about you. Then compare with a partner.

1 This year at school I would like …
2 I'd recommend …
3 I think it's fun …
4 I've always been interested in …

5 Speak

a Work with a partner. Student A: Complete the questions with the correct form of the verbs. Student B: Turn to page 125.

Student A

1 Which sports or hobbies are you good at? … (do)? Why?
2 Which famous person would you like … (meet)? What would you talk about?
3 Which sports or hobbies do you think are difficult … (learn)? Why?
4 Which sports or hobbies would you recommend … (take up) as a child? Why?

b Work with a partner. Ask and answer the questions.

c Tell the class something interesting about your partner.

6 Vocabulary

Sports collocations

a 1.22 Choose the two nouns that match each verb. Then listen and check.

1 *score*	A a goal	B a point	C a match
2 *beat*	A a team	B a game	C a time
3 *win*	A a player	B a match	C a game
4 *break*	A a record	B a rule	C a match
5 *play*	A at home	B a time	C a game
6 *hold*	A a record	B a goal	C a sports event

b Complete the sentences with a verb from Exercise 6a in the correct form.

1. He … his opponent by four points and won the match.
2. The organisers want to … the next Olympic Games in our country.
3. Are your team … at home this weekend or are they playing away?
4. Our team is top of the league. We've … every match this season.
5. She … the world record for 100m. She beat her old time by 0.1 seconds.
6. Their team only needs to … one more goal to win.

Check it out!

- Remember: *practice* is a noun but *practise* is a verb.
  I've got football **practice** every day this week.
  I need to **practise** shooting goals.

c 1.23 Copy the table. Make collocations with *sports*. Then listen and check.

1 ~~centre~~ **2** ~~competitive~~ **3** contact **4** event **5** extreme **6** fan **7** kit **8** individual **9** star **10** team (x2) **11** winter

Adjective/noun + *sport*	*Sports* + noun
competitive sports	sports centre

d Work with a partner. Write down as many examples as possible for each category.

1. individual sports
2. competitive sports
3. extreme sports
4. team sports
5. winter sports
6. sports stars

7 Listen

a 1.24 Listen to four people talking about sport. Match the number of the speaker with the sport.

athletics

yoga

hockey

tai chi

going to the gym

football

Get it right!

Remember to use the verb *do* with *sports* and *exercise*.

✓ *People think I do too much sport/exercise.*
✗ *People think I ~~make~~ too much sport/exercise.*

b 1.24 Listen again and match sentences A–F with the speakers. There are two extra sentences.

Speaker 1; Speaker 2; Speaker 3; Speaker 4;

- **A** Exercise makes me feel energetic.
- **B** I enjoy doing extreme sports.
- **C** I love watching and playing the same sport.
- **D** I would like to find a sport that I enjoy.
- **E** People think I do too much exercise.
- **F** I never did any sport at school.

c Work with a partner and answer the questions.

1. What does sport mean to you?
2. Do you think people can do too much sport? Why? / Why not?
3. Which sports do you think are best for people …

- **A** in their teens?
- **B** who are unfit?
- **C** in their 30s and 40s?
- **D** in their 60s and 70s?

8 Grammar

remember, *stop* and *try* with *-ing* and the infinitive

a Look at the examples and choose the correct words to complete the rules.

*I **remember going** to my first match when I was six.*
*I **remembered to go** to the match yesterday.*
*If I'm working, I **stop to listen** to the match on the radio.*
*I **stop listening** to the radio after the match.*
***Try doing** some exercise.*
***Try to do** some exercise.*

- When we remember something we did in the past, we use *remember* + ***-ing*** / **the infinitive**.
- When we remember something before we do it, we use *remember* + ***-ing*** / **the infinitive**.
- When we stop one activity to do another, we use *stop* + ***-ing*** / **the infinitive**.
- When we stop an activity, we use *stop* + ***-ing*** / **the infinitive**.
- When we make an effort to do something, we use *try* + ***-ing*** / **the infinitive**.
- When we do something as an experiment, we use *try* + ***-ing*** / **the infinitive**.

Grammar reference: page 134

Check it out!

- We can also *try* + *noun* when we do something as an experiment.
  I **tried yoga** to help me relax.

b Complete the sentences so that the second sentence means the same as the first. Use the *-ing* or infinitive form of the verb.

1 I forgot to take my sports kit to school yesterday.
I didn't remember … my sports kit to school yesterday. (take)
2 I don't want to swim any more. I want to have a rest.
I want to stop … a rest. (have)
3 I learned to ride a bike when I was five. I can still remember the experience.
I remember … to ride a bike when I was five. (learn)
4 We train every day because we want to win the league.
We train every day because we're trying … the league. (win)

c Work with a partner. Ask and answer the questions.

1 What do you remember learning as a young child?
2 Which sport or school subject have you tried to get better at? How?
3 Who do you always stop to talk to? Why?
4 Have you tried doing anything new recently? If so, did you like it? Why? / Why not?

Interaction 2 DVD

Making and responding to excuses

a 1.25 Listen to Ed talking to his teacher. What does he want to be excused from? What's his excuse?

b 1.25 Listen again. Which phrases are used to make an excuse (*M*) and which are used to respond (*R*)?

1 I need to talk to you about that.
2 The thing is, I can't …
3 What's the matter?
4 I've got a bit of a problem.
5 It's just that I have to …
6 I'm really sorry.
7 These things happen, I suppose.
8 Thanks for letting me know.

c 1.26 Turn to page 124. Listen to the sentences and repeat them. Practise showing regret or disappointment by using a lower pitch and making your intonation fall at the end of the sentence.

d Work with a partner.
Student A: Turn to page 126.
Student B: Turn to page 128.

Portfolio 2

A fact file

> **Get it right!**
>
> ***Cannot* is always written as a single word.**
>
> ✓ *Players cannot go in all areas of the court.*
>
> ✗ *Players ~~can not~~ go in all areas of the court.*

a Read the fact file and choose the correct information about netball.

- Players cannot touch the other players.
- Netball is mostly played by men.
- Players cannot go in all areas of the court.
- Anyone on the team can score a goal.
- Players can run with the ball.
- There are six people on a team.

FACT FILE

What is netball?

Netball is a competitive team sport which is similar to basketball, but with some differences. It is a non-contact sport which is played by women. It is a fast game which is exciting to watch. Players have to be good at passing the ball quickly.

The game

Netball is played on a court with a net at each end. Players try to score goals by shooting the ball into the other team's net.

The rules

- There are seven players on each team. Each player has a specific position and is only allowed to go in certain parts of the court.
- Only two players on each team can score goals.
- Teams score one point for each goal.
- Players must remember not to run with the ball or hold the ball for more than three seconds.

Major sports events

The most important competition is the Netball World Championship which is held every four years. People enjoy playing netball around the world in countries like Australia, New Zealand, England, Jamaica, Malawi and Fiji.

b Read the fact file again. Choose the features of a fact file below. Which two features do we not include in a fact file?

Fact file features

- boxes
- informal language
- neutral language
- headings
- personal experience
- short sentences
- visuals (*photos, diagrams, etc.*)

c Find out some facts about a sport played in your country. Then write a fact file about the sport. Make sure you include:

- interesting facts about the sport
- the rules of the sport
- short sentences
- headings
- boxes and visuals

d Work with a partner. Read your partner's fact file and answer the questions.

1 What interesting facts did you learn about the sport?
2 Is the information on the fact file organised well?
3 Would you like to watch or play the sport? Why? / Why not?

1

ABOUT THE TRACK WORLD CUP

The UCI Track World Cup Classics is a global four race series that sees the world's best cyclists including household names like Sir Chris Hoy and Victoria Pendleton competing for the points that will ultimately determine qualification for the Olympics. The event takes place in the velodrome at the National Cycling Centre in Manchester, home of British cycling and scene of some of the greatest moments in British cycling over recent years.

4

Manchester will host the final round of the UCI Track Cycling World Cup Classics series this February. Following the three rounds in Melbourne, Beijing and Cali in Colombia, riders will arrive in the North West competing for the points that will decide the World Cup titles.

Don't miss the chance to see some of your Olympic cycling heroes in action.

The event has been a sell out in previous years. Book your tickets TODAY!

5

trackcycling.com/eventinformation/printpage.html

Event information

All times are local

Fri 18/02 10:00	UCI Cycling World Cup Classics Day session Manchester Velodrome-Manchester	£6	Find Tickets
Fri 18/02 19:00	UCI Cycling World Cup Classics Finals Manchester Velodrome-Manchester	£12	Find Tickets
Sat 19/02 10:00	UCI Cycling World Cup Classics Day session Manchester Velodrome-Manchester	£6	Find Tickets
Sat 19/02 19:00	UCI Cycling World Cup Classics Finals Manchester Velodrome-Manchester	£12	Find Tickets
Sun 20/02 09:15	UCI Cycling World Cup Classics World Cup Finale Manchester Velodrome-Manchester	£15	Find Tickets

2

THE ATHLETES

LIZZIE ARMITSTEAD

DOB: 18 December 1988

HEIGHT: 1.68 m

WEIGHT: 57 kg

HOMETOWN: Otley, Yorkshire

EVENTS: Omnium and Team Pursuit

In the summer she's a road racing talent capable of winning over any terrain. In the winter she translates that ability to the velodrome where both Omnium and Team Pursuit seem tailor-made for her versatility, stamina and speed. Having already won world cup rounds in scratch race, points race and team pursuit at the age of 24, Lizzie is a talent who should be making her presence felt on the world stage for years to come.

6

MANCHESTER

Whether you have a ticket for a *Day session* or *Finals*, or were lucky enough to get both, make sure you take advantage of the spare time in between racing to visit the city and experience the many shopping and dining opportunities it offers. Check out the city which is the home of British cycling!

ABOUT MANCHESTER

Inviting, original, edgy, happening, different: spend any time in Manchester and you'll soon see it's a place like no other. This free-spirited city demands your attention, with a warm, no-nonsense welcome and a liberating open-mindedness that challenges you to take part. Manchester has thrown off its grimy industrial image for good and reinvented itself as a truly contemporary metropolis, with landmark buildings, art, culture, entertainment and world-class hospitality in abundance.

Bring your ideas, your energy and your attitude to Manchester, and you'll fit right in. That's what makes this city uniquely MANCHESTER …

3

Cycling in Manchester

Cycling Information

More and more Manchester people are choosing to cycle. It is a great way to get around – being healthy, environmentally friendly, and affordable. More cycle journeys also means reduced traffic congestion and cleaner air. It is one of the most sustainable modes of travel but whilst more people are taking it up it still only accounts for a small amount of commuting trips.

To encourage more Manchester residents to consider cycling the Council is investing considerably in improved infrastructure for cyclists, both on and off-road.

Many journeys to work are ideal for cycling. If you live a reasonable distance from work (up to about five miles), you might find it possible to cycle – even just once a week – which will benefit both your health and the environment, whilst saving you money!

1 Culture UK: Manchester

a Look at the information about the Track World Cup and answer the questions.

1. Where does the final round of the Track World Cup Classics take place?
2. Do tickets usually sell out for this cycling event?
3. How much is a ticket for the last day?
4. How old is Lizzie Armitstead?
5. Is Manchester a good city for eating out?
6. What are some of the advantages of cycling around Manchester?

b Copy and complete the puzzle and find the mystery word.

1. To go to a place in order to see what it's like. (phrasal verb; text 6)
2. To be the place that provides the space for an event. (text 4)
3. The physical or mental strength to keep doing something difficult. (text 2)
4. Specially made for a particular purpose. (text 2)
5. Free time when you're not doing anything. (text 6)
6. Dirty or unclean. (text 6)
7. A special place for indoor cycling races. (text 1; text 5)
8. Lots of cars in one place; busy. (text 3)
9. An event for which no more tickets are available. (text 4)

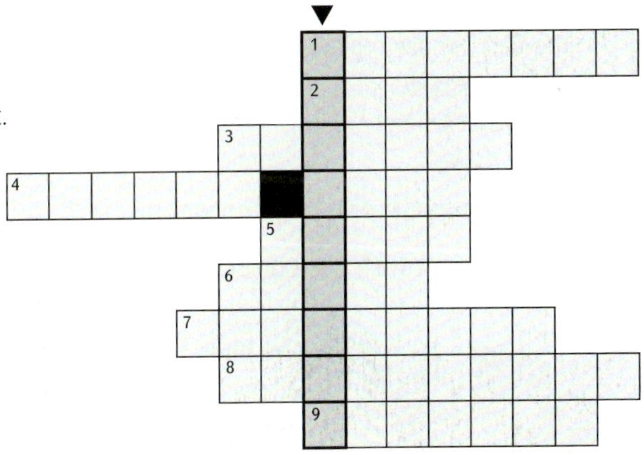

c Work with a partner. Would you like to go to the UCI Track World Cup? If not, which sporting event would you most like to go to? Why?

2 Your noticeboard

A sporting event where you live

a Work in a group. Make a list of some of the sporting events that take place near where you live. Think about:

- events that would be most popular for people your age
- whether people watch the event or take part
- other things a visitor to the event could do

b Make a leaflet to advertise the event in other countries. Include the information from Exercise 2a.

Get it right! 1 and 2

Common errors

1 Verbs ending in *-y*

For verbs with two or more syllables ending in *consonant + -y*:
In continuous tenses, add *-ing*.
✓ *studying* (✗ ~~*studing*~~)
In simple tenses, replace the *y* with *-ied* or *-ies*.
✓ *studies* (✗ ~~*studyes*~~)
For verbs with one syllable ending in *-y*:
In continuous tenses, add *-ing*.
✓ *saying* (✗ ~~*saing*~~)
In the past simple, replace the *y* with *id*.
✓ *said* (✗ ~~*sayed*~~)
In the present simple, add *-s*.
✓ *says* (✗ ~~*sais*~~)

Complete the text with the correct form of the verb in brackets.

I've been [1] … (study) all my life. These days, I am [2] … (try) to learn computer programming. I'm also [3] … (try) to learn Chinese. Everybody [4] … (say) I'm too old and it's easier to learn a language when you're young. I keep telling them they're wrong, but nobody [5] … (pay) attention.

2 *during* or *for*?

Don't use *during* to talk about a length of time, use *for*.
✓ *We have been friends* ***for*** *five years.*
✗ *We have been friends* ~~*during*~~ *five years.*
To talk about something that happens at some time between the beginning and the end of a period of time, use *during*.
✓ *We met several times* ***during*** *the summer.*

Correct three of these sentences.

1 I belonged to a basketball team **during** five years.
2 We played on Fridays **during** the summer.
3 **During** my trip to London, I made new friends.
4 I'll remember this **during** the rest of my life.
5 Look outside! It's snowed **during** the night.
6 If you live in England **during** six months, you will improve your English.

3 *interesting* or *interested?*

Don't confuse *interested* and *interesting.*
Interesting is used to describe something that keeps your attention.
Your training course is very ***interesting****.*
Interested means wanting to know more about something. We use the preposition *in* with *interested*. If it is followed by a verb, we use the *–ing* form.
✓ *I am* ***interested in*** *your training course.*
✗ *I am interested* ~~*on*~~ *your training course.*
✓ *I am* ***interested in joining*** *your club.*
✗ *I am interested* ~~*to join*~~ *your club.*

a Read the conversation with a partner. Correct the mistakes as you read.

A: So, Jane, why do you want to join our club?
B: Well, I've always been interesting in sports.
A: But, what's so interesting about netball?
B: Well, I'm interested on team sports but I'm not interesting in playing contact sports.
A: Ah, that's interested. Are you afraid of being hurt?
B: No, I'm just interested in play skilful fast sports.

b 1.27 Listen and check your answers.

c Do you know other adjectives like *interested* and *interesting* that are similar but don't mean the same. How many can you think of?

4 Say it right!

Linking

a 1.28 We link a consonant sound at the end of a word to a vowel sound at the start of the next word. Listen to the examples and repeat.

They haven't wo**n‿a** ga**me‿a**ll year.
She se**t‿u p‿a n‿o**nline company.

b 1.29 Copy the sentences and mark the consonant to vowel sound links. Then listen, check and repeat.

1 What is netball exactly?
2 This is our ice hockey team.
3 She's online at the moment.

Review 1 and 2

1 Grammar

a Read Jin's message and complete the gaps with a verb in the correct simple or continuous tense in the present or past.

get	write	be	hope	learn

Hi Charlie!

I [1]… to you on my new laptop. I [2]… so happy with it! I [3]… it yesterday as an early birthday present. I [4]… my parents would get me one but I wasn't sure they would. I [5]… how to use it today!

I'll write again soon, Jin

b Put the words in the correct order.

1 the / been / training / for / for / six / has / He / months. / competition
2 he / taken / part / had / in / won / two / Olympic Games / a / before / medal. / He
3 He / the / plan / for / had / months / before / made / decision. / the / thought / he / about /
4 always / I / hated / the / have / at / studying / weekend.

c Complete the dialogue with the verbs in the infinitive or *-ing*.

Jess: I hate [1]… (watch) football on TV but I'm really good at [2]… (play) it. I'd love [3]… (be) a professional footballer one day.

Mark: Well, have you thought about [4]… (join) a club? If you really want [5]… (improve) and you're interested in [6]… (play) professionally, you really should be in a good club.

Jess: You're right, but it's difficult [7]… (become) a professional, especially for girls!

Mark: True. But imagine [8]… (be) one of the best in the world. You would need [9]… (train) really hard to get there. You should go for it!

d Complete the questions with the verb in the *-ing* or infinitive form.

1 Do you remember … (watch) the Olympic Games for the first time?
2 Have you ever stopped … (eat) a particular food because it wasn't good for you?
3 When you're studying hard for exams, do you stop regularly … (have) a break?
4 Do you try … (get up) as soon as your alarm clock goes off in the morning?
5 Have you ever tried … (change) your hairstyle to give yourself a completely new look?

2 Vocabulary

a Complete the sentences with a verb from the box in the correct form.

build turn make speed look come set charge

1 A lot of stories on the internet are … up, they're not true at all.
2 If you can't hear the video, … up the volume a bit.
3 They've … up a blog for their class.
4 She … up the numbers of members of the website really quickly.
5 He didn't … up his laptop before the presentation and it stopped working in the middle of it.
6 The internet makes … up information for school projects really easy.
7 Who … up with the business idea? It's brilliant!
8 He wants to … up his internet connection, it's really slow at the moment.

b Copy and write the missing letters.

1 Big glasses to protect your eyes from snow or water: g_ _ _ _ _ _
2 This is worn to protect your head when you ride a motorbike or do a dangerous sport: h_ _ _ _ _
3 A goal post or a basketball ring has this on it: n _ _
4 You use this to row a boat: o_ _
5 You use this to play tennis: r_ _ _ _ _
6 You use this to play hockey: s_ _ _ _
7 You go ice-skating here: r_ _ _
8 You play tennis here: c_ _ _ _

c Match the sentence halves.

1 He scored …
2 The new player beat …
3 We've only won …
4 He broke …
5 Are they playing …
6 They are holding …

A the world record by 1.3 seconds.
B the first goal after two minutes.
C the grand prix in Monaco this Sunday.
D the club champion in his first match.
E at home this weekend?
F one match so far this season.

3 Multicultural matters

be used to **and** ***get used to***
as*, *like **and** ***such as***
Vocabulary: Extended family; British/American vocabulary
Interaction 3: Empathising

1 Read and listen

a Look at the photos of three teenagers who have moved to live in the UK from other countries. Which countries do you think they came from? How do you think they find life in the UK? Read the text quickly. Were your predictions correct?

Marshal (*right*) and his best friend, Carl.

STARTING OVER IN THE UK

Imran used to think England was a small city in Pakistan; Marshal expected to see snow every day; and Altynay was amazed that people in Britain smiled all the time. All three moved to the UK to join their mothers and begin new lives at the age of eleven. How did they get on in their new country?

Altynay is from Bishkek, the capital city of Kyrgyzstan, in central Asia, where she lived in a tower block with her grandmother and was top of her class at school. She and her mother now live in a tiny village in Yorkshire, in the north of England. Altynay picked up English with a Yorkshire accent in just one year and is now doing extremely well at school. She has a great sense of humour, which she is able to express in English, and lots of friends. In her second year in England she got very homesick, but now she is used to village life, sings in the church choir, and loves wearing fashionable clothes.

Altynay with her British-born baby sister.

Imran came to Peterborough to live with his mum and his stepfather, her British Pakistani second husband. At first he was fascinated by his new environment, but he soon became very homesick. He felt claustrophobic in his small terraced house and couldn't get used to the lack of open space. Although his new home was in an Asian neighbourhood, Imran was bullied at first because he refused to wear jeans and still dressed in traditional Pakistani clothes. However, gradually Imran earned his acceptance, mainly through starting a craze for cricket at his school. Now he speaks English fluently and has got used to life in Britain, while maintaining a close connection to Pakistan. He was very pleased when his family arranged his engagement to a girl in Pakistan.

Imran and his mother.

When Marshal arrived in Newcastle he didn't recognise his mother at the airport. He had to get used to living with her again after five years apart: she had been living in Britain while he was still in Zimbabwe. Marshal loved his school in England, and was impressed by how friendly the teachers were. He had the advantage of already being an English speaker and his good looks and charm helped him make friends quickly. After a few years in the UK, he is extremely popular with girls and wins medals at football tournaments. His ambition is to speak English with a perfect Geordie (north-eastern) accent. Although Altynay, Imran and Marshal have come from very different countries, all three have adapted very successfully to life in the UK and have made their new country their home.

Which is right? Don't look at the text!
His good looks and charm helped him ***do/get/make*** *friends quickly.*

b 1.30 Read the text again and listen. Then answer the questions.

1 Which family members were already in the UK when the teenagers arrived in the country?
2 What is the main difference between Altynay's old home town and her new one?
3 What two things did Imran most dislike about living in Peterborough?
4 How did Imran make friends at school?
5 Why did Marshal easily adapt to school in the UK?
6 Which teenager(s) has/have developed a regional accent?
7 Which teenager(s) has/have kept in touch with their native country?

c Work with a partner. Ask and answer the questions.

1 Who do you think has found it easiest / most difficult to live in the UK? Why?
2 Why do you think people are often homesick when they leave their country?
3 Do you think you would find it hard to live in the UK? Why? / Why not?

2 Grammar

be used to and *get used to*

a Look at the examples and match them with the descriptions of how *be/get used to* are used: *A* or *B*.

1 *Now Altnay **is used to** village life.*
2 *Marshal had to **get used to** living with his mother again.*

A Describes a situation that is now normal or familiar, but wasn't in the past
B Describes a situation in the process of becoming familiar, or less strange or difficult over time

Choose the correct word(s) to complete the rule.

- *be/get used to* is followed by a noun, pronoun, or the ***-ing*** / **infinitive form** of the verb.

Grammar reference: page 133

b Match the sentences (1–4) with their meaning (A–D).

1 I'm used to the hot weather.
2 I'm getting used to the hot weather.
3 I can't get used to the hot weather.
4 I'm not used to the hot weather.

A Hot weather is becoming more and more normal for me.
B Hot weather is normal for me.
C Hot weather is strange for me.
D I've tried to feel comfortable with hot weather, but it's still strange for me.

Check it out!

- Don't confuse *be/get used to* with *used to* + infinitive. We use this for things that happened normally or often in the past but don't happen now.
She **used to drive** to work, but now she goes by train.

c Complete the sentences with *be/get used to* in the correct form.

Zoe is British and has just moved to Brazil.
I'm still [1] ... the number of people in the streets. It's so crowded here compared to home.
I can't [2] ... eating rice and beans all the time. I don't like them.
At home we went to the beach once or twice a year, but now [3] ... going all the time!

Carlos is Colombian and has lived in London for two years.
At first I hated the weather here, but now I [4] ... it.
I'm still [5] ... drinking tea yet. I prefer coffee!
Next year I'm going to university so I'll have to [6] ... living away from my parents.

d Work with a partner. Ask and answer the questions.

1 Is there anything you are getting used to at the moment? If so, what?
2 Is there anything you are used to doing now which you would have found strange a few years ago?
3 What do you think you will have to get used to doing in a few years' time?

3 Vocabulary

Extended family

a 1.31 Match the words (1–6) with the definitions (A–F). Then listen and check.

1 ex-husband
2 great-grandfather
3 half-sister
4 mother-in-law
5 second wife
6 stepbrother

A a sister who shares one parent with you
B the son of your mother or father's new husband or wife
C your husband or wife's mother
D your former husband
E your grandmother or grandfather's father
F your wife from a second marriage

b 1.32 Listen to the questions and choose the correct answer.

1 your stepmother / your aunt
2 your cousin / your second cousin
3 their grandmother / their great-grandmother
4 his ex-wife / his second wife
5 your sister-in-law / your stepsister
6 her stepson / her son-in-law

c Do you know any more words for extended family? Write them in your Workbook (page 116 Exercise 1).

d Work with a partner. Tell your partner four true and two false statements about your family, using words from Exercise 3b. Can they guess which are false?

A: *My great-grandmother is 95.*
B: *True.*
A: *No, it's false! I don't have any great-grandparents. Your turn.*

4 Speak

a Have you ever thought about living in another country? Which country would you most like to live in? Why?

b Imagine that you are going to live in the country you chose in Exercise 4a. Write a list with two answers for each statement (1–6) below, but do not write them in the same order.

1 what you would miss from your own country
2 what you wouldn't miss from your own country
3 people you would miss from your own country
4 people you wouldn't miss from your own country
5 what you would find hard to get used to in the new country
6 what you would like about the new country

c Work in a pair. Look at your partner's list and guess the number from Exercise 4b. Then ask and answer questions about their information.

A: *Why wouldn't you miss that presenter?*
B: *She's always on TV and she's really boring. She has nothing to say.*

d Tell the class about you and your partner's lists. Was any of your information the same? Did you have the same reasons for including it on your list?

5 Listen

a Look at the sentences. Do you think they are true or false?

1 In the UK most secondary school students learn Spanish.
2 Some schools are starting to teach Mandarin Chinese.
3 In the US the most popular foreign language to study in high school is French.

b 1.33 Listen to four students talking about learning foreign languages and see if your guesses in Exercise 5a were correct.

Poppy

Marek

Priti

Justin

Get it right!

We write nationalities and languages with capital letters.
✓ *In the UK most secondary school students learn Spanish.*
✗ *In the UK most secondary schools students learn ~~spanish~~.*

c 1.33 Listen again and choose the correct answer: A, B or C.

1 Most of Poppy's friends think learning languages is …
A difficult **B** unnecessary **C** interesting
2 Marek speaks Polish at home … of the time.
A most **B** some **C** all
3 Marek thinks the most difficult thing about Chinese would be how to …
A write it **B** speak it **C** listen to it
4 When Priti and Anna speak to each other, they use …
A more English **B** more German
C the same amount of English and German
5 What language does Priti sometimes speak at home?
A Urdu **B** Hindi **C** Bengali
6 Justin is learning American Sign Language because it's …
A easy **B** useful **C** enjoyable

d Work with a partner. Do you agree or disagree with the statements? Why? / Why not?

1 Everyone in the world should speak at least two languages.
2 Language learning should be compulsory until the age of 16.
3 The most useful language in the world is English.

Culture Vulture

Did you know that the most popular foreign language studied in UK secondary schools is French, followed by German, Spanish, Mandarin Chinese, Italian and Urdu? What are the most popular foreign languages studied in your country? What language(s) would you like to study?

6 Vocabulary

British/American vocabulary

a 1.34 Match the British and American words with the pictures. Then listen and check.

A 4, 7

1 autumn	**11** holiday
2 biscuit	**12** lorry
3 candy	**13** pants
4 chips	**14** petrol
5 cookie	**15** rubbish
6 fall	**16** sweets
7 French fries	**17** trousers
8 garbage	**18** truck
9 garden	**19** vacation
10 gas	**20** yard

A

B

C

D

E

F

G

H

I

J

b Complete the sentences. Then decide if the speaker is British or American.

biscuits garden gas garbage yard holidays truck chips

1 I'm really full. I had a hamburger and … , then four … !
2 Could you take out the … ? Leave it in the … .
3 My parents are going to put more flowers in the … during the summer … .
4 How much … do I need to put in the … ?

c Change the sentences in Exercise 6b from American to British English or from British to American English.

d Do you know any more words that are different in American and British English? Write them down in your Workbook (page 116 Exercise 4).

Check it out!

- In the UK and the US, *time prepositions* are sometimes used differently.
  at the weekend (UK) / **on** the weekend (US)
  write **to** me (UK) / write ~~to~~ me (US)

e Work with a partner. Ask and answer the questions.

1 Do you prefer British or American English? Why?
2 Do you listen to more British or American music? Give examples.
3 Do you watch more British or American films? Give examples.

7 Pronunciation DVD

British and American pronunciation

a 1.35 British and American pronunciation of the same words is sometimes different. Listen to the words. First you will hear the British pronunciation, then the American.

advertisement adult library magazine tomato vitamins

b 1.36 Listen to the sentences. Write *B* for British pronunciation and *A* for American pronunciation.

1 Look at this magazine article about celebrities. …
2 He can't find the book he wants in the library. …
3 Have you seen this advertisement for vitamins? …
4 You need an adult to supervise you in the laboratory. …
5 Can you water the tomato plants today? …

c 1.36 Listen again and repeat.

d Practise saying the sentences in Exercise 7b to your partner with either British or American pronunciation. Can your partner guess which it is?

8 Grammar

as, *like* and *such as*

a Look at the examples and choose the correct words to complete the rules.

*Maybe I'll study something **like** international business and French.*
*Some people learn ASL because they want to work **as** translators.*
*ASL is regarded **as** a foreign language.*
*I speak English 95% of the time, **like** most of my Polish friends.*
*Students in the US are now studying languages **such as** Chinese or Japanese much more than a few years ago.*
*German is becoming less popular, **as** is French.*

- We use ***as*** / ***like*** to talk about a job or role.
- We use ***as*** / ***like*** after certain verbs, e.g. *use*, *regard*, *accept*.
- We use ***as*** / ***like*** + noun to mean 'similar to something or someone'.
- We use *like* or ***as*** / ***such as*** for giving examples.
- We use ***as*** / ***like*** / ***as*** or ***like*** + subject + verb to talk about things happening in a similar way.

Grammar reference: page 134

Check it out!

- Use *like* to talk about:
  personality: What's she **like**?
  appearance: What does she look **like**?
  likes/tastes: What does she **like**?

b Choose the correct words.

1 I'd like to live in a hot country *as* / *like* Tunisia.
2 When we went camping, we used boxes *as* / *like* chairs.
3 Would you like to work *as* / *like* a language teacher one day?
4 The Ukrainian language sounds *as* / *like* Russian, but it's not the same.
5 If you've learned Latin, languages *as* / *such as* Italian and Romanian are easy.
6 He refers to her *as* / *like* his sister, but she's really his half-sister.
7 Rihanna is nothing *as* / *like* Beyoncé! They're completely different artists.
8 She's going to study law, just *like* / *such as* her mother did.

Get it right!

We never use *like* with *look*/*feel*/*sound* before adjectives.
✓ *She looks kind and friendly.*
✗ *She looks ~~like~~ kind and friendly.*

c Complete the sentences so they are true for you.

1 One day I'd like to work as …
2 I'd like to travel to places such as …
3 My first language sounds a bit like …
4 I listen to songs like …

d Work with a partner. Compare your answers for Exercise 8c.

Interaction 3 DVD

Empathising

a 1.37 Listen to Paola's conversation with Lara and Sam. What's her problem? How does she feel at the end of the conversation?

b 1.37 Listen again and put the sentences in the order you hear them.

1 Things will get better, you'll see.
2 You'll feel better soon.
3 It must be very difficult.
4 You mustn't let it get you down.
5 I know how you feel.
6 Everyone feels a bit homesick at first.
7 Being homesick can be awful.

c 1.38 Turn to page 124. Listen to the sentences and repeat them. Practise using the weak forms of the modals.

d Work with a partner.
Student A: Turn to page 126.
Student B: Turn to page 129.

Portfolio 3 A webpage for a school exchange

a Look at the article from a school website and match headings to the paragraphs.

1 eating **2** getting around **3** the school **4** the weather **5** fun things to do

Coming to Lancaster

http://interactive.cambridge.org

Coming to Lancaster

Home | Our school | About us | Events | Contact us

A ...

Our school is quite big, but very friendly. It is for boys and girls from 11 to 18 years old. Our facilities include sports fields and a gym, besides a theatre for plays and concerts and a professional recording studio. We have links with schools all around the world, in countries such as Lithuania, Vietnam and South Africa, and we often have exchange trips with them.

B ...

Lancaster is a small city but there's a lot to do here. There are cinemas, music venues and a theatre. We're also very near the sea and the Lake District National Park is only half an hour away. If you like the outdoors, you can enjoy activities like walking, climbing and sailing.

C ...

In the north of England the weather changes quickly and can be wet and windy. This might be a shock at first, but you'll soon get used to it! You should be prepared for everything. Bring jumpers for the cold, an anorak for the rain and T-shirts for when it's warm.

D ...

British food has a bad reputation, but really it's very tasty! We love food from all over the world, so you're sure to find a restaurant in Lancaster that you like. Choose from Chinese, Italian, Indian, Thai ... anything you want! British families usually have toast or cereals for breakfast, a sandwich or salad for lunch and their main meal in the evening.

E ...

You can get around easily by bus, bike or on foot. Lancaster is on a main train line and Manchester is less than an hour away. London is two and a half hours away by train, or four hours by coach.

b Read the article again and write down examples of ...

1 giving advice, **2** making suggestions, **3** empathising, **4** giving examples, **5** positive verbs, adjectives and adverbs.

Get it right!

***To** talk about walking to a place, we use **go ... on foot**, or **walk**.*

✓ *Every day I go to school on foot.*

✓ *Every day I walk to school.*

✗ *Every day I go to school ~~walking~~.*

✗ *Every day I go to school ~~by foot~~.*

c Write an article for your school webpage for exchange visitors to your school. Make sure you include:

- four or five topics from the box
- positive verbs and adjectives
- advice and suggestions for visitors
- things that might be difficult for foreigners to get used to

your school the weather in your area local food things to do in your town daily routines transport the area round your town your own ideas

d Read your partner's article. Would it be helpful to a foreign exchange visitor? Has your partner included positive verbs, adjectives and suggestions in their article?

is a
rican
untry
f ten
s and
ories.
n the
art of
nent,
from
lantic
n the
to the
Ocean
west,
hward
Arctic
anning
ver 9.9
square
etres,
is the
econd-
country
al area,
ommon
with the
tates is
est land
order in
e world.

1 Growing up in multi-racial Canada

Vancouver: one of the top immigrant destinations in Canada.

Canada has a very high number of young immigrants. In 2008 only 56% of Canadian teenagers were born in the country; the other 44% were mainly from South Asian countries (China, India, the Philippines), but also from the USA, the UK and France, among other places. Young people are also the happiest people in Canada. In 2009 a staggering 96% of Canadians aged 12 to 19 reported they were highly satisfied with life!

Why is this? Reginald Bibby, a professor at the University of Lethbridge, in Alberta, set up Project Teen Canada to find out how the cultural changes in Canadian society are affecting teens. He found that many have more inter-racial friendships and more tolerant attitudes than their parents to foreigners. He also puts the high level of teenage happiness down to plenty of funding for schools and other youth institutions, open-minded parents, and access to new technology.

2 Adjusting to a new country

Nathalie Lozano arrived in Vancouver as a refugee from Colombia when she was 14 years old. It was the middle of a school year and it was a very difficult experience for her. Although Nathalie spoke little English, it was her responsibility as the only child to help her parents, who had no English at all.

'Money was tight and I was the one going to the banks, arranging the accommodation, paying all the bills, dealing with the manager and the landlord, at age 14,' says Nathalie, now a youth worker with the Immigrant Services Society of British Columbia. 'It kind of forced me to grow up.' But there were pleasant surprises too: she hadn't expected to find Vancouver so multicultural and liberal.

Nathalie now helps other young immigrants.

3 Cosmopolitan teens

Yvonne Hebert, a sociologist at the University of Calgary, describes today's Canadian teens as cosmopolitan. 'They see themselves as citizens of the world,' she says. 'They're far more likely to get involved socially and volunteer than their parents.'

Seventeen-year-old Omar Bainto is definitely an example of this type of multicultural teenager. His father came to Canada from the Philippines and his mother is Canadian. Omar spends his free time volunteering, reading, going to the cinema with friends, hanging out with his girlfriend and applying for university scholarships. He says that he and his friends are generally happy, apart from a little stress at school.

Toronto-born Vinay Virmani, 19, is another 'citizen of the world'. He comes from an Indian family but is brilliant at the Canadian national sport of ice hockey.
He is about to take the lead role in *Breakaway*, a film he wrote himself about Sikh ice hockey players in Toronto. Bollywood star Akshay Kumar will produce the film, described as a comedy about the cultural conflicts faced by an Indian immigrant family in a new country. The film's message is: You don't have to give up your identity and cultural values to achieve your dreams. This could be a good motto for Canada.

Vinay is an expert hockey player.

1 Culture World: Canada

a Before you read the article, choose the statements you think are true. Then read the article quickly and check your predictions.

1 Middle-aged Canadians are happier than young people.
2 More than 40% of Canadian teenagers were not born in Canada.
3 Only native Canadians play ice hockey.
4 Immigrants to Canada come mostly from Asia.

b Read the article again and answer the questions.

1 How is immigration changing the attitudes of Canadian teenagers?
2 What reasons does Reginald Bibby give for teenage happiness in Canada?
3 Why did Nathalie have a difficult time when she arrived in Vancouver?
4 How and why did Nathalie have to help her parents?
5 Why is Omar a good example of a cosmopolitan Canadian teenager?
6 The text refers to three of Vinay's talents. What are they?

c Find the word(s) in the article that mean …

1 happy, content (text 1)
2 the head of department at a university (text 1)
3 there wasn't enough money (text 2)
4 shelter, or somewhere to live (text 2)
5 having experience from many parts of the world (text 3)
6 disagreements between people (text 3)

d Work with a partner. Ask and answer the questions.

1 Do you agree with Reginald Bibby about the reasons for teenage happiness?
2 Would you like to emigrate to Canada? Why? / Why not?
3 What advice would you give a friend who was going to move to Canada?

2 Your project

Emigrants from your country

a Work in a group. Make a list of …

- places people from your country emigrate to
- their reasons for emigrating
- what jobs they do in different countries
- what they bring back to your country (customs, food, etc.)

b Make a poster about emigrants from your country. Include …

- a map of the world, or part(s) of it
- the information from Exercise 2a
- pictures or photos

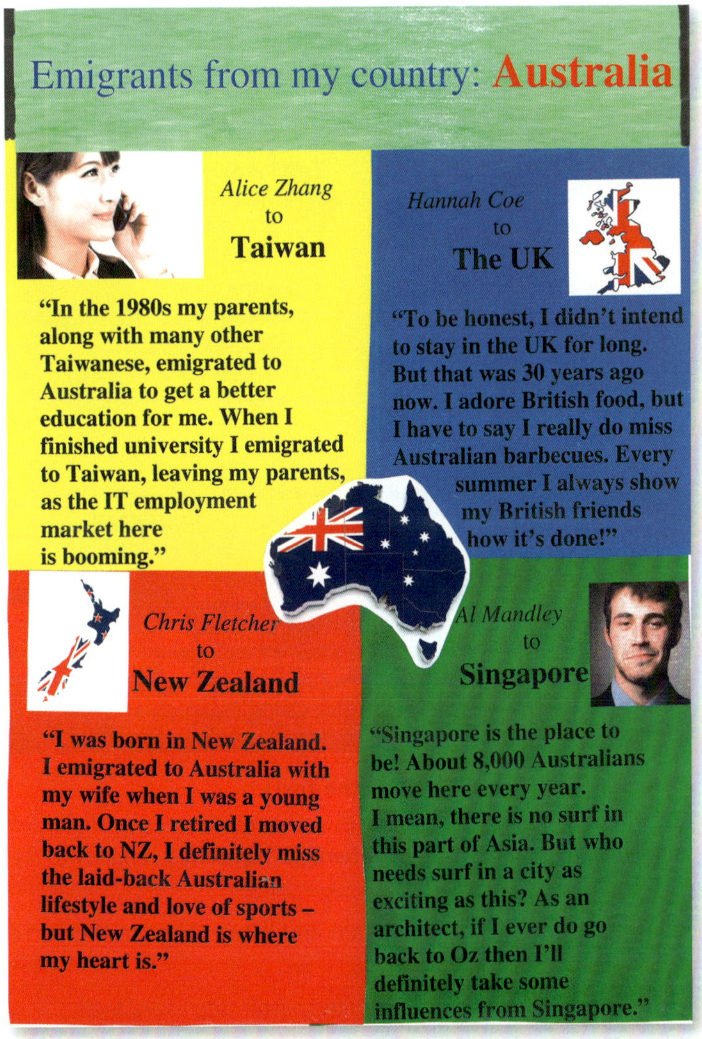

4 Adrenaline rush

Adverbs
Making comparisons
Vocabulary: Verbs of fear; Expressions of fear
Interaction 4: Listening actively

1 Read and listen

a Look at the photo. Where do you think it was taken? Why do you think people enjoy scary rides? Read the text quickly and check your ideas.

THE ATTRACTION OF FEAR

'Absolutely brilliant! The best thing I've ever done! Let's do it again!' shouts Laura who's still shaking after her rollercoaster ride. Her friend sitting next to her just giggles. Rewind a few minutes and while Laura is waiting for the ride to start, the anticipation of what's about to happen creates butterflies in her stomach. As the rollercoaster climbs higher and higher, her heart beats quickly and she starts to sweat. Suddenly, without warning, the ride shoots down incredibly fast, making her scream in terror. Yet Laura and so many other people choose to go on rollercoasters for fun.

So why do we happily put ourselves into situations where we know we're going to feel really scared? Why do we often choose to repeat the experience? The reason we look for fear may be physical, emotional, chemical or even genetic.

American psychologist Frank Farley believes that certain people are natural thrill-seekers and love the adrenaline rush they feel when they do activities like sky diving or bungee jumping. Rather than being scared, they enjoy the physical reactions such as sweaty hands or a rapid heartbeat. Other research into the human brain suggests that surviving a risky situation makes us feel good because the feeling of fear is normally followed by a feeling of euphoria or intense happiness. However, a study in the USA by investigators Eduardo Andrade and Joel B. Cohen indicates a different reason. They say that people are able to feel both negative and positive emotions at the same time, so someone doing something frightening, like watching a horror movie, is happy to feel scared.

Terrifying attractions like rollercoasters play with our fear of heights, falling, and, most importantly, with the fact that we can't control a situation. When the human body is in a dangerous situation, the brain releases a chemical called adrenaline. Adrenaline prepares the body to fight or to run away, commonly referred to as 'fight or flight'. The fact that you can't get off the roller coaster confuses the brain as the body can't respond naturally. Adrenaline also produces endorphins, chemicals which make us feel good, which is why people often want to get straight back on a ride as soon as it finishes.

Laura is not entirely sure why, but as soon as the ride stops, she can't wait to get back on it again. And as she sits down on the ride for the second time, she starts to feel butterflies in her stomach once more.

Which is right? Don't look at the text!
Terrified/Terrifying *attractions like rollercoasters play with our fear of heights.*
Someone doing something ***frightening/frightened*** *is happy to feel scared.*

b 2.2 Read the text again and listen. Choose the correct answer: A, B or C.

1 At the beginning of the rollercoaster ride Laura feels ...
A sad. **B** happy. **C** scared.

2 According to Frank Farley, some people are addicted to ...
A danger. **B** extreme sports. **C** adrenaline rushes.

3 According to research, people can feel negative and positive emotions ...
A at the same time. **B** one after the other. **C** one at a time.

4 In a dangerous situation the human body ...
A can react in two different ways. **B** loses control. **C** slows down.

5 One effect of adrenaline is that it can make us feel ...
A good. **B** angry. **C** tired.

c Work with a partner and answer the questions.

1 Have you ever been to a theme park? Did you enjoy it? Why? / Why not?

2 What do you think rollercoasters will be like in the future?

3 When was the last time you had butterflies in your stomach?

2 Vocabulary Verbs of fear

a 2.3 Match the words with the sounds (1–6).

1 shout

gasp giggle scream shout stutter whisper

b 2.4 Listen and check your answers.

c Work with a partner. Take turns to make the noises in Exercise 2a. Can you guess your partner's noise?

d 2.5 Match the words (1–5) with the definitions (A–E). Then listen and check.

1. beat fast
2. breathe quickly
3. shake
4. shiver
5. sweat

A shake slightly
B make small, quick movements
C when your heart pumps blood quickly around your body
D when moisture comes out through your skin
E take air in and out of your lungs fast

e Choose the correct word.

1. You were *shaking* / *screaming* for so long my ears hurt!
2. I was still *shivering* / *beating* with fear when the ride finished.
3. That film was so funny! I couldn't stop *sweating* / *giggling* the whole way through.
4. The kitten is frightened. Look, it's *whispering* / *shaking*.
5. When we got to the top of the rollercoaster my heart started *beating* / *shouting* really fast.
6. He definitely sounded scared because he was *breathing* / *shivering* more quickly than normal.

f Work with a partner. Ask and answer the questions.

1. Has something ever made you scream?
2. What makes you shiver?
3. What makes your heart beat fast?
4. When do you whisper?

Check it out!

- Many sound words can be a *noun* and a *verb*.
  a **scream** – to **scream**
  a **giggle** – to **giggle**

3 Pronunciation DVD

Stressing adverbs and adjectives

a 2.6 To show strong feelings or opinions we often add extra stress to adverbs and adjectives. Listen to the sentences.

It was <u>absolutely</u> <u>brilliant</u>!

The rollercoaster was <u>terrifying</u>!

b 2.7 Listen and write the words which have extra stress in each phrase. Then listen, check and repeat.

1. That ride is so scary!
2. It goes incredibly fast!
3. It made me feel really sick!
4. I'm definitely not doing that again!
5. The water ride is totally amazing!
6. Suddenly, everything went completely black.

c In pairs write a dialogue about a trip to a theme park or a place where you had a really good time. Include adjectives and adverbs in the dialogue. Read your dialogue to the class with extra stress on the correct words.

A *I went to an amazing water park last weekend.*

B *What was it like?*

A *It was absolutely brilliant!*

B *Why? What did you do?*

Get it right!

Don't use *very* with adjectives that show strong feelings.

✓ *The rollercoaster was absolutely terrifying.*

✗ *The rollercoaster was ~~very~~ terrifying.*

Culture Vulture

Did you know that the world's longest rollercoaster is 2479m long? Have you ever been on a rollercoaster? Which theme parks are there in your country? Which are the most popular?

4 Grammar

Adverbs

a Look at the examples and choose the correct answers to complete the rules.

> ***Absolutely** brilliant!*
> ***Suddenly**, without warning, the ride shoots down **incredibly fast**.*
> *It confuses the brain as the body can't respond **naturally**.*
>
> - Adverbs may describe a **noun / verb**, an adjective or another adverb.
> - The irregular adverbs *fast*, *early*, *late* and *hard* are **the same as / different from** their adjective forms. The adverb form of *good* is *well*.
> - Emphatic adverbs like *absolutely*, *completely*, *totally*, *entirely* usually go before a verb or **an adjective / another adverb**.
> - The adverbs *extremely* and *incredibly* usually go **before / after** an adjective or another adverb.
> - The adverbs *suddenly* and *personally* often go at the **beginning / end** of a sentence.

Grammar reference: page 135

b Complete the sentences with the adverb form of the adjective.

easy fast incredible quiet personal total

1. Shhh! You're shouting! Speak … !
2. She arrived … late today – an hour after the class started!
3. I'm always terrified when I go in the car with him. He drives too … .
4. I'm not very good at French, so I want a simple book I can read … .
5. **A:** … , I thought the film was a complete waste of time!
   B: I … agree!

c Change the adjectives into adverbs and put them in the correct place in the sentence.

1. The new ride goes fast, up to 160km/h. (incredible)
2. The rollercoaster began to move. (sudden)
3. He rode his bike across the ice. (careful)
4. You're right! (absolute)
5. Does he speak Spanish? (good)

> **Get it right!**
>
> **When the adjective ends in '-*l*', the adverb ends in '–*lly*'.**
> ✓ *Would you ever touch a really big snake?*
> ✗ *Would you ever touch a ~~realy~~ big snake?*

d Complete the sentences with your own ideas or opinions.

1. I totally believe that it is a good idea to have … in schools.
2. Generally, theme parks are …
3. One thing I do well is …
4. Once, I completely forgot to …

5 Speak

a Work with a partner. Student A: Put the words into the correct order to make questions. Student B: Turn to page 125.

Student A

1. go / Would you ever / bungee jumping ?
2. a motorbike / dangerously / Would you ever / without a helmet / ride ?
3. touch / snake / really big / a / Would you ever ?
4. on a / rollercoaster / Would you ever / completely alone / go ?
5. sing / your friends / in front of / Would you ever / loudly ?
6. a forest / at night / Would you ever / through / slowly / walk ?

b Work with a partner. Ask and answer the questions. Ask Why/ Why not? Use the language below to help you answer.

☺ Definitely! / Absolutely! / I'd love to!
😐 Maybe / I'm not sure / I might if …
☹ Definitely not! / Absolutely not! / No way!

A: *Would you ever touch an extremely big snake?*
B: *Absolutely not!*
A: *Why not?*
B: *Because it would feel disgusting.*

c Compare your answers with another pair. Did you give similar or very different answers? Why? / Why not?

6 Vocabulary

Expressions of fear

a 2.8 Complete the expressions with the words in the box. Then listen and check.

1 blood	**2** breath	**3** butterflies	**4** heart
5 leaf	**6** life	**7** seat	**8** skin

A If you **frighten the** … **out of someone**, you scare someone a lot.
B If you **shake like a** … , you shake with fear.
C If you almost **jump out of your** … , you suddenly jump because you're scared.
D If something **makes your** … **run cold**, it scares you a lot.
E If you **have** … **in your stomach**, you feel nervous and scared.
F If you're **on the edge of your** … , you're ready for something exciting or scary to happen.
G If your … **misses a beat**, you suddenly feel scared or excited.
H You **hold your** … when you wait for something scary or exciting to happen.

> **Get it right!**
>
> - With parts of the body we always use *my*, *your*, *his*, *her*, etc. to show who they belong to.
>
> ✓ He jumped out of **his** skin.
>
> ✗ ~~He jumped out of the skin.~~

b Complete the sentences with the correct form of the expressions in Exercise 6a.

1 I was so nervous before my Maths exam this morning I had … in my stomach.
2 His heart missed a … when the other team scored a goal.
3 Everyone nearly jumped out of their … when they heard the explosion.
4 Don't scare me like that! You frightened the … out of me!
5 When he heard there had been an accident, his … ran cold.
6 We all held our … while they told us who the winner was.

c Write three true and three false sentences about yourself using the expressions in Exercise 6a. Read your partner's sentences and guess which are true and which are false.

A: *I get butterflies in my stomach before all my exams.*
B: *True.*
A: *No, it's false!*

> **Get it right!**
>
> **The verb is *to breathe*; the noun is *breath*.**
>
> ✓ *I was so scared that I could not breathe.*
>
> ✗ *I was so scared that I could not ~~breath~~.*

7 Listen

a 2.9 Listen to a film expert talking about techniques used in films to scare people. Write the films he mentions.

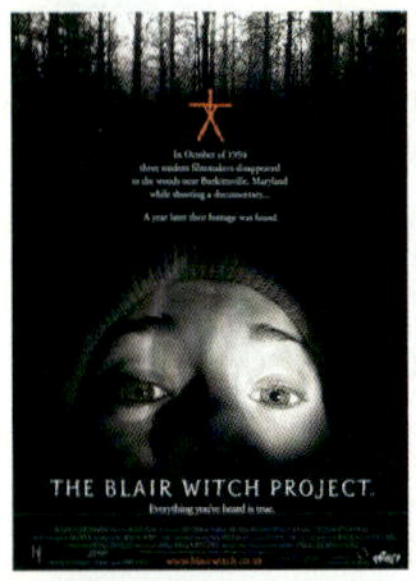

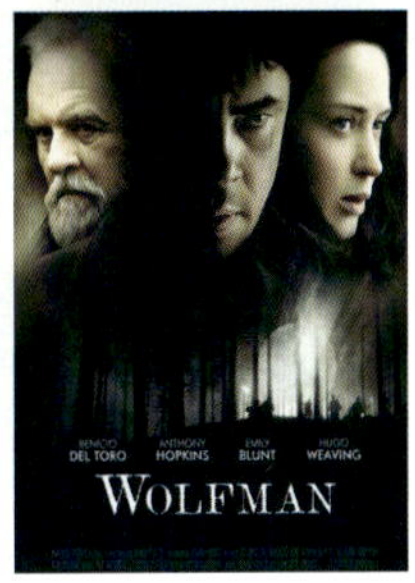

b 2.9 Listen again. Are the sentences *right* (✓) or *wrong* (✗)? Correct the wrong sentences.

1 Successful horror films always use expensive special effects.
2 It's scary when the victim doesn't know that the killer is behind them.
3 In *Jaws* we watch the action through the victim's eyes.
4 It's often scarier when the audience can't see what is happening.
5 Music is always better than silence for scaring audiences.

c Work in a group. Ask and answer the questions.

1 Which do you think are the scariest techniques used in films?
2 What's the scariest film you've ever seen? Why was it scary?

8 Grammar

Making comparisons

a Look at the examples and choose the correct words to complete the rules.

Gradually, the camera gets ***closer and closer****.*
It's ***cheaper than*** *using lots of special effects.*
You can make blood ***more cheaply****.*
Silence can be ***as scary as*** *music.*
The more unexpected *the event is,* ***the more frightening*** *it will be for the audience.*

- We use **adjectives only** / **adjectives or adverbs** to make comparatives.
- We repeat comparatives when something **doesn't change** / **changes continuously**.
- We use *as* + adjective or adverb + *as* when two things are **alike** / **different**.
- We use *the* + comparative + subject + *the* + comparative when one thing **depends** / **doesn't depend** on another.

Grammar reference: page 135

Check it out!

- *a bit, a little, slightly* + *comparative* = a small difference between two things.
  The original film is **a bit scarier than** the remake.
- *far, much, a great deal* + *comparative* = a big difference between two things.
  It's **a great deal scarier** when they use background music.

b Choose the correct word(s).

1 Vampires appear in horror films *a lot* / *more frequently* than any other character.
2 I think that *Jaws 2* is *slightly* / *as* scarier than *Jaws*, but not much.
3 The *modern* / *more modern* the film is, the *good* / *better* the special effects are.
4 The remake of *Frankenstein* is not as *good* / *better* as the original.
5 Horror films are becoming *a great deal* / *more and more* popular thanks to good marketing.

c Complete the text with the correct form of the words in brackets.

Horror films today are as [1] ... (popular) as they were 100 years ago and many old films are being remade. Even though technology is getting more and [2] ... (advanced), a remake is not always [3] ... (good) than the original. For example, The Wolfman (2010) tells a far [4] ... (detailed) story than The Wolf Man (1941) and is a great deal [5] ... (long). Many believe that the [6] ... (advanced) the technology is, the [7] ... (good) the special effects are, but the transformation from man to wolf in the 1941 film is as [8] ... (realistic) as in the modern version. Critics also say that the original film is much [9] ... (scary).

d Work with a partner. Do you agree or disagree with the statements? Why? / Why not?

1 Black and white films are not as good as colour films.
2 Special effects in films are getting better and better all the time.
3 Vampire films are far scarier than zombie films.
4 Watching horror films alone is more frightening than watching them with other people.

Interaction 4 DVD Listening actively

a 2.10 Listen to Anya and Leo talking about a film. Why does Anya get annoyed with Leo?

b 2.10 Copy the table and put the phrases in the correct column. Then listen again and check.

1 Say that again ... 2 Hang on a sec! 3 Carry on ...
4 No way! 5 You're kidding! 6 Go on ...
7 If you let me get a word in, I'll tell you!
8 Let me finish, will you?

Interrupt and show interest	Tell someone to continue	Show you want to continue

c 2.11 Turn to page 124. Listen to the sentences and repeat them. Emphasise the key words to show that you want to continue speaking or that you want the other person to speak.

d Work with a partner.
Student A: Turn to page 126. Student B: Turn to page 129.

Portfolio 4

Beginning a story

a Read the beginning of a story. What language has the writer included to make it feel like a horror story? What do you think is going to happen next?

The shed

'Thanks for letting me borrow your tent,' said Mark. 'It's so much better than my brother's. His isn't even waterproof', he explained. It had rained non-stop on his camping trip and Mark and his brother had got completely soaked.

'No problem, although I'm not sure where it is', said Alice. She thought for a minute. 'Oh hang on, it might be in the shed. Let's go and look for it.'

Outside it was dark and was raining heavily. Alice and Mark ran quickly to the shed and Alice pushed open the old, wooden door. She tried the light switch, but nothing happened.

'That's odd,' she thought. 'The light worked last time I was here.'

'We need a torch,' said Mark.

'Hang on! I'll go and get ... Ahhhhhhhh!' screamed Alice. Something touched her face and she saw a huge insect as big as a rat run across the floor.

'Wh-wh-what was that?' she stammered. 'Mark?' she whispered. But Mark didn't reply.

'Where are you, Mark?' shouted Alice desperately, shivering with fear. Suddenly, the door slammed shut and Alice was in complete darkness. Her heart was beating fast and her blood ran cold as something ran over her foot. She tried to move, but couldn't. She was paralysed with fear, and screamed as loudly as she could ... but no one replied.

b Read the beginning of the story again and write examples of the language we use in a horror story:

- verbs and expressions of fear
- adjectives and adverbs to give detail
- narrative tenses (past simple, past continuous, past perfect)
- direct speech

c Write the beginning of a horror story. Write 120–180 words. Make a plan before you write. Make sure you include:

- the main characters in a realistic situation
- a good setting – the place, the time (day or night) and the weather
- scary surprises
- examples of horror story language (see Exercise b)

d Read the beginning of your partner's story. What examples of horror story language from Exercise b has he/she used? Have they used any examples of direct speech? What do you think is going to happen next?

ILLEGAL COPY
2.12
CRAZY
CARL WISEMAN
RUBY RED
HOW DOES IT FEEL TO BE BRITAIN'S HIGHEST-PAID ACTRESS WHEN YOU'RE ONLY 20?
WHAT CAN YOU TELL US ABOUT CRAZY?
DO YOU KNOW YOU'VE JUST REACHED 7,000,000 TWITTER FOLLOWERS?
I KNOW YOU'RE ALL DESPERATE TO SPEAK TO RUBY, BUT LET'S HAVE ONE QUESTION AT A TIME.
HI RUBY. IT'S DAN BLACK FROM TOP MUSIC MAGAZINE.
ARE YOU GOING TO RETURN TO MUSIC ANY TIME SOON?
I'M HOPING TO GO BACK INTO THE RECORDING STUDIO THIS SUMMER, ONCE I'VE FINISHED PROMOTING CRAZY.
AND IS IT TRUE YOU AND CARL WISEMAN ARE IN A RELATIONSHIP?
YOU KNOW, DAN, YOU SHOULDN'T BELIEVE EVERY RUMOUR YOU HEAR.
SO, IS YOUR ANSWER YES OR NO?
OK, DAN, THANKS FOR THAT QUESTION. LET'S HEAR FROM SOMEONE ELSE NOW …
AFTER THE PRESS CONFERENCE.
I'VE JUST BEEN ON THE PHONE WITH THE STUDIO EXECUTIVES. THEY AREN'T HAPPY.
THEY THINK PEOPLE ALREADY KNOW YOU'RE GOING OUT WITH CARL.
IT WASN'T MY IDEA TO KEEP IT SECRET, KAREN. I DON'T UNDERSTAND WHAT THE PROBLEM IS.
WELL, GET USED TO IT. THEY WANT IT TO BE A SURPRISE FOR THE FANS AT THE PREMIERE.

IT'LL GET EVEN MORE PUBLICITY FOR THE FILM.
BUT I'M TIRED OF PRETENDING ALL THE TIME.
YOU JUST HAVE TO WAIT ONE MORE WEEK.
OK. I'LL SEE YOU TOMORROW.
WHERE ARE YOU GOING NOW?
I'M HAVING ANOTHER 'SECRET' DINNER WITH CARL. AND I'M ALREADY LATE!
DON'T BE LONG, DARLING.
OK, I'LL BE THERE AS SOON AS I CAN.
OH NO! NOT AGAIN! WELL, THEY WON'T CATCH ME TODAY!
WHAT THE …?
WHAT …? WHERE AM I?
DON'T WORRY, DEAR. YOU'RE IN HOSPITAL.
WHAT? WHAT HAPPENED? HOW LONG HAVE I BEEN HERE?
YOU HAD A TERRIBLE ACCIDENT. YOU'VE BEEN UNCONSCIOUS FOR THREE WEEKS.
WILL I BE OK? DOES CARL KNOW I'M HERE? WHERE'S MY MOBILE?
THE DOCTOR WILL BE HERE TO SEE YOU IN THE MORNING. BUT NOW YOU NEED TO GO BACK TO SLEEP.
GOODNIGHT, SANDRA.
SANDRA?!

Get it right! 3 and 4

Common errors

1 Comparing things

Don't use *as* on its own for comparing things or people.

The expressions *as … as* and *the same as* are followed by a noun or noun phrase.

✓ *Rihanna isn't **as tall as** Beyoncé.*

✗ *Rihanna isn't tall as Beyoncé.*

We usually use *like* for saying things are similar:

✓ *Rihanna is tall **like** Beyoncé.*

✗ *Rihanna is tall ~~as~~ Beyoncé.*

We use *like* after verbs for the senses, e.g. *look, feel, sound, taste, smell*, which are followed by a noun.

✓ *Rihanna **looks like** my cousin.*

✗ *Rihanna **looks ~~as~~** my cousin.*

Choose the correct comparison.

1 English isn't *as easy / as easy as* French.
2 London isn't hot *like / as* Tunisia.
3 Rihanna doesn't look *like / as* Beyoncé.
4 Rihanna doesn't sound as good *like / as* Beyoncé.
5 Your jacket looks the same *like / as* my brother's.

2 never or ever?

Don't confuse *ever* and *never*.

Ever means 'at any time'.

✓ *Have you **ever** been on a rollercoaster?*

✓ *She has**n't ever** been on a rollercoaster.*

Never means *not ever*. It isn't used with *not*.

✓ *She has **never** been on a rollercoaster.*

✗ *She ~~hasn't never~~ been on a rollercoaster.*

Notice the position of *ever* and *never* with the verb *be*.

✓ *She **is never** afraid of being alone.*

✗ *She ~~never is~~ afraid of being alone.*

a Complete the text with *ever* or *never*.

Until last year, I had [1] … travelled to a foreign country, and I hadn't [2] … stayed with an English family. I was nervous but when I met my host family, I felt much better. They had [3] … met someone from Spain and they hadn't [4] … been abroad either! It was the best holiday I have [5] … had.

b 2.13 Listen and check your answers.

c Talk to your partner about occasions when you did something for the first time. Use the following prompts:

The first time I ever … ; Before then I had never … ; Have you ever … ?.

3 Make something happen!

Use expressions with *make* correctly and use the correct word order.

- *make* + *somebody/something* + infinitive without *to*

  ✓ *The rollercoaster **made her scream**.*

  ✗ *The rollercoaster made her ~~to~~ scream*

  ✗ *The rollercoaster made her ~~screaming~~.*

- *make* + *somebody/something* + adjective

  ✓ *Technology **makes our life easier**.*

  ✗ *Technology makes ~~easier our life~~.*

a Choose the correct form of the verb.

1 Surviving a risky situation makes us *feeling / to feel / feel* good.
2 Has something ever made you *screaming / to scream / scream*?
3 It makes my heart *beating / to beat / beat* faster.

b Put the words in the correct order.

1 cheaply / make / blood / we can / These / days
2 want / Film makers / to make / famous / their movies
3 in the city / will make / cycling / Cycle paths / easier and safer

4 Say it right!

/ɔː/ in the letters 'au', 'aw' and 'a'

a 2.14 We often pronounce the letters 'au', 'aw' and 'a' with the sound /ɔː/ Listen to the examples and repeat.

August law ball

b 2.15 Copy and complete the words with the letters 'au', 'aw' or 'a'. Then listen, check and repeat.

sm_ll t_lk _ful _tumn c__ght f_ll __dience p_ l_nch

Review 3 and 4

1 Grammar

a Complete the sentences with *be/get used to* or *used to* in the correct form.

1 He lived in China. Now he lives in Brazil and he adapted quickly to life there.
He … live in China. He … living in Brazil quickly.

2 Last year she worked in the day, now she has to work at night and she doesn't sleep well.
She … work in the day, but now she works at night and she still hasn't … it.

b Complete the sentences using *as*, *like* or *such as* and the words from the box.

> the weather forecast predicted   Facebook
> a teacher   one of the best golfers in the world
> my sister

1 He'd like to work … when he finishes university.
2 Everyone says I look … .
3 What do you think about social network sites … ?
4 Seve Ballesteros was regarded …
5 Look! It's raining, … .

c Choose the correct adjectives and adverbs from the box to complete the sentences.

> usual/usually   careful/carefully   total/totally
> sudden/suddenly   easy/easily

1 I think it's … ridiculous that there's been a … ban on mobile phones at school.
2 … he felt a pain in his chest. He couldn't believe it was so … !
3 … he has lunch at 1 o'clock so it wasn't … for him to eat at 3pm.
4 She finds driving … , so she'll … pass her test first time.
5 Be … ! You've got to measure the quantities … or the recipe won't work.

d Choose the correct words in the dialogue.

A: It's getting harder and *harder / more hard* to get a job these days, isn't it?
B: It really is. It must be one of the *worst / bad* times in recent years to look for work.
A: The problem is that there are *fewer / less* jobs and *far / much* more people with qualifications.
B: Tell me about it! I think it's only going to get *more / as* difficult as time goes on.
A: Listen to us! We're so pessimistic. Maybe it's not as bad *like / as* we think!

2 Vocabulary

a What relation to you is …

1 … your mother's new husband?
2 … your step-father's daughter from his first marriage, before he married your mother?
3 … your sister's husband?
4 … your father's new wife's son?
5 … your cousin's cousin?
6 … your grandmother's mother?

b Write the American equivalent of these English words.

1 rubbish	4 autumn	7 chips
2 sweets	5 holiday	8 lorry
3 trousers	6 petrol	

c Match the two parts of the sentences.

1 I couldn't write my name
2 She ran up the stairs so she
3 After half an hour running in the sun
4 My heart was beating
5 They started giggling
6 He whispered the answer to the question

a he was sweating a lot.
b because my hand was shaking so much.
c when they saw what he was wearing! It was so funny.
d was breathing quickly.
e to his partner, but the teacher heard him.
f so fast I could feel my chest moving.

d Choose the correct word to complete the sentences.

1 They were *scared / frightened* stiff at the end of the film.
2 You frightened the *death / life* out of me!
3 After the accident, she was shaking like a *tree / leaf*.
4 He didn't realise that she was at home and he jumped out of his *body / skin* when he saw her.
5 Watching the news sometimes makes my *blood / sweat* run cold.
6 When the policeman arrived at the door she broke out in a cold *sweat / gasp*.
7 Before giving a presentation he gets *butterflies / caterpillars* in his stomach.
8 I was on the edge of my *chair / seat* waiting for the results of the blood test.
9 She's so in love, her *heart / stomach* misses a beat when she sees him.
10 I held my *air / breath* when the car hit the wall.

5 Man and beast

Expressing contrast
Reflexive pronouns and *each other*
Vocabulary: The animal kingdom; Physical habits
Interaction 5: Challenging someone's ideas

1 Speak

a Work in a group. Look at the pictures of the ten most endangered species in the world. Do any of them live in your country? Have you ever seen any of them?

b Imagine you are part of an organisation that campaigns to protect endangered species. Discuss each animal in the pictures and then decide which two you are going to campaign to save.

c Work with a partner from a different group. Explain your group's decision about which two animals to save.

d As a class, can you agree on the two animals to save? Why? / Why not?

2 Vocabulary

The animal kingdom

a 2.16 Match the words with the definitions. Then listen and check.

1 cage **2** endangered **3** habitat **4** hunt **5** rare **6** sanctuary **7** species **8** survival **9** tame **10** wild

A animals or plants which may not exist soon because there are very few left
B a family of animals or plants which have similar characteristics
C animals or plants that live independently of people in natural conditions
D not wild or dangerous
E the natural environment in which an animal or plant usually lives
F protection or a safe place for animals or birds
G to chase and try to catch an animal, for food, sport or money
H very unusual or uncommon
I a space surrounded by bars to keep animals in
J the state of continuing to live or exist

b Complete the sentences with a word from Exercise 2a.

1 The lions in the zoo are so … they let people get really close to them.
2 Experts believe that animals are usually happier living in their natural ….
3 Keeping a wild snake in a small … is cruel!
4 His uncle … birds and deer for sport in the winter.
5 A tiger is an extremely … animal. There are only a few left living in Asia.
6 The … of the African rhinoceros depends on how much it is protected from hunters.

c Do you know any more words for the animal kingdom? Write them in your Workbook (page 118 Exercise 1).

3 Read and listen

a Work with a partner. In what kind of jobs do people work with animals? Make a list. Read the text quickly. Which animals are mentioned in the text?

The Animal People

Kevin Richardson

Kevin Richardson is a South African zoologist and animal behaviour scientist who has spent many years living with lions in an animal sanctuary outside Johannesburg. He has established such love and trust with the animals that he is considered to be one of the family. Kevin never worries about the danger of being so close to the lions, though if you watch him lie down with three or four huge lions, you wonder if maybe he should! He knows their personalities in the same way as a mother knows about her children, and has written books and made documentaries about his experiences. His fascinating film, *White Lion*, follows the story of how a very special lion survived in spite of the problems he faced.

Ruth Muñiz López

The harpy is the largest and most powerful eagle on earth. It weighs up to nine kilos and eats monkeys for its lunch! It is also extremely rare and in danger of extinction. Ruth Muñiz, a Spanish biologist, is the director of the Harpy Eagle Conservation Programme. She has worked for many years in the rainforests of Ecuador, leading teams to help research and protect the birds. Although Ruth's work involves climbing trees and catching the eagles, she has never had a serious injury. She took part in a pioneering expedition in 2007 which involved catching a wild harpy eagle and tagging it with a GPS system. Her job is a real challenge that is only for experts!

Shaun Ellis

Shaun Ellis, 'the wolfman', has spent his life studying wolves and has lived with wild packs for long periods of time. In order to be accepted he acts like them, eats with them and communicates with them by howling. When the beasts eat, Shaun joins in too, but his meat has been specially cooked for him and placed inside a plastic bag! The National Geographic has made a film about Shaun's experiences. *A Man Among Wolves* is about how he managed to integrate himself in a pack and what he learned about wolves during this time. Even though he has been badly scratched on several occasions, he has never been seriously hurt. Nowadays Shaun runs courses on wolf pack management at an animal park in the UK.

Timothy Treadwell

For thirteen seasons Timothy Treadwell, a bear enthusiast and eco-warrior, lived with grizzly bears in the Katmai National Park in Alaska. His aim in living with the bears was to protect them from hunters. As part of this work he set up The Grizzly People, an organisation dedicated to bear protection. Despite the fact that Timothy had a deep understanding of bears, his story ended in tragedy. In 2003, new bears that he and his girlfriend didn't know moved into the area where they were living and killed them both. His story has since been made into a film called *Grizzly Man* which uses some of the scenes that Timothy filmed when he was observing the bears.

Which is right? Don't look at the text!

*He has spent many years **to live/living** with animals in an animal sanctuary.*

*Shaun Ellis has spent his life **studying/to study** wolves.*

b 2.17 Read the texts again and listen. Write the name(s) of the correct person from the text.

Who ... T.Treadwell K.Richardson Shaun Ellis

1 ... has had films made about their lives or the animals they work with?
2 ... works with an animal that is in danger of extinction? Ruth Muñoz
3 ... has taken part in a unique conservation project? Ruth Muñiz
4 ... protected animals from hunters? Timothy Treadwell
5 ... has made a film about a very special animal? Kevin Richardson
6 ... behaves like the animals they work with to be accepted by them? Shaun Ellis

c Work with a partner. Do you think it is a good thing that the people in the texts spend so much time with animals? Why? / Why not? Would you like to do any of their jobs?

4 Grammar

Expressing contrast

a Look at the examples and choose the correct words to complete the rules.

> *Kevin never worries about the lions, **though** you wonder if he should!*
> ***Although** Ruth's work involves catching the eagles, she has never had a serious injury.*
> ***Even though** he has been badly scratched, he has never been seriously hurt.*
> ***Despite** the fact that Timothy had a deep understanding of bears, his story ended in tragedy.*
> *A very special lion survived **in spite of** the problems he faced.*

- We use *though*, *although* and ***despite*** / ***even though*** + subject + verb.
- We use *despite* and ***in spite of*** / ***although*** + noun or a pronoun.
- We sometimes use ***the fact that*** after *despite* and ***in spite of*** / ***even though***.
- We don't usually use ***although*** / ***though*** at the beginning of a sentence.

Grammar reference: page 135

Get it right!

Despite **is not followed by** ***of.***

✓ *She was tired despite the fact that she had gone to bed early.*

✗ *She was tired despite ~~of~~ the fact that she had gone to bed early.*

b Choose the correct words to complete the sentences.

1 *In spite of* / *Although* his injury, he continued working with wild animals.
2 *Even though* / *Despite* she doesn't really like animals, she always watches nature programmes on TV.
3 She was tired all day *despite* / *even though* the fact that she had gone to bed early.
4 *Although* / *Despite* he loved animals, he continued to eat meat.
5 The eagle died, *in spite of* / *even though* he was treated by the team.

c Make one sentence from two. Change the sentence structure when necessary.

1 She visited the sanctuary. She's scared of crocodiles. (even though)
She visited the sanctuary even though she's scared of crocodiles.
2 He woke up at 6am. His alarm was set for 8am. (although)
3 He's never been bitten. He works with snakes. (despite the fact that)
4 He was determined to film the lions. It was very dangerous. (in spite of the fact that)
5 I work in the same zoo as my friend. I hardly ever see her. (though)
6 She wants to have a pet monkey. It's not recommended. (even though)

d Complete the sentences so they are true for you, then compare your answers with a partner.

1 Despite the fact that it's expensive, one day I would love to …
2 Even though it was really difficult, I …
3 In ten years' time I hope to … although I know …
4 In spite of the fact that it's not very good for me, I …

5 Vocabulary Physical habits

a 2.18 Match the words with the pictures. Then listen and check.

1 blink 2 burp 3 chew 4 hiccup 5 rub 6 scratch 7 sneeze 8 yawn

b 2.19 Listen and number the sounds in the order you hear them.

1 sneezing

hiccuping chewing burping yawning scratching sneezing

c Choose the correct word to complete the sentences.

1 In some countries it's polite to *burp* / *chew* after a meal.
2 She was so tired she *blinked* / *rubbed* her eyes and made them red.
3 He was *scratched* / *rubbed* by a cat and had to go to hospital.
4 Watching lions *rub* / *chew* the meat was quite a scary sight.
5 When I'm tired I can't stop *burping* / *yawning*.
6 Looking into the sun always makes me *blink* / *hiccup*.

FUNDACIÓ MONA Centre de Recuperació de Primats

Get it right!

We never use the auxiliary verb *be* with *agree* or *disagree*.

✓ *I agree that wild animals should never be kept as pets.*

✗ *I ~~am~~ agree that wild animals should never be kept as pets.*

6 Listen

a 2.20 Listen to Miranda's presentation about a primate sanctuary. Number the pictures in the order you hear them.

b 2.20 Listen again. Choose the correct answer: A, B or C.

1 Who runs the MONA Foundation?
A volunteers **B** a business **C** the government

2 In which part of Spain is the MONA Foundation?
A north-west **B** north-east **C** south-west

3 Which of these 'jobs' for primates does Miranda not mention?
A actors **B** models **C** babysitters

4 Why do people tend to abandon pet primates?
A because they destroy their homes
B because they get bored with them
C because they kill other pets

5 How are new primates introduced to the others in the group at MONA?
A quickly **B** gradually **C** they are always kept separately

6 What did Miranda do at the end of her visit to the MONA Foundation?
A she fed a monkey **B** she became a volunteer
C she gave money to the foundation

c Work with a partner. Ask and answer the questions.

1 Have you ever visited an animal sanctuary?
2 Which animals do you think need the most protection from humans?
3 Would you like to volunteer to work with animals? Why? / Why not?

7 Pronunciation DVD

Pronunciation of *ea*

a 2.21 The same letters can often be pronounced in different ways. Listen to the pronunciation of the letters *ea* in these words.

/iː/ beast /e/ head /eɪ/ break /ɪə/ year

b 2.22 Copy the table and put the words in the box in the correct column, then listen and check.

steak hear teach bread
seal cheat breath weather

/iː/	/e/	/eɪ/	/ɪə/
beast	head	break	year

c 2.23 Choose the word with a different vowel sound. Then listen, check your answers and repeat.

1	ready	real	read *(past)*
2	dear	meat	meal
3	breathe	mean	dead
4	clean	near	clear
5	sweat	reach	beach
6	dream	team	fear

d Write the words in Exercise 7c in the table in Exercise 7b.

8 Grammar

Reflexive pronouns and *each other*

a Look at the examples and underline the reflexive pronouns.

Some of the monkeys hurt themselves.
He only liked being by himself.
There's space for them to relax and play with each other.

Choose the correct words to complete the rules.

- Reflexive pronouns and *each other* always come **before** / **after** the verb. They can be the direct or indirect object of the verb or they can follow a preposition.
- We use a reflexive pronoun when the person or thing we are referring to is also the **subject** / **object** of the verb.
- We use *each other* for an action which each person in a pair or group does to the other(s) in the group.

Grammar reference: page 135 and 136

b Copy and complete the table with the reflexive pronouns.

singular	m…	yourself	him… / herself / itself
plural	ourselves	your…	themselves

c Complete the sentences with a reflexive pronoun or *each other*.

1 People who work too hard can make … ill.
2 He's so selfish, he only thinks about … .
3 Anne and Nicola see … twice a week.
4 I didn't know him, so when we met … for the first time we both introduced … .
5 Friends often send … emails or messages to say happy birthday.

d Complete the sentences with a verb from the box in its correct form and a reflexive pronoun.

look at   scratch   behave   defend   enjoy   blame

1 I really … on holiday this summer, I had a great time!
2 The head teacher told them to … or they wouldn't be able to go to the end-of-year party.
3 We … because we were covered in mosquito bites and didn't have any cream.
4 Most animals try to … when they are in danger.
5 She's so vain. She's always … in the mirror.
6 I try not to … for the accident, because it wasn't really my fault.

Interaction 5 DVD

Challenging someone's ideas

a 2.24 Listen to Anna and Emily discussing the treatment of circus animals. Which animals do they mention?

b 2.24 Listen again and choose the word you hear.

1 You're not *serious / crazy*, are you?
2 Do you really *mean / think* that?
3 I can't believe what I'm *seeing / hearing*!
4 Have you considered the *fact / detail* that …?
5 Don't change the *subject / topic*.
6 You have to look at it from both *angles / sides*.
7 I guess I can *understand / see* your point.

c 2.25 Turn to page 124. Listen to the sentences and repeat them. Practise challenging other people's ideas using rising intonation and expressing strong opinions with falling intonation.

d Work with a partner.
Student A: Turn to page 127.
Student B: Turn to page 129.

Culture Vulture

The RSPCA (Royal Society for the Prevention of Cruelty to Animals), set up in 1824, is one of the biggest animal charities in the world. Are there any similar organisations in your country? Do you think these organisations are important?

Portfolio 5 An opinion essay

a A group of students have recently had a class discussion about whether or not wild animals should ever be kept as pets. Read their notes on the topic. Which ones do you agree with?

Nobody should keep wild animals as domestic pets

Agree
- can be illegal
- a home usually doesn't have enough space for a wild animal
- animals grow!
- will the animal be happy away from its natural surroundings?

Disagree
- can be original and fun!
- if you love them, why not?
- for some people, the animal is their passion, an important part of their lives.

b Read Simon's essay and choose the ideas from Exercise a that he mentions.

Nobody should keep wild animals as domestic pets

1 Nowadays it seems to be in fashion to keep wild animals as pets. Monkeys, snakes, lizards, endangered birds and even tigers are sold, often illegally, as pets. In spite of the fact that many people are aware of the problems of keeping wild animals as pets, the trend is increasing and it's easier than ever to buy exotic pets online, and keep them in your home.

2 In my view, despite the fact that they can be very cute, wild animals should never be kept as pets. Wild animals need to be in their own habitat and usually they are happier in the company of other animals, where they can play with each other, rather than in the company of humans. Even though they *can* live in a cage on their own, we must take into account that in these circumstances they simply don't have the space they need in order to develop naturally.

3 However, on the other hand, many people think that it's fine to have wild animals at home. These people often think that they themselves can give the animal love and care that they won't find in the wild. For many exotic pet owners, the animals are their passion. In reality they often find that as the animal grows they cause chaos and destruction, and the animals are often abandoned or given away to an animal sanctuary.

4 To conclude, I strongly believe that the laws should be stricter and that it should be totally illegal to keep any wild animals as domestic pets. In my opinion it's simply not fair on the poor animals!

c Read the essay again. Match the paragraphs with the functions.

A Explain why you agree or disagree
B Conclude with your opinion and/or a suggestion
C Give some contrasting information
D Introduce the topic

d Now write an essay to give your opinion on one of the topics below, or a topic of your choice. Choose something you feel strongly about.

- Foxhunting / bullfighting / dog racing / an animal event from your country should be banned.
- Looking after a pet is a good experience for a young child.
- It's more important to support a charity that works with people, than one that works with animals.
- English is a useful communication tool.

Make sure you:
- make notes before you start writing
- organise your paragraphs as in Exercise c
- give reasons why you agree/disagree with something
- include phrases to give your opinion

e Work with a partner. Read each other's essays. Do you agree or disagree with their ideas?

I'm Like a Bird

1 Song

a Work with a partner. Look at the pictures. Who loves who in each picture? Give examples of songs in English that could match pictures A–D.

A 

B 

C 

D 

b 2.26 Listen to the first verse and chorus of the song. Which picture in Exercise 1a best matches the song's theme?

c 2.27 Listen to the first verse of the song again and put the lines in the correct order.

Though my love is true
That I won't ever change
You're lovely but it's not for sure
Though my love is rare
You'll never ever fade
You're beautiful, that's for sure

d 2.28 Complete the end of the song with the words in the box. Then listen and check your answers.

tears tell goodbye through
years scared well me

Your faith in me brings me to 1 …
Even after all these 2 …
And it pains me so much to 3 …
That you don't know me that 4 …
And though my love is rare
Though my love is true

It's not that I wanna say 5 …
It's just that every time you try to tell me that
you love 6 …
Each and every single day I know
I'm going to have to eventually give you away
And though my love is rare
And though my love is true
Hey I'm just 7 …
That we may fall 8 …

e 2.29 Listen to the whole song again. Which is the best summary of the song in your opinion? Why?

1 The singer is in love with the person she is singing to, but she doesn't want to continue the relationship because she is frightened that it won't work out.
2 The singer isn't in love with the person she is singing to and is trying to get out of the relationship without hurting the other person.
3 The singer is confused about what she wants in life. She doesn't have any roots and doesn't want a committed relationship with anybody.

2 Sound check

a 2.30 Listen to the chorus of the song and write the stressed words.

I'm like a bird, I'll only fly away (four words)
I don't know where my soul is, I don't know where my home is (four words)
(and baby all I need for you to know is) (three words)

b 2.31 Read and sing the chorus as you listen. Copy the intonation of the stressed words.

I'm like a bird, I'll only fly away
I don't know where my soul is, I don't know where my home is
(and baby all I need for you to know is)
I'm like a bird, I'll only fly away
I don't know where my soul is, I don't know where my home is
(and baby all I need for you to know is)

African

Latin

3 Musical notes

Music around the world

NELLY FURTADO

Nelly Furtado was born in Canada, but her parents are immigrants from the Azores, which is part of Portugal. She grew up in Victoria, British Columbia, Canada with a lot of Hindi and Punjabi-speaking friends. Nelly sings both international pop music and Latin music. She sings in English, Portuguese, Spanish and Hindi.

Asian

Get it right!

We use the auxiliary verb *be* before *born*.
✓ *Nelly Furtado was born in Canada.*
✗ *~~Nelly Furtado born~~ in Canada.*

a 2.32 Listen and write the types of music in the order you hear them.

African Asian Europop Latin

1 … 2 … 3 … 4 …

b Work in a group. Ask and answer the questions.

1 Which types of music from Exercise 3a are popular in your country?
2 Do you listen to music from different countries? Which ones?
3 Which musicians in your country sing/play different types of music? Do any musicians sing in more than one language?

Euro pop

6 Take action

Future review
Future perfect and future perfect continuous
Vocabulary: Campaigning; Phrasal verbs with *take*
Interaction 6: Persuading people to do things

1 Vocabulary Campaigning

a 2.33 Match the words with the definitions. Then listen and check.

1 campaign **2** charity **3** flyer
4 make a donation **5** raise awareness
6 raise money **7** support **8** voluntary work

A different activities to achieve a specific aim
B to increase people's knowledge about something
C an organisation that helps people, animals, etc.
D to agree with an idea, or give help to a group or a person
E to give money to an organisation
F a piece of paper with information about an event or organisation on it
G to make money for an organisation
H unpaid work to help a group or individual

Check it out!

- We often add *-er* or *-or* to a word to make a noun for a person.
  campaign → campaign**er** visit → visit**or**

b Complete the sentences with words from Exercise 1a.

1 He wants to work for a … after university.
2 She gave me a concert … in the town centre.
3 We are going to ask the headteacher to … our campaign for less homework.
4 He gave a talk to raise … about using plastic bags.
5 Let's try to … some money for the sports centre.
6 Would you like to … a donation to our school trip fund?

c Do you know any more campaign words? Write them in your Workbook (page 119 Exercise 1).

d Work with a partner. Ask and answer the questions below, and ask follow-up questions.

1 Do you support any charities? Which one(s)?
2 Have you ever raised money for anything? What for? What did you do?

2 Listen

a Work with a partner. What is there for teenagers to do in your town? Do you think there are enough places for young people to meet?

b 2.34 Listen to an interview with Liz Shepherd. What is she campaigning for? Has the campaign been successful?

c 2.34 Listen again. Are the sentences *right* (✓) or *wrong* (✗)? Correct the wrong sentences.

1 Liz's home town is an awful place to live.
2 The police often ask teenagers to stop hanging about in the street.
3 A TV programme has given money to the campaign.
4 The town council is supporting the café.
5 Customers can play pool in Barcode.
6 Barcode is open from 5.30pm at the weekend.

d Work in a group. Ask and answer the questions.

1 Would you like to go to a youth café? Why? / Why not?
2 Are there any similar places in your town? Do you think there should be?

Culture Vulture

Did you know that in Britain there is an event called *Red Nose Day* to raise money for charities in Africa and the UK? In 2011 people donated over £75 million to *Red Nose Day* in one night. What are the most popular charities in your country? Are there any special charity days?

3 Grammar Future review

a Look at the examples and choose the correct words to complete the rules.

We're ***opening*** *the café in October.*
We ***'re going to see*** *it later this week to get some ideas.*
*I'****ll get*** *you one, if you like.*
And what exactly ***will*** *the youth café* ***look*** *like?*
*Hopefully in a few months we'****ll be chilling out*** *in our own space.*
So when ***will*** *you* ***be opening*** *your café, do you think?*
It's ***going to be*** *absolutely amazing.*

We use …

- the present continuous for **predictions about / arrangements in** the future.
- *will* and *going to* for **predictions about / arrangements** in the future.
- ***will / going to*** for future plans that are already decided.
- ***will / going to*** for decisions made at the time of speaking (e.g. offers).
- the future continuous for things that will **finish / be in progress** around a specific time in the future.
- the future continuous for future events that **are arranged / are not arranged**.

Grammar reference: page 133

b 2.35 Joe and Kerry are going to a music festival. Choose the correct words. Then listen and check your answers.

Kerry: So, do you know who [1]*you will / you're going to* see yet?
Joe: I've decided on a few things. [2]*I'll go / I'm going to* see Bloc Party on Friday at 3 o'clock.
Kerry: Oh, my train gets in at 3.30pm, so I [3]*won't make / won't be making* that. I'm still not sure about what to do on Friday.
Joe: On the website it says Arcade Fire [4]*will perform / will be performing* on the Friday. [5]*I'll / I'm going to* check again for you if you like.
Kerry: OK. [6]*I'll / I'm going to* meet Lena and Molly at lunchtime though.
Joe: What [7]*are you guys going to / will you guys* do on Saturday evening?
Kerry: Jessie J [8]*will sing / will be singing*, so we're going to that! Do you want to come with us?
Joe: Maybe, but Muse [9]*will be playing / will play* at the same time. I think I'd rather see them.

Get it right!

All days of the week and months of the year begin with a capital letter.
✓ *I'm still not sure what to do on Friday.*
✗ *I'm still not sure what to do on ~~friday~~.*

c Complete the sentences so they are true for you, then compare with a partner.

1 At school tomorrow morning we'll be …have math class
2 At the weekend I'm going to …meet up, with my family
3 At 7pm tomorrow I'll probably …studing
4 This time next year I …will be studing

4 Speak

a Work in a group. You are going to plan your ideal youth café. Discuss the questions.

1 Where are you going to open your café?
2 How are you going to raise money for it?
3 Who will the café be for?
4 What furniture and electrical equipment will you get?
5 What activities and events will you be having?
6 What days and times will the café be open?

b Tell the class about the plans for your youth café and listen to the other groups. Which café would be the most fun? Why?

5 Read and listen

a Work with a partner. How many ways of promoting a campaign can you think of? Read the text quickly. How many of your ideas are mentioned?

Battlefront

http://interactive.cambridge.org

Get campaigning with BATTLEFRONT

***Battlefront* is a TV programme which helps 14–21-year-olds turn their ideas for campaigns into reality by using TV, social networking sites and online videos.**

New technology is making it easier than ever for young people to take up campaigning. One campaigner working with *Battlefront* is Aimee Nathan, 17, from London, who will soon have been campaigning for six months. Aimee is trying to stop people using disposable coffee cups. These are non-recyclable due to their plastic covering, so they end up in landfill sites. Aimee worked out that if just 1,000 people bring their own mugs with them when they buy coffee, by the end of a year, one coffee shop will have saved 5.5 tonnes of waste and 125 trees. Highlights of her campaign included appearing on TV and getting a crowd of people, including a famous model, to take their own mugs to a coffee shop. Aimee's Facebook page played a big part in publicising the event.

Another *Battlefront* campaigner, Manpreet Darroch, 19, from Birmingham, became aware of the importance of road safety when several people he knew were killed or injured in road accidents. He was shocked to discover that traffic accidents are the biggest cause of death for 15–19-year-olds worldwide: about 7,000 people under 25 will have lost their lives on the road by the end of next week. Manpreet decided to focus his campaign on the danger of crossing the street while listening to an MP3 player. He has used Twitter in his campaign, spoken at political meetings and made a video for the *Battlefront* website. He is now hoping to work with musicians to make his message go viral!

Aimee's successful coffee cup stunt

Manpreet appearing on a local TV programme

So how can you get your campaign to take off?

Have a clear message
Keep your message nice and simple, like Manpreet's: 'Tune into Traffic'.

Accept offers
If anybody offers you a hand, take them up on it! You'll need extra help for things like putting up posters and giving out flyers.

Get celebrities on board
Aimee wanted Lady Gaga to take part in her campaign because celebrities can help a campaign become popular.

Organise a stunt
A stunt is an unusual event to attract attention. Aimee covered Trafalgar Square in London with 'a sea of coffee cups', which the public was invited to take away.

Be persistent
Campaigns take time, so don't give up, keep going! Your family and friends will be supporting you.

BATTLEFRONT
The campaigns will soon be ending on TV, but they won't have finished online!

Get it right!

We use the preposition *in* with *take part*.

✓ *Aimee wanted Lady Gaga to take part in her campaign.*
✗ *Aimee wanted Lady Gaga to ~~take part on~~ her campaign.*
✗ *Aimee wanted Lady Gaga to ~~take part of~~ her campaign.*

b 2.36 Read the text again and listen. Are the sentences *right* (✓), *wrong* (✗) or *doesn't say* (–)?

1 Young people find it easier to campaign nowadays.
2 Hundreds of young people campaign with *Battlefront*.
3 Aimee wants people to use their own coffee cups to save money.
4 More young people die in traffic accidents than due to any other cause.
5 Lady Gaga helped Aimee with her campaign.
6 *Battlefront* campaigns usually finish in a short time.

c Work with a partner. Ask and answer the questions.

1 Do you think Aimee's and Manpreet's causes are good ones? Why? / Why not?
2 Would you be interested in taking part in a TV programme like *Battlefront*? Why? / Why not?
3 What would you raise money for if you were campaigning? How would you campaign?

6 Grammar

Future perfect and future perfect continuous

a Look at the examples and choose the correct words to complete the rules.

Future perfect

By the end of a year, we ***will have saved*** *5.5 tonnes of waste and 125 trees.*

About 7,000 people under 25 ***will have lost*** *their lives on the road.*

The campaigns ***won't have finished*** *online.*

Future perfect continuous

Aimee ***will*** *soon* ***have been campaigning*** *for six months.*

- We use the future perfect to show that an action will take place **before** / **after** a certain time in the future.
- The action **will** / **won't** be completed before this later time.
- We use the future perfect continuous to show that an action will be in progress up to a certain time in the future.
- Often the action **will be completed** / **will still be happening** at this later time.
- We often use these tenses with *by*. *By* + time means '**after** / **not later than** this time'.

Grammar reference: page 134

b Complete the sentences with the future perfect or the future perfect continuous form of the verb.

1. I … (finish) the posters by 5 o'clock.
2. At the end of June I … (learn) Chinese for three years.
3. When will you … (write) your presentation?
4. They … (mend) my bike by Saturday morning.
5. By midnight I … (work) on my essay for six hours without a break!
6. She … (clean up) the mess from the party by the time her parents get home.

Check it out!

- Use *for* for lengths of time.
  We'll have been learning English **for** three years.
  Use *during* for within a period of time.
  The café is open **during** the summer.

c Work with a partner. Take turns to make and answer questions using the words in the box.

Will	we people politicians scientists engineers (other)	find build end invent solve (other)	world poverty a way we can live to be 150 undersea houses cities on another planet (other)	by next year? 2015? 2020? 2050? (other)?

A: *Will scientists have discovered a way we can live to be 150 by 2020?*

B: *I don't think so, but maybe they will by 2030.*

7 Pronunciation DVD

Elision in future forms

a 2.37 Listen to the pronunciation of the strong and weak forms of the sentences.

They're going to buy it now. /gəʊɪŋ tuː/ They're going to buy it now. /gənə/

We will have been there for three years. /wɪl həv biːn/

We'll have been there for three years. /wiːləvbɪn/

b 2.38 Listen and write the number of words in the sentences.

1 … **2** … **3** … **4** … **5** … **6** …

c 2.38 Listen, check your answers, and repeat.

8 Vocabulary

Phrasal verbs with *take*

a 2.39 Look at the examples and match the phrasal verbs with *take* with the definitions. Then listen and check.

1 I think I'm going to **take up** karate at a sports club.
2 I really hope my campaign is going to **take off**!
3 Sometimes it can be difficult to **take in** a lot of information.
4 Thanks for offering to help me. I'll **take** you **up on** it!
5 If you don't like the photo I tagged on Facebook, I'll **take** it **down**.
6 **Take away** this leaflet so you can read it later.
7 I know you're upset, but don't **take** it **out on** me!
8 This project is going to **take up** a lot of my time.

A to understand completely
B to accept somebody's offer
C to start doing a new activity
D to become successful (used for things)
E to treat somebody badly because you are unhappy
F to occupy time or space
G to remove something (general)
H to remove something from a wall or a website

b Complete the sentences with a phrasal verb from Exercise 8a in the correct form.

1 Lots of people are going to the new club. It has really … .
2 Did you … everything he said? There were too many numbers for me!
3 I share a room with my brother but he … all the space!
4 He's going to … capoeira. There's a beginners' class starting next week.
5 When my sister's in a bad mood, she shouts and … it … me!
6 Will you help … the rubbish … after the party?
7 You've put a terrible photo of me on the school website! Can you … it … , please!
8 I think I'll … you … your offer to help me.

c Do you know any more phrasal verbs or expressions with *take*? Write them in your Workbook (page 119 Exercise 1).

d Work with a partner. Ask and answer the questions and give more information.

1 Have you taken up a new activity this year?
2 Have you taken someone up on an offer recently?
3 Which subjects do you find it hard to take in?
4 Has anyone taken out their bad mood on you in the last few days?
5 Can you think of anyone whose career has taken off recently?

Interaction 6 DVD

Persuading people to do things

a 2.40 Danny, Lola and Marcus are planning a campaign to raise money for a new sports centre. Match their initials (*D*, *L* or *M*) to the job(s) they decide to do.

Make a poster
Write to a newspaper
Go on TV
Organise an event

b 2.40 Listen again and match the two parts of the sentences.

1 You'd be good at
2 Well, I really wanted
3 Why don't you
4 You'd be
5 How do you feel about
6 I'm not very good at
7 You're so much better

A great on TV.
B writing the letter?
C speaking in public.
D doing that sort of thing.
E at writing than me.
F to organise the event.
G have a go at making it?

c 2.41 Turn to page 124. Listen to the sentences and repeat them. Practise being persuasive by stressing the adjectives or adverbs.

d Work in a group of three.

Student A: Turn to page 127.
Student B: Turn to page 129.
Student C: Turn to page 131.

Portfolio 6

A report

a Teenagers in your area have been complaining that they have nowhere to go. The council has asked for a report on the existing youth centre so that they can improve it or start a new one. Read the report and put paragraphs A–E in order.

1 D

b Match the underlined phrases in the report with their functions.

A explaining the purpose of the report
B talking about the overall impression
C stating the biggest problem
D giving ideas for improvements (three expressions)
E concluding or summarising

Check it out!

- Start with the *purpose* and end with the *conclusion*.
- Use *formal language*.
- Use *headings* for each section of the report.
- Have a maximum of five or six *paragraphs*.

c We often use formal language in reports. Find formal ways of saying the following in the text.

1 I think we should pay the people who work in the centre more.
2 I think we need things to do and places to sit.
3 We need a way of playing or listening to music so we need sound equipment.

Report on our youth centre

A ...
Our youth centre today
[1]In general, our youth centre creates a good impression. It is in a very central location in the town and has plenty of space for young people to meet. There is a kitchen and some drinks machines and the building is being redecorated. By the end of next month the council will have redecorated the building and installed new pool tables.

B ...
Conclusion
[2]To sum up, our youth centre has a lot of potential, but we should spend more money on it and think about the kinds of activities young people really want to take part in.

C ...
Recommendations
[3]The main drawback is that the youth centre does not open for very long. It is closed most weekends and in the school holidays, when this is precisely the time it should be open. [4]I would recommend more funding of staff for the centre.

D ...
Purpose
There have been a lot of complaints about the youth centre in our town. [5]The aim of this report is to assess the current situation and to make suggestions for improving the centre.

E ...
Further suggestions
[6]I would also suggest having more types of games in the centre and some sofas to provide more seating. Many people would like to be able to play or listen to music in the centre, so sound equipment [7]would be useful.

d Your local council wants to improve facilities in your town for young people. Write a formal report about how one of the places in the box can be made more appealing to teenagers. You can make recommendations.

a sports centre   a museum   an arts centre   a youth centre / café

Make sure you include:
- paragraph headings
- some of the phrases in Exercise b
- phrases with *would* for your recommendations

e Read your partner's report. Is it organised in a logical way? Is the language formal enough?

1

The red squirrel is our only native British squirrel but is at serious risk of extinction if population numbers continue to decline. The main cause of this decline is competition with the American grey squirrel, an introduced species which is larger than the red and better able to survive harsh weather and occasional food shortages. It also breeds more successfully and quickly out-competes its red cousin for food.

Cumbria is one of the few counties in the country where red squirrels can still be seen and the Save our Squirrels (SOS) project is working to protect and increase numbers. The project supports networks of volunteers who assist with population surveys and monitoring. They provide education programmes and web-based teaching materials for schools, and work to raise the profile of the red squirrel through educational walks, talks and events for the wider community, their website and local media.

2

The town of Egremont in Cumbria celebrates crab apple time with a unique day of quirky events that are topped off with the World Gurning Championships.

Contestants put their heads through a horse collar and have a set time in which to contort their faces in the scariest, most grotesque, silliest expression possible. The person who gets the most applause for pulling an ugly face wins!

The event attracts camera crews from all over the world. The Egremont Crab Fair dates back to 1267 to celebrate the time when the local Lord of the Manor wheeled a cart of crab apples through the village of Egremont as a goodwill gesture to the poor.

Crab apples have a sharp taste and it is said the gurning competition originates from the faces the locals made when they bit into the sour apples.

3

Love your Lakes: a campaign to get phosphates out of the Lake District

Tourism is the lifeblood of an area as ruggedly beautiful as the Lake District, with its mountains, wooded valleys and lakes attracting eight million visitors a year. The closure of the lakes would hit local businesses badly. However due to a sudden explosion of blue-green algae in the Lakes, many have recently been closed for recreational use.

A dynamic campaign, Love Your Lakes, has been set up to tackle one significant cause of this algae problem: phosphates in laundry and dishwashing detergents.

The National Lottery-funded campaign is encouraging locals, businesses and visitors to switch to phosphate-free laundry and dishwasher products.

'We've mail-shotted 5,000 homes with an eye-catching leaflet to raise awareness and provide information on phosphate-free products,' says Amy McLoughlin, sustainable tourism adviser for Nurture Lakeland. The charity has also worked with 250 accommodation-providers to help them reduce their impact, and attended numerous community events and co-ordinated projects with local schools.

4

Cumbria Soaring club

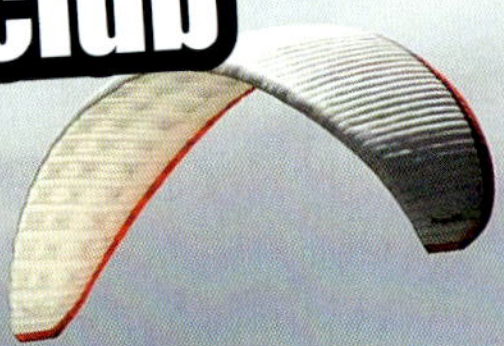

JOIN US

New members of the Cumbria Soaring Club are very welcome. Normally we would expect you to have a Club Pilot rating from the BHPA before you join the club. We don't teach you to fly; that's the job of the flying school - details of which can be found on the links page. We can help you through the transition from flying school to flying at our sites. During the flying season, we run coaching days for low airtime pilots.

RULES OF FLYING IN THE LAKES

- All land in the Lakes is owned by someone
- Valley land is valuable. Treat it with care and stick to the footpaths
- The walls have taken centuries to evolve. They take a lot of work to rebuild. Don't climb over them.
- Lambing time is the main time in the year when the farmer makes his money - don't fly if a site is closed
- There are some rare birds nesting in the Lakes – keep away from nesting sites

MEMBERSHIP FEES

The costs of membership are as follows:
£20 for a 'Full' member
£22 for 'Family Membership' (2 people - partners/spouse/father and daughter/mother and son etc.)
Please make cheques payable to 'Cumbria Soaring Club'.
Please note - you must be a member of the British Hang Gliding and Paragliding Association (BHPA) before you join the CSC.

1 Culture UK: Cumbria

a Look at the information about Cumbria and answer the questions.

1. What is the main industry in the Lake District (the large national park in Cumbria)?
2. What is one of the main causes of algae in the lakes?
3. Why are American grey squirrels a threat to native red squirrels?
4. What can volunteers do to help the SOS project?
5. Why shouldn't you climb over walls in the Lake District?
6. What is the difference in price per person between a Cumbria Soaring Club family member fee and a full member fee?
7. How can you win the World Gurning Championship?
8. What is the possible connection between crab apples and 'gurning'?

b Copy and complete the crossword and find the mystery phrase.

1. To twist into an unnatural shape. (text 2)
2. A sport where you fly in the sky. (text 4)
3. To produce young animals. (text 1)
4. A piece of paper with information on it. (text 3)
5. The period when sheep give birth. (text 4)
6. Unusual in an interesting way. (text 2)
7. A place where birds lay eggs. (text 4)
8. Most frightening. (text 2)

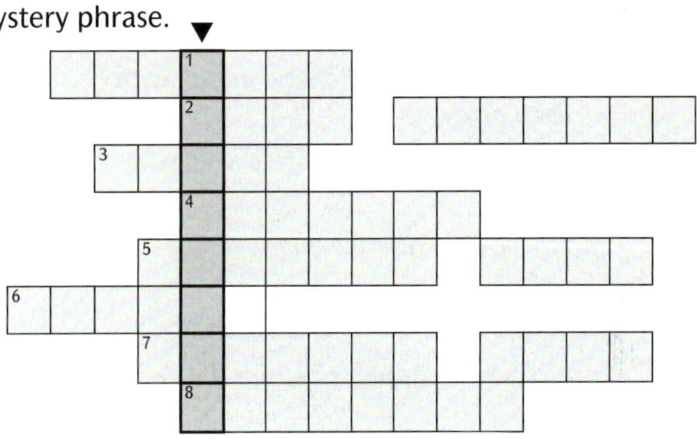

c Work with a partner. Which areas in your country are national parks? What can you do there? Are there any threats to these areas? If so, what?

2 Your noticeboard

A local campaign

a Work in a group. Plan a campaign for your town/area. Think about:

- the type of campaign
- the name of the campaign
- why the issue is important
- ways of getting publicity for the campaign
- how to get people involved in the campaign
- ways of raising money

b Make a plan of action for the campaign. Include the information from Exercise 2a and pictures or photos if possible.

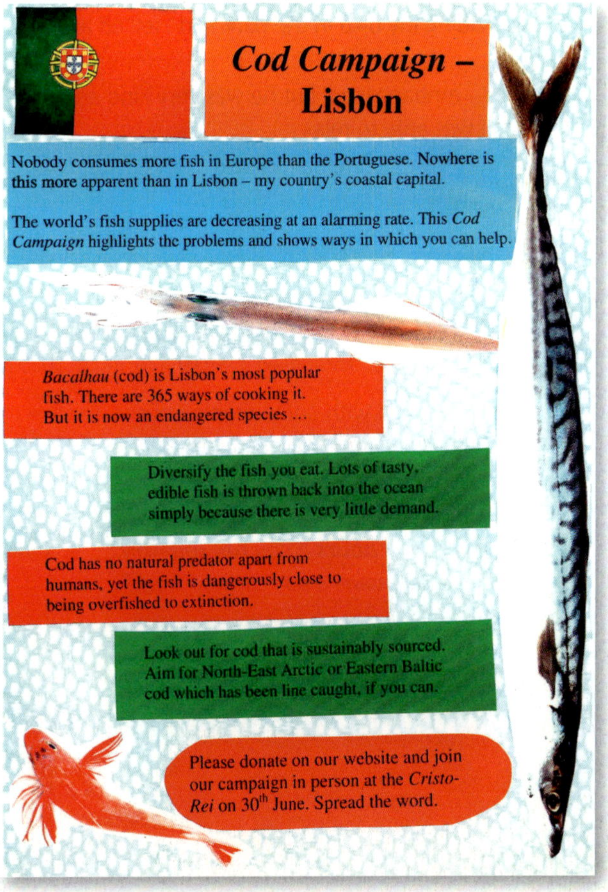

Get it right! 5 and 6

Common errors

1 Reflexive pronouns

Remember:

Some verbs take a reflexive pronoun when the subject of the verb is also the object:

enjoy, scratch, behave, hurt, look at

✓ *I* ***enjoyed myself*** *at the wedding.*

Some verbs usually take *each other* as their object:

get on with, meet, get in touch with, get to know

✓ *My sister and I don't always* ***get on with each other****.*

Some verbs do not usually take a reflexive pronoun:

relax, feel, apologise, reproduce, resist

✓ *At weekends I like to* ***relax****.*

✗ *At weekends I like to relax ~~myself~~.*

a Complete the sentences with a reflexive pronoun, *each other* or – (nothing).

1 Rory and I go to the same school but we didn't get to know … until the summer.
2 I was riding my bike in the park and I fell off and hurt … .
3 I felt … embarrassed, but he was very kind and soon I was able to relax … .
4 We went to the cinema the next weekend and we really enjoyed … .
5 I think we will meet … again next Saturday.

2 *how much* or *how many*?

Use *How much* with uncountable nouns:

✓ ***How much time*** *do you need?*

✗ *How ~~many time~~ do you need?*

Use *How many* with countable nouns:

✓ ***How many hours*** *a day can you work?*

✗ *How ~~much hours~~ a day can you work?*

a Read the interview with a campaigner and find four mistakes. Correct them.

A: So, Jane, how much months have you been campaigning?

B: We've been campaigning for five months.

A: And how much money have you raised in that time?

B: By March, we will have reached our target!

A: How much people have helped you with your campaign?

B: We've had a lot of help. It's amazing how many time people have devoted to the campaign, and how much money we've raised. I'm just so happy when I think how much animals we will have saved!

b 2.42 Listen and check your answers.

3 Say it right!

/aʊ/ in the letters 'ou' and 'ow'

a 2.43 We often pronounce the letters 'ou' and 'ow' with the sound /aʊ/. Listen to the /aʊ/ sounds in the example then repeat.

They found the crowd shouting in the south of the town.

b 2.44 Which word in each group doesn't have the /aʊ/ sound? Listen and check.

1 sound ground group shout
2 out about mouse could
3 show brown house how
4 owl cousin cow crown
5 found mouth town touch

Review 5 and 6

1 Grammar

a Choose the best ending for the sentences: A or B.

1 We decided to go to the coast despite
A the dark clouds in the sky.
B the fact that dark clouds in the sky.

2 My Dad bought us a dog even though
A not liking them. **B** he doesn't like them.

3 I'm going to save up for a video camera although
A the expense. **B** it's very expensive.

4 She managed to get into university in spite of
A her poor marks. **B** she got poor marks.

5 He speaks excellent Russian in spite of
A he's never been to Russia.
B never having been to Russia.

b Complete the sentences with the correct reflexive pronoun, *each other*, or nothing.

1 Tom and Mark used to talk a lot in class, but now they behave … .
2 We've known … since we were six.
3 I washed … , got changed, and rushed out.
4 At exam time she always gets stressed and makes … ill.
5 My mother and my aunt phone … every Sunday.
6 Sit down, relax … and have a cool drink.

c Choose the correct form of the verb.

Alex: So, what are your plans for next year?
Sami: 1 *I'm going to apply / I apply* to university, but first 2 *I'm going / I'll go* to visit my cousins in Australia.
Alex: Cool! When 3 *will you go / are you going* there?
Sami: I think 4 *I'll go / I go* in April.
Alex: Oh, 5 *I'll be travelling / I'll travel* in Indonesia then - we could meet up!
Sami: Well, 6 *I'm working / I'll be working* in a café in Sydney and 7 *I probably won't have / I probably won't be having* enough money to get to Indonesia.
Alex: That's OK. 8 *I'll get / I'm getting* a cheap ticket and come and see you.

d Complete the sentences with the future perfect or future perfect continuous form of the verbs.

run work not finish close

1 Hurry up, or the shop … by the time we get there.
2 By next year my grandfather … in the same factory for forty years.
3 I'm too tired to concentrate. I … my homework by tomorrow morning.

2 Vocabulary

a Complete the sentences with animal kingdom vocabulary.

1 Animals have to fight for … in the wild.
2 … animals which may not exist soon.
3 Some people keep birds or small animals in a … .
4 An animal's … is where it usually lives.
5 If an animal lets you touch it, it is … .
6 A … is a safe place for animals and birds to live.
7 A … is a similar group of animals.

b Use the words in the box to answer the questions.

scratch yawn sneeze burp
blink rub chew hiccup

What do people (sometimes) do …
1 when the sun is in their eyes?
2 if they have an itch?
3 when they are tired?
4 before they swallow food?
5 if their arm hurts?
6 if they have air in their stomach?
7 if they eat or drink too quickly?
8 when they have a cold?

c Complete the sentences by changing the word in brackets to another word in the same word family.

1 My sister's going to do some … (volunteer) work in the holidays.
2 Leonardo Di Caprio made a big … (donate) to the NGO.
3 I've been an active … (campaign) for three years.
4 There's a talk this evening to raise … (aware) about homelessness.
5 Ben's going to work for an educational … (organise).
6 With this .... (fly) you can get in for free.

d Replace the underlined words with a phrasal verb with *take* in the correct form.

1 I'm going to <u>start</u> skiing next winter.
2 His career has really <u>become successful</u> recently.
3 Please <u>delete</u> that photo of me and Jon from your album. We're not friends any more.
4 I had to stop doing gymnastics. It was <u>using</u> too much time.
5 I'm starving. I'll <u>accept</u> that offer of a sandwich.
6 I know your team lost, but don't <u>get annoyed with</u> me.

7 Self-image

Passive review
***have/get* something done**
Vocabulary: Describing clothes and materials; Body idioms
Interaction 7: Comparing two photos

1 Read and listen

a Look at the pictures. What kind of people do you think the bedrooms belong to? What kind of music do they like? What hobbies do they have? Read the text quickly and check your answers.

What your taste says about you

Is your personality exposed to the world by your possessions? Sam Gosling, a psychologist at the University of Texas at Austin, thinks so. [1] … He says he can usually tell what kind of person uses the space just by looking at their things.

Sensitive people, for example, like dark, moody colours. They will often have posters of romantic films and will play sad music. Extroverts love bright colours and need constant stimulation from other people, action films, or video games.

We applied interpretations from Gosling's book, *Snoop: What Your Stuff Says About You*, to two volunteers. They both agreed that the descriptions matched their personalities pretty well.

Julia's room is full of books and magazines, and is very colourful. There is a vibrant pink chair, an orange and yellow spotted carpet and pink flowers on the wall above the bed.

Open people often have lots of books, posters and CDs etc. in their rooms, and they love discovering new things. [2] …

In Frank's room everything has been neatly organised and looks a bit impersonal. A few prizes from tennis competitions can be seen on the wall, and the colours are mainly neutral: white, beige and green.

Conscientious people like rules and order, so they are very tidy. [3] …

Another fascinating study, conducted by Heriot-Watt University in Edinburgh, shows a clear connection between musical taste and personality. According to the study, indie music listeners are creative, but not very hard-working; while lovers of pop music are hard-working, but not very creative. It also found that both jazz and classical music lovers are innovative and self-confident. [4] …

Perhaps the most common indicator of taste is what we wear. If you wear bright colours and flowery patterns, it's a signal that you don't want to be part of the crowd. People who like old clothes can look as if they don't care enough to try and look smart. [5] … Casual dressers, for example those who favour classic white T-shirts, are regarded as being relaxed and sincere. The drawback is that always dressing in this way will be seen as boring by some people. [6] …

Which is right? Don't look at the text!
Perhaps the most common indicator of taste is what we ***use/wear/dress***. (regarding clothes)

b Read the text again and complete it with sentences A–F.

A Similarly, Goth or punk clothes can give the impression that the wearers are angry or depressed.
B They are often interested in art and likely to be creative themselves.
C So be careful about what you buy, listen to or wear: these things send out strong messages about your personality!
D They are very concerned with getting work done on time and their taste in art is traditional, or even old-fashioned.
E He has been studying people's things and how they are arranged in their offices, cars or bedrooms.
F However, classical music fans are introverts, whereas jazz fans are extroverts, like rap lovers.

c 3.2 Read the text again and listen. Check your answers to Exercise 1b.

d Work in a group. Ask and answer the questions.

1. Do you agree with Sam Gosling that you can tell a lot about a person from their bedroom? Why? / Why not?
2. What kind of music do you like? What do you think this says about your personality?
3. Do you think that the way you dress is important? What do you think clothes say about personality?

2 Vocabulary

Describing clothes and materials

a 3.3 Copy the table and put the words in the correct column. Then listen and check.

1 baggy **2** checked **3** flowery **4** plain **5** scruffy **6** short-sleeved **7** spotted **8** striped **9** tight **10** trendy

Pattern	Opinion	Size and shape

b Do you know any more words for describing clothes and materials? Write them in the table in your Workbook (page 120 Exercise 1).

c 3.4 Listen and choose the correct adjectives.

1 The T-shirt is too *flowery / plain*.
2 Bryan doesn't look *scruffy / trendy*.
3 The curtains are *spotted / striped*.
4 Steph doesn't think the jacket is *tight / trendy*.
5 The cushion they buy is *striped / checked*.
6 The jeans are *baggy / tight*.

Check it out!

- Use *-ish* and *-y* if you're not sure exactly what colour something is.
  It's **green-ish**.
  It's **greeny-blue**/**bluey-green**.

d Work in a group. Describe the following things using the adjectives in Exercise 2a. Can the group guess what you are describing?

- your favourite item of clothing
- an object in your room
- a present you got for your birthday
- an item of clothing belonging to someone in your family

Get it right!

We never make adjectives plural. Do not add an 's'.
✓ *The jeans are tight.*
✗ *The jeans are ~~tights.~~*

3 Grammar Passive review

a Look at the examples and choose the correct words to complete the rules.

*He has been studying people's things and how they **are arranged**.*
***Is** your personality **exposed** to the world by your possessions?*
*It **has been** neatly **organised**.*
*A few prizes from tennis competitions **can be seen** on the walls.*
*Another fascinating study **was conducted** by Heriot-Watt University.*
*Always dressing in this way **will be taken** as a lack of creativity by some people.*

- In **a passive / an active** sentence the cause of the action (the agent) is often obvious, unknown or unimportant.
- Most tenses have a passive form. We use a form of the verb ***be* / *do*** + past participle.
- We can also use a modal (*will*, *can*, *should*, etc.) + be + **past simple / past participle.**
- If we want to say who or what did the action we add ***with* / *by*** + the agent.

Grammar reference: page 136

b Rewrite the sentences in the passive.

1 Cleaners clean the school every evening.
The school … .
2 The designer showed his collection of clothes at the fashion event.
The new collection of clothes … .
3 The authorities will close the airport because of fog.
The airport … .
4 Designers have used the internet to share ideas for a long time.
The internet … .
5 Men first wore jewellery to bring them luck in battle.
Jewellery … .

c Complete the text with verbs in the active or passive form.

Fashion facts

Perfume [1] … (first, make) by the ancient Egyptians.

The Romans used umbrellas as protection against the sun. Sometimes they [2] … (dye) these in the colours of chariot teams.

In 16th century England, everyone over the age of seven had to wear a hat on Sundays. People without hats [3] … (fine) the equivalent of about £30.

Worldwide, women [4] … (throw away) at least seven times as much clothing as men.

4 Speak

a You have been asked to think of six things which represent teenagers from your country for a time capsule. The things must be about the size of a book, or smaller, and will have recorded explanations of what they are used for. Make your list.

b Work with a partner. Explain your choices and together choose the six most important things from both your lists. Practise the explanations of what the things are used for.

it's used to … it's used for … it has been sold … it was invented … it's bought by …

c Work in a group. Explain your list from Exercise 4b with your partner. Make a final list of six choices as a group.

A: *I think we should send a computer mouse. We spend a lot of time online every day but a computer would be too big for the capsule.*

B: *OK. The explanation could be: this is a small electronic object. It's used to control a computer …*

d Compare your group's final list with the class. Has each group chosen the same things for the time capsule?

5 Listen

a 3.5 Listen to a radio programme about a body art exhibition. Choose the things that the presenter talks to people about.

tattoos

clothes

jewellery

piercings

hairstyles

make-up

b 3.5 Listen again and complete the sentences. You can use words you hear in the listening, or your own words.

1 The Tattoo and Body Art Expo is in … .
2 Gothic jewellery is inspired by … .
3 Red is the most popular … .
4 Rawiri is a Maori from … .
5 Some Maori women have tattoos called *moko*, on their … .
6 If you have a tattoo done, it's very important to think about … .
7 A tattoo is for … .
8 You have to be … to get a tattoo.

c Work with a partner. Ask and answer the questions.

1 Would you like a tattoo, a piercing or dyed hair? Why? / Why not?
2 What do you think influences fashion for body art in your country: celebrities, films, music or other things?
3 What do you think will be fashionable in the future?

Culture Vulture

Did you know that a survey of US Girl Scouts (aged 13–17) found that 75% said fashion was 'really important' to them? How important is fashion to teenagers in your country? Is fashion as important to boys as to girls?

6 Pronunciation DVD

Intrusive /j/, /r/ and /w/

a 3.6 We sometimes add extra sounds between words to make it easier to pronounce them. Listen to the words separately, then together.

body art → body art /j/ here at → here at the Expo /r/ who aren't → people who aren't /w/

b 3.7 Listen and write the sound you hear between the underlined words.

1 They aren't very expensive.
2 She loves drama and music.
3 You open it at the side.
4 I can see it.
5 It's a good photo opportunity.
6 We saw Andrew in the park.

c Follow the /j/ sounds to find a way through the puzzle. You can move up or down ⇕ and left or right ⇔. Work with a partner and say the words.

→ He is here.	She's crazy about rap.	I'm meeting Zara at two.
Zoo animals.	Baby elephants.	That's so easy.
Africa and Asia.	She earns a lot.	In my opinion …
It's too expensive.	You are kind.	Three or four.
So do I.	Here and now.	He isn't coming. ↓

d 3.8 Listen and check your answers.

7 Grammar

have/get something done

a Look at the examples and choose the correct word(s) to complete the rules.

*I **had** my hair **cut** by that hairdresser with the pink hair.*
*You can also **have** your hair **dyed** at the Expo.*
*Sometimes they **have** their lips **coloured** blue.*
*Is **getting** a tattoo **done** very expensive?*

- We use *have/get* + object + past participle when **we do something ourselves / somebody does a service for us**.
- If we want to identify the person who does the service, we use ***by / for***.

Grammar reference: page 136

Check it out!

- It is important to think about who does an action in a sentence.
  I **cut** my hair. = I did it myself
  I **had**/**got** my hair **cut**. = somebody else cut my hair

b Complete the sentences using the verbs and words in brackets.

get / repair get / cut have / build have / deliver have / paint

1 My hair's really long. I must … (it).
2 He's taken his bike to the shop to … (it).
3 Our house is a mess at the moment. My parents … (it).
4 They haven't got a car, so they … (their shopping).
5 My grandparents are going to … (a conservatory).

c Work with a partner. Ask and answer the questions.

1 How often do you get your hair cut?
2 Have you had anything done at the dentist's recently?
3 If you were going to have your bedroom redecorated, what would you have done?
4 Do you know anyone who has had a tattoo done?

8 Vocabulary

Body idioms

a 3.9 Look at the idioms and match them with the definitions. Then listen and check.

1 Can I **be nosy** and have a look?
2 I **set my heart on** going to university in London.
3 Men are often covered in moko **from head to foot**.
4 It **costs an arm and a leg**.
5 Stop complaining. You're being **a** real **pain in the neck**.
6 Oh dear, I **put my foot in it** there! I shouldn't have said that.
7 He's always talking about his good marks. He's so **big-headed**.
8 That can't be true! You'**re pulling my leg**!

A to think you are more important or clever than you really are
B to be very expensive
C to be very interested in other people's business
D all over the body
E to joke with or tease somebody
F to be very annoying
G to want something very much
H to say something by accident which upsets somebody else

b Complete the gaps with an expression from Exercise 8a in the correct form.

1 I've got so much homework, I can't go out. It's … .
2 I shouldn't have mentioned his ex-girlfriend. I think I … .
3 He keeps … because I'm short and my surname is Long.
4 He's so … ! He's always asking me personal questions.
5 She's really … going to that concert. She'll do anything to get a ticket.
6 I can't afford to join the gym now they've put the prices up. It … .
7 She's so … , she never stops talking about how clever she is.
8 We got caught in the rain. I was soaked … .

c Do you have any similar body idioms in your language?

d Work with a partner. Ask and answer the questions.

1 Have you ever put your foot in it with a friend or someone in your family?
2 Who is the nosiest person you know?
3 What do you think costs an arm and a leg?

Interaction 7 DVD

Comparing two pictures

a 3.10 Listen to Jasmine and Luca comparing two photos in an English exam. Who does the task better? Why?

b 3.10 Listen again and choose the sentences you hear.

1 One similarity is that both pictures …
2 They both seem to be of …
3 One big difference is that one picture …
4 It's messy, whereas the other bedroom is very tidy.
5 It looks like it has been cleaned recently.
6 It appears to have been designed by a professional.
7 This room is much messier than the other one.

c 3.11 Turn to page 124. Listen to the sentences and repeat them. Practise using the correct stress in longer sentences.

d Work with a partner.

Turn to page 131.

Portfolio 7

A magazine article

a Read the magazine webpage and choose the best title for the article.

- My lucky leather jacket
- My favourite accessory
- My embarrassing jacket

Fashion First!

http://interactive.cambridge.org

Fashion First: Write it!

Tell us about your favourite possession (an item of clothing or jewellery, a game, a poster, etc)

- Describe it and tell us why it's important to you
- Upload a photo or a drawing of your possession
- More articles will be posted next week

Prizes for the best articles!

http://interactive.cambridge.org

Home | Articles | Blog | Contact

Search

My favourite possession is old, worn and cracked. It's my much-loved biker jacket. It's made of thick black leather and it has a silver zip and a silky red lining. It's a real biker's jacket and it used to belong to my mother when she was young, so it's very old now!

Why do I love my jacket? Because it was my mother's and because it is very practical. You don't need to iron it and you never need to get it cleaned. It keeps me warm and dry, so I wear it all the time, except in the summer. Another thing is that leather jackets never go out of fashion and you can wear them with jeans or with skirts and dresses.

A couple of months ago I was in a café and I left the jacket on the back of my chair by accident. I realised what I had done when I was on the bus and I thought I'd lost it forever. At that moment, a young guy jumped onto the bus, holding my jacket. He had chased me down the road with it! We started chatting and I made a new friend. Now I think of it as my lucky jacket.

b Read the article again and find examples of …

1. physical description of the possession.
2. reasons why the writer likes the possession.
3. a personal story.
4. a question to involve the reader.
5. an interesting first sentence.

Check it out!

- Use interesting *adjectives* and *adverbs*. Try not to repeat the same language, even if you are describing the same object.
  old/worn/cracked/much-loved/lucky + jacket

c Write an article about one of your favourite things for the magazine. Make sure you include:

- adjectives in the description of the possession
- personal feelings, opinions or a story
- an interesting title and first sentence

d Read your partner's article. Does it contain personal details? Does it use descriptive adjectives well?

JAMAICA: Clothes and culture

(1) Jamaican clothing is a fantastic fusion of traditional and western cultures. The Caribbean island's cultural variety is reflected in all aspects of Jamaican life and especially in the clothes that Jamaican people wear. In addition to its rich cultural diversity, Jamaica's tropical climate plays a significant role in defining what people wear.

(2) Traditional clothing

Traditional clothing is made from lightweight materials such as cotton or linen in bright, vibrant colours. Women often wear handmade clothes made from calico, a type of printed cotton cloth with a striped pattern and colourful headscarves. Men opt for jeans or light-coloured trousers, short-sleeved shirts and sometimes a bandana on their heads. The quadrille dress, which is the national costume of Jamaica, is worn for special celebrations and traditional dancing. The cotton dress has a similar pattern to Scottish tartan.

Quadrille dancing in traditional Jamaican dress

(3) Attitude

The carefree attitude of this Caribbean island has undoubtedly influenced Jamaican clothing. Usually bright and colourful, comfortable clothing is a must and lightweight fabrics are favoured over heavy ones. Beachwear is also a significant part of Jamaican attire and Jamaican coastlines are packed with people wearing western-style swimming costumes, shorts and flip-flops.

Casual Jamaican beachwear

(4) Rastafarianism

The Rastafarian movement started in Jamaica, and Rastafarian-inspired clothing, with its characteristic three colours of red, green and gold, is widespread on the island. Rastafarian or Rasta clothing is made from natural materials such as cotton, wool or fibres from the hemp plant.

One immediately recognisable Rasta accessory is the 'rastacap', or 'tam', the knitted hat which is worn over dreadlocks. Rasta clothing is often associated with both fans and musicians of reggae music, such as the legendary Bob Marley.

Legendary Bob Marley covered his dreadlocks with a Tam

(5) Fashion shows

Jamaica holds two prestigious fashion events every year: the Caribbean Fashion Week and Style Week Jamaica. The events attract international designers who come to see the latest trends and styles from the Caribbean. They also give local Jamaican designers a chance to share their talent with the rest of the world. Young designers are also being featured on reality TV shows in Jamaica like *Mission Catwalk*, which aims to discover talented local designers and help them to enter the international world of fashion. Among Jamaica's successful fashion designers is Bob Marley's daughter, Cedella, who has created her own fashion label, *Catch a Fire*, named after one of her father's albums, and whose clothing is also inspired by him.

Fashion designer Cedella Marley (right)

1 Culture World: Jamaica

a Before you read, choose the things you think influence the clothing people wear in Jamaica. Read the article and check your answers.

> hot weather hurricanes
> the world of business
> a variety of cultures
> the Rastafarian movement
> football an easy-going attitude
> supermodels

b Read the article again and answer the questions.

1 Why is Jamaican clothing usually made from light fabrics?
2 Which three types of headwear are mentioned in the text?
3 Which five materials used to make clothes and accessories are mentioned in the text?
4 When do Jamaicans usually wear more traditional clothing?
5 Where can you find many people wearing western clothing?
6 Which colours are associated with Rastafarianism?
7 Which two fashion events are held in Jamaica every year?

c Find the word(s) in the article that mean ...

1 a combination of different things. (Text 1)
2 lively, bright and full of energy. (Text 2)
3 to choose. (Text 2)
4 the typical national dress of a country. (Text 2)
5 a long stage where models walk in a fashion show. (Text 5)

d Work with a partner. Ask and answer the questions.

1 Which information about Jamaica in the article did you find most interesting?
2 Have you ever listened to reggae music? Which songs or singers do you know?
3 What kind of clothes worn in Jamaica would you most like to wear?

Get it right!

We spell *comfortable* with 'm'.

✓ *Bright and colourful, comfortable clothing is a must.*
✗ ~~confortable~~

2 Your project

What people wear in my country

a Work in a group. Make a list of the clothes and accessories people in your country wear:

> in summer in winter on special occasions
> on holiday as the national dress in any other situations

b Make a poster about what people wear in your country. Include descriptions of the:

- clothes and accessories
- materials
- colours and patterns
- situations they are worn in
- people who wear them
- types of music that influence clothing
- most important fashion events or fashion designers

c Illustrate your poster with pictures or photos.

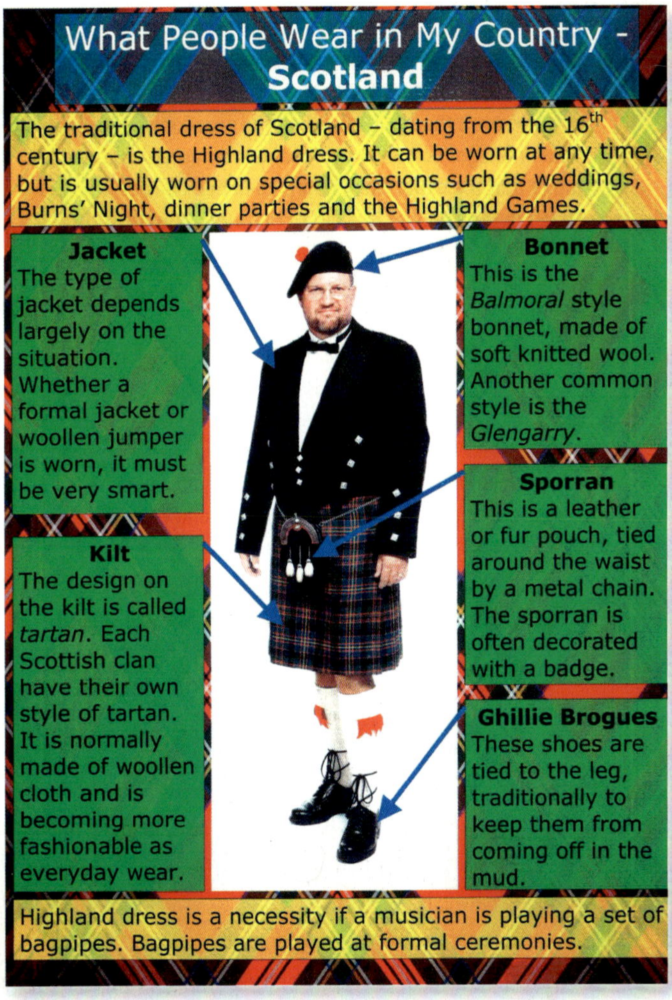

8 Something for nothing

Third conditional review
Expressions of purpose, reason and result
Vocabulary: Phrasal verbs and expressions with *give*; Numbers and symbols
Interaction 8: Talking about money

1 Read and listen

a Look at the pictures of Mark Boyle. What do you think his book might be about? Read the text quickly and check your ideas.

THE MONEY-LESS MAN

Can you imagine washing in an ice-cold river in winter and cleaning clothes by hand? Cycling for miles in the rain and cooking outdoors? Never going shopping, eating in a restaurant or travelling on public transport? That's exactly what Mark Boyle did when he lived without money for a year. However, even though he finished the year-long experiment some time ago, he hasn't yet reached for his wallet once! He admits that the experiment might have been easier if he'd started in the summer instead of the winter, but he didn't ever consider giving up.

Mark studied Economics and then worked in business for several years before realising he wanted to try and make a change in the world. He had been an eco-warrior for some time before deciding to give money-less living a go. He was given an old caravan to live in, and before beginning the experiment he bought solar panels to ensure he would have enough energy to run his laptop and a lamp. If Mark hadn't had any electricity, he wouldn't have been able to share his experience with the world via his blog, w*The Freeconomy Community*. His caravan is on a friend's farm, where he works part time in order to 'pay' for the space.

Eating without spending any money is a challenge, but Mark never goes hungry. He is a vegan and he grows his own fruit and vegetables. He also forages for wild foods like nuts and collects waste food from supermarkets and shops in the nearest town. There is so much food thrown away by supermarkets that he often gives away the extra to people who need it.

One of the first observations that Mark made after a few weeks of money-less living was that everyday tasks take a lot longer. Washing clothes by hand can take all morning, and preparing a simple meal can take hours. Mark believes, however, that not depending on other people or technology makes him appreciate everything more.

If Mark had experienced a lot of difficulty during his experiment, he would have been happy when it was over. However, he has no plans to return to a life with money. He has written a book about his money-less year, and the profits will be given to his charity, the *Freeconomy Charitable Trust*, which is working towards setting up money-less villages around the country for people who want to live in an alternative way.

Mark's experiences have made a lot of people think twice about their relationship with money; he has certainly given the experiment his all. How do you think you would feel about money-less living?

Which is right? Don't look at the text!
*Before **begin/beginning/to begin** the experiment, he bought solar panels.*

b 3.12 Read the text again and listen. Choose the correct answer: A, B or C.

1. How does Mark get around?
   A On public transport **B** By cycling and walking **C** In friends' cars
2. Mark's caravan has …
   A a bathroom. **B** some electricity. **C** a cooker.
3. What does Mark do when he has too much food?
   A throws it away **B** gives it to people **C** sells it at a local market
4. What will Mark do with the money he makes from his book?
   A buy himself a house **B** give it to his charity **C** give it away
5. Which of the following has Mark *not* done?
   A started a blog **B** published a book **C** made a film

c Complete the sentences so they are true for you. Then compare your sentences with a partner.

1. The idea of living without money is ...good
2. In ten years' time I think Mark will ...still living like now
3. If I tried to live without money, I would ...die
4. In my opinion, Mark's experiment is ...hard

2 Grammar

Third conditional review

a Look at the examples and answer the questions.

*If Mark **had experienced** a lot of difficulty during his experiment, he **would have been** happy when it was over.*

1 Did Mark experience a lot of difficulty during the experiment? NO
2 Was he happy when the experiment was over? NO

*If Mark **hadn't had** any electricity, he **wouldn't have been able to share** his experience with the world.*

1 Did Mark have electricity? YES
2 Was he able to share his experience? YES

*The experiment **might have been** easier if he'**d started** in the summer.*

1 Did he start the experiment in the summer? NO
2 Which modal verb is used instead of *would*? Why? Might because is a verb of posibility

Choose the correct word(s) to complete the rules.

- We can use the third conditional to talk about situations that **happened** / **didn't happen** in the past that might have been different.
- The third conditional is formed with *if* + **past perfect** / **present perfect** + *would have* + *past participle*.
- We **can** / **can't** use other modal verbs instead of *would* in third conditional sentences.

Grammar reference: page 137

b Read these sentences separately, with both of the possible modal verbs. How does the meaning change?

1 They **would/might** have won the match if it hadn't started raining.
2 They **would/could** have saved lots of money if they'd gone by bus.

Check it out!

- The contraction *'d* can be two different words: If I'd (**had**) known you were hungry, I'd (**would**) have made you a sandwich.

c Write sentences that have a similar meaning to the first. You can change the order of the ideas.

1 He planned to save his birthday money but he spent it all on a new jacket.
If he hadn't …
2 You studied lots for an exam and you passed with a good mark.
You wouldn't …
3 They fell asleep in the sun and got really burnt.
If they hadn't …
4 She felt sick after eating a whole box of chocolates.
She wouldn't …

d Work in a group. Ask and answer the questions.

What would you have done if …

1 … you'd arrived for English class today and your teacher hadn't been there?
2 … you'd woken up and seen half a metre of snow on the ground?
3 … you'd met your favourite actor/singer on the way to school?
4 … you'd found out last night that you'd won £100,000?

3 Speak

a Work with a partner. You are going to role play an interview between a journalist and Mark Boyle from Exercise 1. Student B: Turn to page 125.

Student A: You are a journalist. Prepare at least six questions to ask Mark. Use the ideas below to help you.

- Friends and family – reactions?
- Daily routine
- Good/bad things about new life
- Future plans
- Things you miss
- Entertainment

b Student A: Interview Student B.

c Tell the class about any interesting questions or answers from the interview.

4 Vocabulary

Phrasal verbs and expressions with *give*

a 3.13 Match the phrasal verbs or expressions with *give* with the definitions. Then listen and check.

1 He often **gives away** the extra food.
2 I need to **give back** the shirt I borrowed.
3 She **gave in** and admitted she was wrong.
4 Mark has **given** money-less living **his all**.
5 He had never ridden a horse before, but he decided to **give it a go**.
6 He **gave his opinion** on the new government.
7 Laura **gave out** flyers to her school's charity event.
8 Shall I **give you a hand** with your homework?

A to finally agree to something you originally didn't want to do
B to say what you think about something
C to hand something to each person in a group
D to help somebody with something
E to put a lot of effort into doing something
F to return something to someone
G to attempt to do something
H to give something to somebody else voluntarily

b 3.14 Complete these quotes with a phrasal verb or expression with *give*. Then listen and check.

1 'Always give … things you borrow, or you will lose friends!'
2 'Give a … to someone in need. You never know when you might need one yourself.'
3 'If everyone gave … 10% of their earnings to charity, the world would be a better place.'
4 'If at first you don't succeed, try, try and try again. Never give … !'

c Work in a group. Do you agree with the quotes in Exercise 4b? Why? / Why not? Re-write the quote, using a phrasal verb or expression with *give*.

d Do you know any more phrasal verbs and expressions with *give*. Write them in your Workbook (page 121 Exercise 1).

Check it out!

- There are lots of ways of saying *give*:
  donate = to give money to charity
  award = to give money / a prize to someone
  present = to officially give someone something, usually at a ceremony
  provide = to give a service

5 Listen

a What do you need most in order to have a good time at the weekend? Work in a group and put the things in the boxes in order from the most to the least important.

friends technology money music food
family transport other (you decide)

b 3.15 Listen to a podcast about things to do for free in London. Number the pictures in the order you hear them.

A

B

C

D

c 3.15 Listen again and match the correct speaker (1–4) with each sentence (A–E). There's one extra sentence.

A I love listening to music, however much it costs.
B I think it's difficult to have fun in a city without spending any money at all.
C I'm surprised more people don't go to this event.
D I spend less money because of my favourite sport.
E I've made lots of new friends thanks to this free activity.

d Work with a partner and answer the questions.

1 Would you like to do any of the free activities mentioned in the podcast? Why? / Why not?
2 What would you have said if you'd been asked what people can do for free in your town?

6 Grammar

Expressions of purpose, reason and result

a Look at the examples. Match the headings (*purpose*, *reason* or *result*) to the expressions.

The parks in London are great ***for*** *skating.*
I go during the week ***so that it's*** *less crowded.*
I go regularly ***so as to get out*** *of the office for a while.*
Last week we didn't go ***due to*** *bad weather,* ***so we went*** *on Sunday instead.*

- **Reason** (what caused the action to happen)
- **Result** (the effect of the action)
- **Purpose** (a person's aim when taking an action)

…
for + noun or *-ing*
to / in order to / so as to + infinitive
so that + subject + verb (often with *can/could* or *will/would*)
…
due to + noun or *-ing*
as a result of + noun or *-ing*
…
so + subject + verb
therefore + subject + verb

Grammar reference: page 136

Get it right!

We only use *for* + *-ing* to talk about purpose when we are referring to the use that something has.
✓ *That machine is great for making ice cream.*
✗ *I travelled across town ~~for buying~~ my favourite ice cream.*
✓ *I travelled across town to buy my favourite ice cream.*

b Rewrite the two sentences to make one, using the word in brackets.

1 I travelled across town. I bought my favourite ice-cream. (to)
2 He ran to the bus stop. He didn't want to miss the bus. (so)
3 We did research. We know a lot about teenagers' spending habits. (as a result of)
4 She always rides a bicycle. She saves money. (in order to)

c Complete the email with language from the box.

to give | due to | therefore | to inform | as a result of

Dear Sir / Madam,
I am writing [1] … you that I am not happy with the service I received in your restaurant yesterday. I am a regular customer and arrived with a client at 1pm. [2] … having to wait for 20 minutes, our meeting was delayed. [3] … the delay, my client was late for his next appointment. [4] … I would like to suggest you reorganise your reservation system [5] … priority to business meetings.
Yours faithfully,
Emily Phillips

d Work with a partner. Ask and answer the questions.

1 What could you do in order to improve your level of English?
2 How could you try and save more money every month?
3 Have you ever failed an exam as a result of not studying enough?

7 Vocabulary

Numbers and symbols

a 3.16 Listen to the introduction of *Money Matters* again and write down the numbers you hear.

b 3.17 Match the words to the symbols. Then listen and check.

1	degree	A	+
2	divided by	B	–
3	equals / is	C	x
4	kilogramme	D	÷
5	minus	E	=
6	multiplied by / times	F	%
7	oh / zero / nought / nil	G	°
8	percent	H	.
9	plus	I	0
10	point	J	kg

c 3.18 Match the sentence halves. Then listen and check.

1 Their new car
2 It was −22.3°C
3 15 x 70 =
4 His phone number
5 Jack gets paid £6.73 per hour
6 On the 15th of each month
7 44% of the population
8 Milan won the match

A for his job. That's £53.84 a day.
B voted in the election.
C cost €11,899.
D against Genoa 4–0.
E is 01737 245819.
F my aunt gives me £20 pocket money.
G on the coldest day last year.
H 1050

d 3.19 Listen and write down the numbers you hear.

1 …
2 …
3 …
4 …
5 …
6 …

8 Pronunciation DVD

Large numbers

a 3.20 When we say large numbers, the speaker has to pause in certain places. Listen to these examples.

Call me later on 01834 | 875 | 291.

It cost $13, | 456, | 822.

b 3.21 Copy and listen to these number. Draw a line where the speaker pauses. The first one is done for you.

1 020 | 8863 | 2197
2 132480
3 6976200000
4 003465874983
5 8743695211

c Work in pairs. Take turns to dictate and write numbers from the lists. The writer must have their book closed and write the number down.

Phone numbers:

Large numbers:

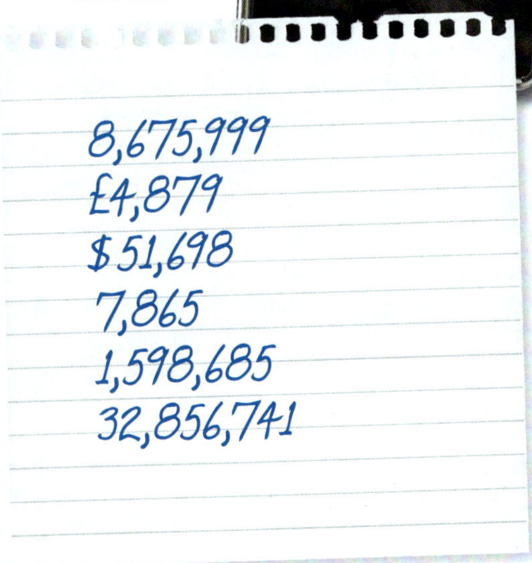

Interaction 8 DVD

Talking about money

a 3.22 Listen to Sally and Mel shopping in a market. Which T-shirt does Sally buy? Why is she angry at the end of the conversation?

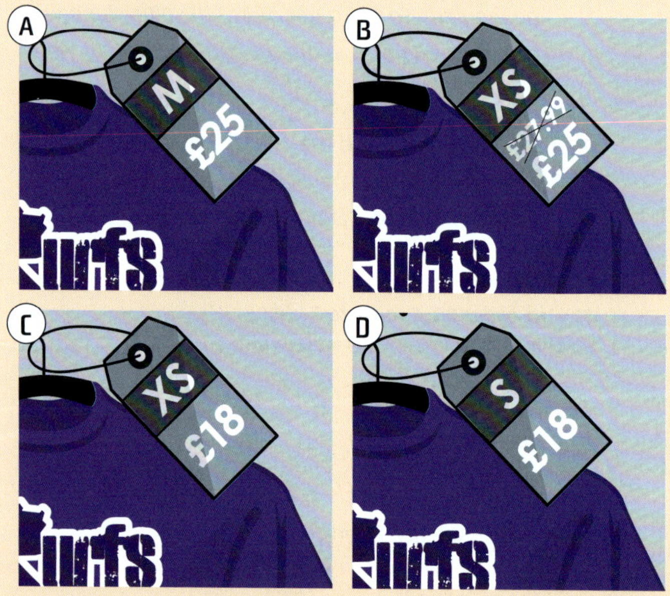

b 3.22 Listen again and put the sentences in the order you hear them.

H, …

A Can you afford it?
B What a rip-off!
C That's a bargain.
D You owe me seven.
E There's ten pounds off.
F I can't afford it.
G Could you lend me seven pounds?
H It's reduced by 10%.
I I promise I'll pay you back.

c 3.23 Turn to page 124. Listen to the sentences and repeat them. Practise using linking between consonant sounds and vowel sounds and the intrusive /w/ between words.

d Work with a partner.

Student A: Turn to page 127. Student B: Turn to page 130.

Culture Vulture

In the UK most teenagers get some pocket money from their parents, but 71% of parents ask their children to do some jobs around the house in order to get pocket money. Do you get pocket money? Do you have to do any household jobs to get it?

Portfolio 8

Writing about survey results

a In a survey for *MoneyTime* business magazine, ten teenagers were given £20 each and told to buy whatever they wanted. This bar chart shows what they decided to spend the money on. Look at the article and read the analysis below. Who spent the most money in each category? If you were given £20, what would you spend it on?

An analysis of teenagers' spending for *MoneyTime* magazine

From the bar chart, I can immediately see that the majority of teenagers spent most of their money on clothes and accessories. Almost everybody, with the exception of Lynn, spent money on this, but only a few people spent more than 50% of their money.

Everyone except Paula spent more than £2 on food and drink. Lynn spent more than the others on food and snacks, a total of £16. On average the girls spent more than the boys on food and snacks.

Out of the ten teenagers, only one of them, Paula, spent nothing on going out. Jenny spent the most on this, but the majority spent less than a quarter of their money on going out. I wouldn't have been surprised if more of them had spent more money in this category!

Over three-quarters of the ten people in the survey spent some money on other things. Most people spent money in each of the four categories. Lynn and Paula were in the minority because they only spent their money on two different things. If we had been able to ask the teenagers exactly what they had spent their money on in the 'other' category, it might have been interesting.

Due to the fact that there aren't too many differences between what the boys and girls spent their money on, we can conclude that they generally have quite similar spending habits.

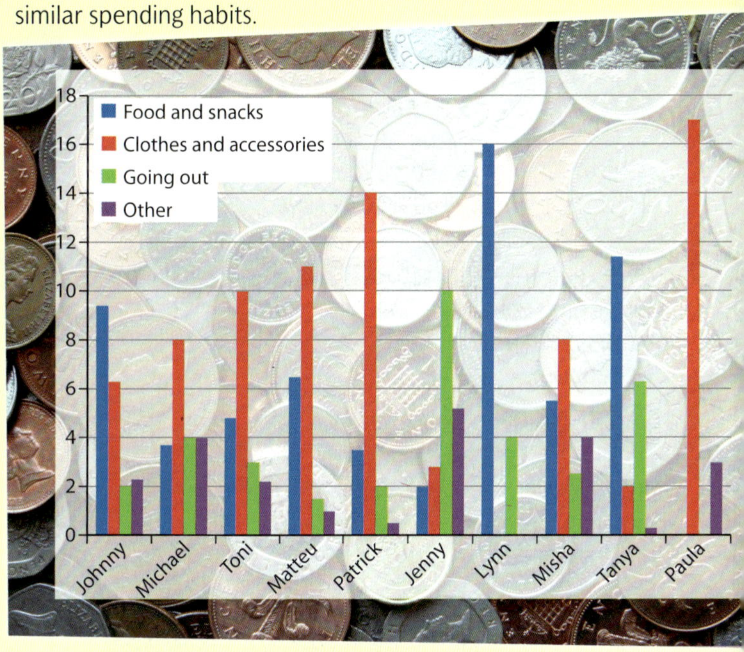

b Read the text again and write the words that mean the same as …

1 more than 75%
2 no more than one or two
3 most people
4 more than half
5 in a group with very few people

c Now look at this pie chart that shows how an average British family spends their annual income. Write a short text to describe it.

d Swap your text with a partner. Have they made any factual mistakes in their survey results?

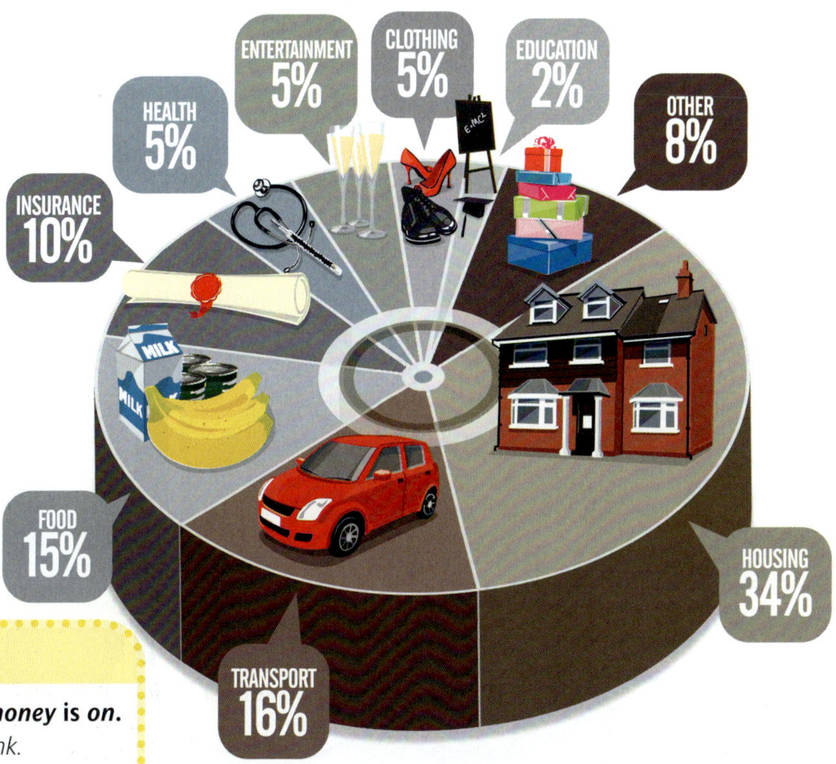

Get it right!

The correct preposition to use with *spend money* is *on*.

✓ *Everyone spent more than £2 on food and drink.*

✗ *Everyone spent more than £2 ~~for~~ food and drink.*

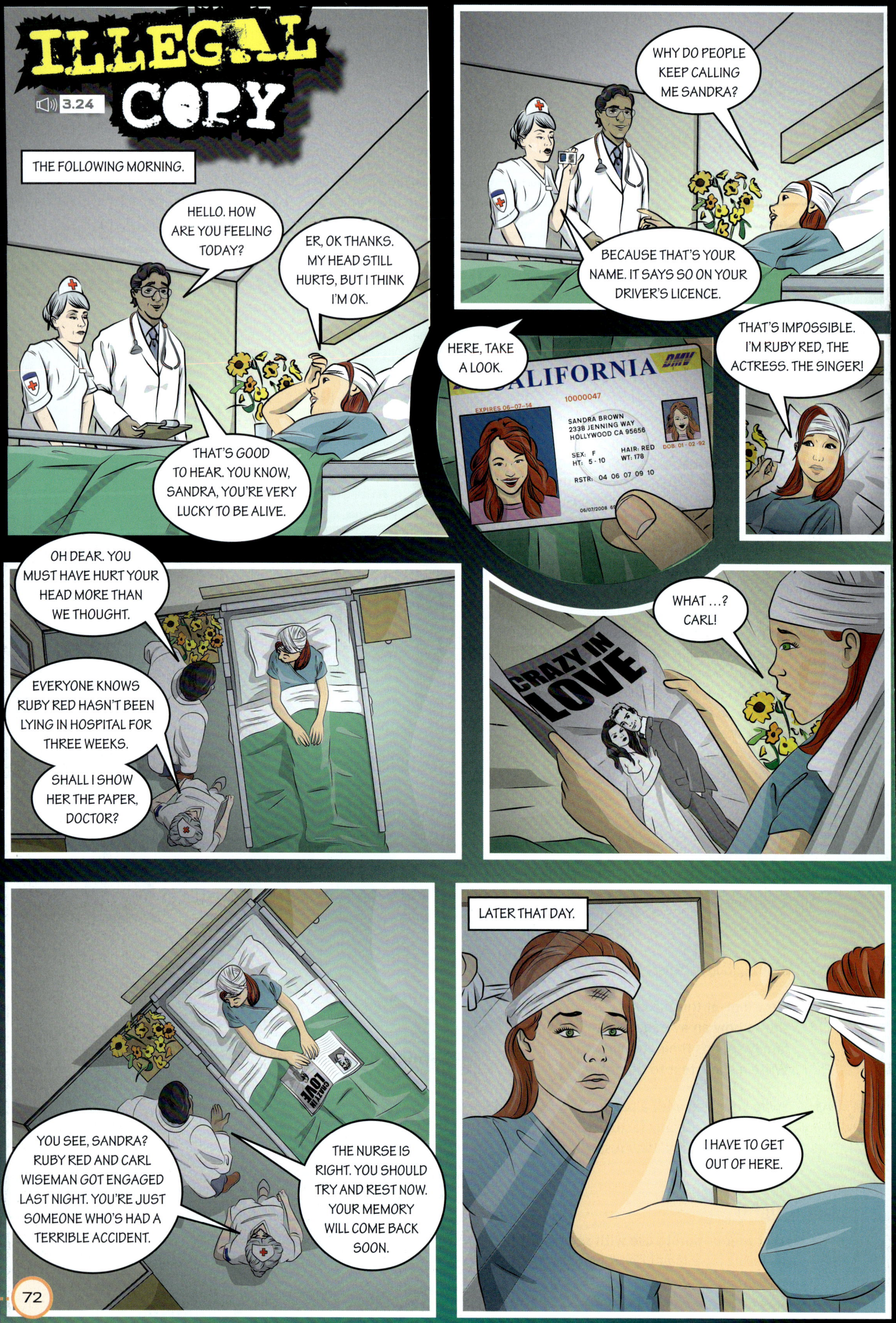

ILLEGAL COPY
3.24
THE FOLLOWING MORNING.
HELLO. HOW ARE YOU FEELING TODAY?
ER, OK THANKS. MY HEAD STILL HURTS, BUT I THINK I'M OK.
THAT'S GOOD TO HEAR. YOU KNOW, SANDRA, YOU'RE VERY LUCKY TO BE ALIVE.
WHY DO PEOPLE KEEP CALLING ME SANDRA?
BECAUSE THAT'S YOUR NAME. IT SAYS SO ON YOUR DRIVER'S LICENCE.
HERE, TAKE A LOOK.
CALIFORNIA DMV
10000047
EXPIRES 06-07-14
SANDRA BROWN
2338 JENNING WAY
HOLLYWOOD CA 95656
SEX: F HAIR: RED
HT: 5-10 WT: 178
DOB: 01-02-92
RSTR: 04 06 07 09 10
THAT'S IMPOSSIBLE. I'M RUBY RED, THE ACTRESS. THE SINGER!
OH DEAR. YOU MUST HAVE HURT YOUR HEAD MORE THAN WE THOUGHT.
EVERYONE KNOWS RUBY RED HASN'T BEEN LYING IN HOSPITAL FOR THREE WEEKS.
SHALL I SHOW HER THE PAPER, DOCTOR?
WHAT ...? CARL!
CRAZY IN LOVE
YOU SEE, SANDRA? RUBY RED AND CARL WISEMAN GOT ENGAGED LAST NIGHT. YOU'RE JUST SOMEONE WHO'S HAD A TERRIBLE ACCIDENT.
THE NURSE IS RIGHT. YOU SHOULD TRY AND REST NOW. YOUR MEMORY WILL COME BACK SOON.
LATER THAT DAY.
I HAVE TO GET OUT OF HERE.

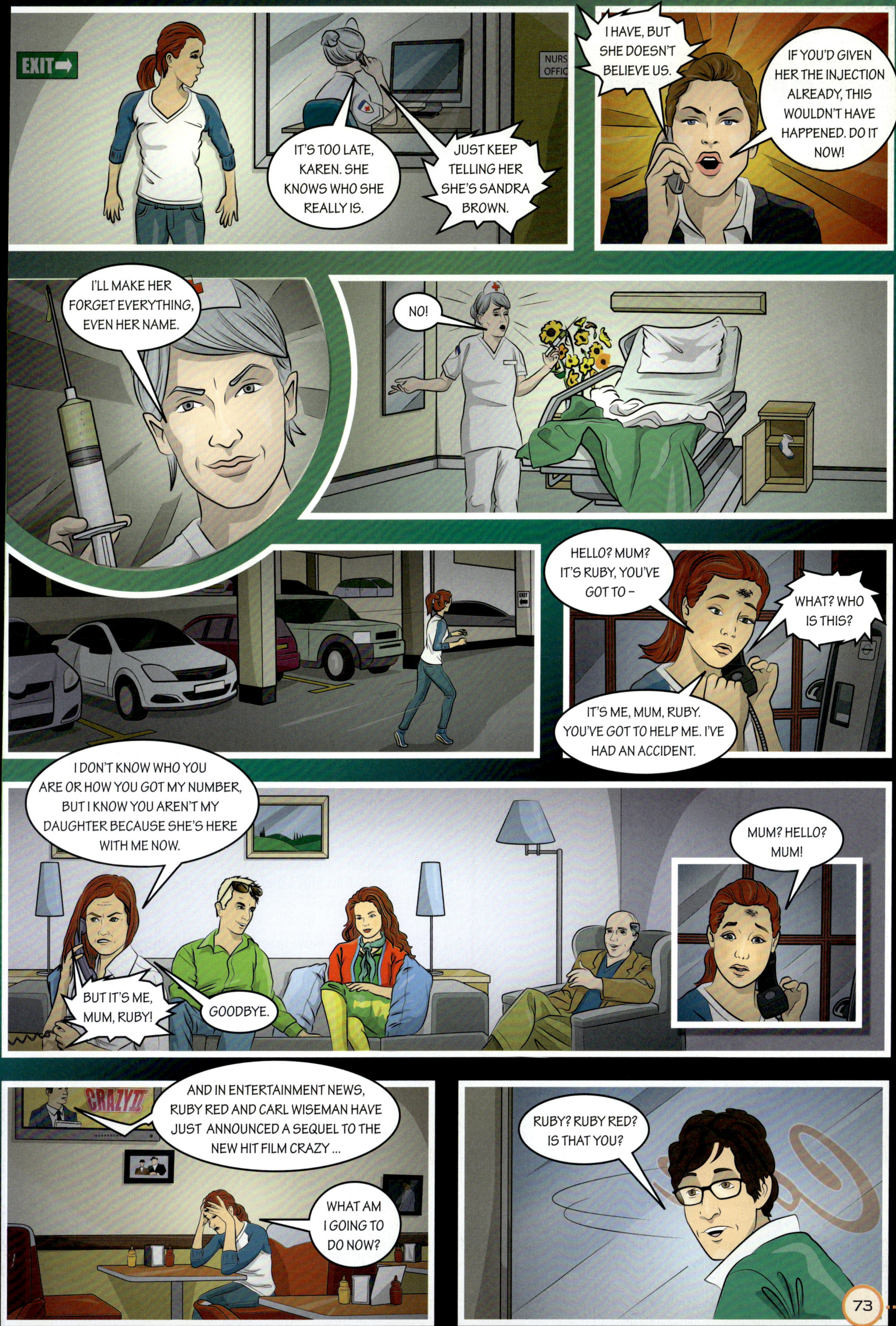
EXIT
IT'S TOO LATE, KAREN. SHE KNOWS WHO SHE REALLY IS.
JUST KEEP TELLING HER SHE'S SANDRA BROWN.
I HAVE, BUT SHE DOESN'T BELIEVE US.
IF YOU'D GIVEN HER THE INJECTION ALREADY, THIS WOULDN'T HAVE HAPPENED. DO IT NOW!
I'LL MAKE HER FORGET EVERYTHING, EVEN HER NAME.
NO!
HELLO? MUM? IT'S RUBY, YOU'VE GOT TO –
WHAT? WHO IS THIS?
IT'S ME, MUM, RUBY. YOU'VE GOT TO HELP ME. I'VE HAD AN ACCIDENT.
I DON'T KNOW WHO YOU ARE OR HOW YOU GOT MY NUMBER, BUT I KNOW YOU AREN'T MY DAUGHTER BECAUSE SHE'S HERE WITH ME NOW.
BUT IT'S ME, MUM, RUBY!
GOODBYE.
MUM? HELLO? MUM!
CRAZY II
AND IN ENTERTAINMENT NEWS, RUBY RED AND CARL WISEMAN HAVE JUST ANNOUNCED A SEQUEL TO THE NEW HIT FILM CRAZY ...
WHAT AM I GOING TO DO NOW?
RUBY? RUBY RED? IS THAT YOU?

Get it right! 7 and 8

Common errors

1 *its* or *it's*?

Don't confuse *it's* and *its*.

Use *it's* as a contraction of *it is* or *it has*.

✓ ***It's*** *my much-loved biker jacket.*

✗ *~~Its~~ my much-loved biker jacket.*

Use *its* to talk about something that belongs to something.

✓ *The dog is playing with **its** ball.*

✗ *The dog is playing with ~~it's~~ ball.*

a Complete the text with *it's* or *its*.

My favourite possession is my suitcase. [1] … old and dirty, but I love [2] … colour and the fact that [3] … always been with me on my travels. [4] … not very fashionable and [5] … handle is nearly broken, but I love it.

b For each time it is used, decide whether *it's* is short for *it has* or *it is*.

2 *Why did you do it?*

Use the correct expressions to explain your reason for doing something.

Use *to / in order to / so as to* + infinitive

✓ *I am writing **to apply** for the job you advertised.*

✗ *I am writing ~~for applying~~ for the job you advertised.*

Use *so that* + subject + verb

✓ *We keep animals in zoos **so that we can** protect them.*

✗ *We keep animals in zoos ~~for protecting~~ them.*

Choose the correct answers.

1 We went to the countryside for relaxing / to relax.
2 I am writing to thank / so that thank you for your hospitality.
3 I had to work hard for passing / to pass my exams.
4 I am saving all my money so to buy / to buy a new computer.
5 You should go to England for improve / so that you can improve your English.

3 Expressions with *most*

Don't confuse expressions for talking about the majority of something.

Use *the most* + adjective to make the superlative:

✓ *Sally bought **the most expensive** T-shirt.*

✗ *Sally bought most expensive T-shirt.*

Use *most* + plural noun to talk about the majority of a group:

✓ ***Most people*** *like going shopping.*

✗ *Most ~~of~~ people like going shopping.*

Use *most of* + *the* / possessive adjective + noun to talk about almost all of something:

✓ ***Most of the money*** *was spent on clothes.*

✗ *~~The~~ most of the money was spent on clothes.*

✗ *Most of money was spent on clothes.*

a Read the text and correct the five mistakes.

Most of people like going shopping, but not me! Most time, I would prefer to stay at home. But sometimes I enjoy going shopping for books. I love reading, so that's most interesting kind of shopping for me. Most my friends prefer shopping for clothes, but I spend most of the my money on books.

b 3.25 Now listen and check your answers.

4 Say it right!

Word stress

a 3.26 Correct word stress is important for comprehension. Listen to the words and repeat.

restaurant comfortable variety

b 3.27 Copy the words in your notebook and mark the word stress. Then listen, check and repeat.

alternative business chocolate creative innovative vegetables

Review 7 and 8

1 Grammar

a Complete the sentences. Use the verbs in the correct form of the passive.

1 The first blue jeans … (make) in the USA by Levi Strauss.
2 Kilts look like checked skirts. They … (wear) on special occasions by Scottish men.
3 The bikini … (invent) in the 1950s. It … (name) after two Pacific islands.
4 In the future, intelligent fabrics … (use) to make clothes.
5 Silk … (make) from the cocoon of the silk worm, and … (use) to make beautiful clothes.

b Complete the second sentence. Use *have/get* + object + past participle.

redecorate pierce repair cut rebuild

1 Your hair is a bit long.
Why don't you … ?
2 Our living room is a terrible colour.
My parents should … .
3 Pearl wants to wear a ring in her nose.
She's going to … .
4 My computer's broken down.
I'll have to … .
5 Our garden shed has fallen down.
We're going to … .

c Write sentences that have a similar meaning to the first using the third conditional. You can change the order of the ideas.

1 I didn't save any money. I couldn't buy a computer.
2 The rain was heavy. The river flooded.

d Choose the correct word(s).

1 We went to London *for visiting / to visit* the British Museum.
2 My grandmother paid for extra Maths classes *so that / due to* I'd pass my exam.
3 The airport is closed *due to / because* fog.
4 I want to get there early *so as to / in order* be first in the queue.
5 He's gone to the park *to / for* a run.
6 There are now very few young children in the village. *Consequently / As a result of*, the school will be closing.
7 *Due / As a result of* the heavy rain, there were a lot of problems with flooding.

2 Vocabulary

a Complete the sentences.

trendy scruffy plain striped
short-sleeved baggy

1 I don't like patterned clothes, I prefer … things.
2 Do you like … trousers or tight ones?
3 Big sunglasses are … at the moment.
4 He's not allowed to wear … shirts at work.
5 You can't go to the dance like that. You look really … !
6 Traditional fishermen's sweaters are … .

b Complete the sentences with body idioms.

1 He thinks he's so clever, he's so …
2 I bet that was expensive. It must have cost …
3 All his clothes are black; he wears black …
4 She's so annoying, she's a real …
5 Whoops, I've … . I shouldn't have said that.
6 You really want that, don't you? You've …
7 You're making fun of me. Stop …
8 That's none of your business! Don't …

c Match the two parts of the sentences.

1 Why don't you give up?
2 I can't lift this on my own,
3 She wanted to win so
4 I'm not sure I can solve that problem,
5 Jan's giving away lots of her clothes.
6 In the main square they're giving out
7 Don't lend Sophie any more books,
8 In the end I gave in

A can you give me a hand?
B she never gives things back.
C Do you want any?
D because I was so tired.
E You'll never manage to mend it.
F she really gave it her all.
G free tickets for the new film.
H but I'll give it a go.

d Complete the words for the symbols.

1	3 x 4	three _ _ m _ _ four
2	60%	sixty _ _ _ _ _ _ t
3	0	n _ _ _ _ _
4	7 – 5	seven _ i _ _ _ five
5	38°	thirty-eight _ e _ _ _ _ _
6	2 + 2	two _ _ _ s two
7	= 4	_ q _ _ _ _ four
8	9.1	nine _ o _ _ _ one

9 Keep your cool

should*, *ought to* and *had better
Expressing wishes and regrets
Vocabulary: Adjectives of character; Expressions for arguments
Interaction 9: Negotiating and responding

1 Read and listen

a Work with a partner. Think of four reasons why teenagers argue with their parents. Read the text quickly. Are any of your ideas mentioned?

TV highlights this week

HOUSE RULES

Lara's parents have lost count of the number of times she has stormed out of the house without permission when she is angry. At school it's a similar story and the argumentative teenager has been expelled from three schools. Image-obsessed Dean, 17, spends more time on his hair than on his schoolwork. He is disrespectful of rules and boundaries and argues with his brothers and sisters. Used to getting her own way all the time, Abi, 16, is completely spoilt. But despite being given everything she wants, she is impossible to live with.

However, rebellious teenagers in New Zealand had better watch out! Parents who believe it's time their children stopped behaving so badly are turning to the reality TV show *House Rules* for help. Desperate parents hand over their troublesome children to new families in other parts of the world such as the USA, Ireland or South Africa for a week in an attempt to improve their behaviour. The series explores the way out-of-control teens handle a completely different environment with parents who think that teenagers ought to be disciplined and respectful at all times. Lara, Dean and Abi are filmed as they learn to live by completely new rules. And if you thought *your* parents were strict, think again; the rules are tough for everyone in the new houses, and the punishments even tougher.

As well as helping out around the house, the teens are not allowed to be rude or stay out late. They must tell their 'new parents' where they are at all times and had better not break any of the rules. If they do, they are grounded or have other privileges taken away. Some of the new parents even believe they should control the music their children listen to or which sites they visit online, and know all their computer passwords.

Abi goes to live with the Roberts family in South Carolina, USA, who believe in strict discipline and hard work. Mum, Annette, admits her rules are tough and that she can be very strict. However, she talks to her children so that they understand why she wants them to do things. During her stay with the new family, Abi changes. The trip opens her eyes to how other people live and shows her that life at home really isn't so bad. The shock treatment appears to work and she is extremely enthusiastic about her old life when she returns home to New Zealand. It seems that the rude, spoilt teenager people once knew is long gone. Her parents hope that the new Abi is here to stay. But can Lara and Dean manage to turn their lives around too?

b 3.28 Read the text again and listen. Are the sentences *right* (✓), *wrong* (✗) or *doesn't say* (–)?

1 Lara's bad behaviour has affected her life at home and at school.
2 Abi behaves well when she is given what she wants.
3 Parents choose the family their teenage children stay with.
4 The teenagers follow the same rules as the children of the families they are living with.
5 The teens can only listen to music or use the internet if their new parents are in the same room.
6 Abi's behaviour improved after going to South Carolina.

c Work in a group. Ask and answer the questions.

1 Do you think reality TV shows like *House Rules* can help improve people's behaviour?
2 Do you think people can change after living a different life for one week? Why? / Why not?
3 How strict do you think rules at home should be?

Culture Vulture

Did you know that reality TV shows like *House Rules* are popular in Australia, Denmark and Germany? Are there any similar programmes in your country? Are they popular? Who watches them?

2 Vocabulary

Adjectives of character

a 3.29 Match the adjectives 1–10 with the definitions A–J. Then listen and check.

1 aggressive	**2** cheerful
3 enthusiastic	**4** imaginative
5 jealous	**6** rebellious
7 reliable	**8** smart
9 spoilt	**10** stubborn

Someone who ...

A is happy.
B can be trusted and depended on.
C breaks rules and doesn't like authority.
D thinks of new and interesting ideas.
E is angry or unhappy because someone else has something they want.
F is very clever or intelligent.
G is determined to do what they want.
H can be angry or violent with people.
I shows a lot of interest and excitement in something.
J behaves badly because they are always given or allowed to do what they want.

b Are the adjectives positive or negative? Write + or – next to the words in Exercise 2a.

c Choose the correct adjective.

1 Adriana is *spoilt* / *stubborn*. She always gets everything she asks for. Her parents never say no to her.
2 Mike is very *reliable* / *aggressive*. If he says he'll do something, he'll do it. You can trust him completely.
3 If you're looking for ideas, ask Henry. He's *imaginative* / *cheerful*, I'm sure he'll think of something great.
4 Dan can get *rebellious* / *aggressive* when he argues with his brother and shouts a lot.
5 My teacher was very *jealous* / *enthusiastic* about my idea for the project. She said it was very interesting.
6 Naomi is so *smart* / *argumentative*. She always knows the answer to everything.

Check it out!

- You can use *un-*, *dis-*, *im-* and *ir-* to make opposite adjectives.
unimaginative, **un**reliable, **un**friendly
disrespectful, **im**polite, **ir**responsible

d Do you know any more adjectives to describe character? Write them in your Workbook (page 122 Exercise 1).

e Work with a partner. Ask and answer the questions.

1 Who are the most reliable people you know? Why?
2 Which characteristic is more negative, being spoilt or being stubborn? Why?
3 Which jobs need imaginative people?
4 What makes you feel cheerful?

3 Pronunciation DVD

Unstressed vowel sounds /ə/ and /ɪ/

a 3.30 80% of unstressed vowel sounds have an /ə/ sound and 10% have an /ɪ/ sound. Listen to the words.

/ə/: parents permission agree
/ɪ/: behave discipline image

b 3.31 Copy the table. Listen and write the words in the column corresponding to the unstressed vowel sounds.

jealous strictest respect argument imaginative reliable punish advice

/ə/	/ɪ/

c 3.32 Listen, check your answers, and repeat.

d Follow the /ə/ sounds and find your way through the puzzle. You can move up or down ⇕, left or right ⇔. Work with a partner and say the words.

→ temper	aggressive	behave	become	invisible
stubborn	message	sister	Ireland	answer
internet	music	expression	interesting	different
famous	another	control	before	again ↓

e 3.33 Listen and check your answers.

4 Grammar *should, ought to and had better*

a Look at the examples and choose the correct words to complete the rules.

- *Rebellious teenagers in New Zealand* ***had better watch out!***
  They ***had better not break*** *any of the rules.*
  Parents think that teenagers ***ought to be*** *disciplined and respectful.*
  Parents believe they ***should control*** *the music their children listen to.*

- We use *should* and *ought to* to give advice and express strong obligation.
- *Ought* is followed by the infinitive **with** / **without** *to*.
- We use *had better* to give advice in the form of a warning. If the advice is not followed, there **will** / **won't** be a negative consequence.
- *Had better* is followed by the infinitive **with** / **without** *to*.

Grammar reference: page 137

Check it out!

- We say *it's time someone did something* when we want to criticise their present behaviour.
  It's time their children **stopped** behaving badly.
  It's time you **started** studying.

b Choose the correct word(s) to complete the sentences.

1 The children had *better* / *better not* keep secrets from their parents or they'll be in trouble.
2 You *ought* / *should* to listen to him more carefully and not be so argumentative.
3 *It's time he* / *He'd better* did more work for his exams. He failed everything last time.
4 You'd *better* / *should* say sorry for being rude, or he won't talk to you again.
5 She *better not* / *shouldn't* leave the room without permission, it's disrespectful.
6 *They ought to* / *It's time they* talk to each other calmly instead of shouting all the time.

c Complete the second sentence so it means the same as the first.

1 You'd better behave if you want to go out.
You should ... behave better if you want to go out
2 It's time you were more reliable.
You ought ... to be more reliable
3 She shouldn't tell anyone the news yet.
She'd ... better tell " " " "
4 You'd better start helping around the house, if you want us to get on well together.
It's time ... you started helping

d Complete the sentences so they are true about you. Then compare with your partner.

1 I should …
2 My parents think it's time I …
3 My teacher sometimes tells me '*You'd better* …'
4 Sometimes I think I shouldn't …
5 I believe people ought to …

Get it right!

***Should* is followed by the infinitive without *to*.**
✓ *She shouldn't tell anyone the news yet.*
✗ *She shouldn't ~~to~~ tell anyone the news yet.*

5 Speak

a Read the problems and number them in order from the most to the least serious.

Problem spot

I keep getting into trouble in German class because I speak in English all the time. But I don't understand the teacher when she speaks in German! 2

I need a new mobile phone, but my parents won't buy me one as my old phone still works. They say I'm spoilt! 3

I got caught cheating in a maths exam and my maths teacher wants to talk to my parents. They're going to go mad! 1

I want a computer in my room. My parents say no as there is a family computer in the living room, but I think I should have my own. 4

b Work with a partner. Tell your partner your order and explain your reasons. Decide on a new order that you both agree on.

A: *I think that Eric's problem is the most serious because …*
B: *But it's not as serious as cheating in an exam because …*

c Discuss possible solutions to the problems. Use *should*, *ought to*, *had better* or *it's time*.

Jacob should get a job so that he can buy …

d Tell the class which problems you thought were the most serious and explain your solutions.

6 Vocabulary

Expressions for arguments

a 3.34 Match the two parts of the sentences. Then listen and check.

1 If you **keep your cool**,
2 If you **lose your temper**,
3 If you **wind someone up**,
4 If you **storm out**,
5 If someone **gets on your nerves**,
6 If you **see someone else's point of view**,
7 If you **keep the peace**,
8 If you **lose it**,

A you annoy them intentionally
B he/she annoys you a lot.
C you stop being able to control your emotions and shout or cry.
D you stay calm during an angry situation.
E you stop other people fighting or arguing.
F you suddenly become angry.
G you leave the room suddenly and angrily.
H you understand his/her opinion.

b Complete the text with words from the expressions in Exercise 6a in the correct form.

In our house, whenever we have an argument, it's always my older brother who [1] … peace. He's very good at [2] … other people's points … and never [3] … his temper. My twin sister, on the other hand, is argumentative and always [4] … everyone up, which is really annoying. I can be very stubborn though, so sometimes we find it hard to get on. It also really [5] … nerves when she keeps taking my things and I usually [6] … it and then [7] … out. Even though we're twins, we're totally different – sometimes she's impossible to live with!

c Do you have any similar expressions for arguments in your language?

d Work with a partner. Ask and answer the questions.

1 When you have an argument do you usually keep your cool or lose your temper?
2 Who winds you up or gets on your nerves? Why?
3 Do you find it easy or difficult to see someone else's point of view during an argument? Why?

7 Listen

a Work with a partner. Ask and answer the questions.

1 How often do you argue with your parents?
2 What do you argue about?
3 What do you do during an argument?

b 3.35 Listen to Dr Murray talking about how to argue. Write the advice she gives.

keep your cool
lose your temper
leave the room
storm out
count to ten in your head
wind someone up
keep the peace
stay in control
see other points of view

c 3.35 Listen again and complete the sentences. You can use your own words.

1 Dr Murray thinks that there are … ways of arguing.
2 Most arguments happen because both people … .
3 In an argument you should … for decisions you don't agree with.
4 It's important to listen to everyone and not interrupt or … in an argument.
5 If you are going to lose your temper, count to ten or … .
6 Don't argue about …, just the important things.

d Work in a group. Ask and answer the questions.

1 Do you agree with Dr Murray's advice? Why? / Why not?
2 Which advice will you try next time you have an argument? Why?
3 What other advice do you have for keeping calm during an argument?

8 Grammar

Expressing wishes and regrets

a Look at the examples and choose the correct words to complete the rules.

Many people ***wish they knew*** *how to stay in control in an argument.*
I wish they would see *things from my point of view.*
Maybe ***I shouldn't have said*** *that.*
There are lots of good ideas ***I should have thought*** *about when I was younger.*
If only I'd learned *a few rules earlier!*

- We use *wish/if only* + past simple to talk about a **present** / **past** situation which we would like to be different but can't change.
- We use *wish/if only* + *would* + infinitive when we want an action to happen now or in the **future** / **past** but we can't make it happen.
- We use *wish/if only* + past perfect to talk about a situation in the **present** / **past** that we regret but can't change.
- We use *should have* + past participle for things we **did** / **did not** do and we regret now.
- We use *shouldn't have* + past participle for things we **did** / **did not** do and we regret now.

Grammar reference: page 138

b Read the first sentence, then complete the second sentence so that it has a similar meaning.

1. Jake failed his exam because he didn't study for it.
   He should … for the exam.
2. Maia's mum won't let her walk home from school with her friends.
   She wishes her mum … her walk home with her friends.
3. Lindsay had an argument with her best friend and told everyone her secret.
   She shouldn't … everyone her friend's secret after the argument.
4. You are grounded so you can't go to the party.
   If only you … grounded, you could go to the party.
5. Lucia left her PE kit at home yesterday so couldn't play in the volleyball match.
   If only she … her PE kit at home.
6. Paula got really scared when she watched the horror film alone.
   She shouldn't … the horror film alone.

Check it out!

- *I wish + could*
  We often use **I *wish* + *could*** to talk about things we want to be different in the present or future.
  I *wish* I ***could*** talk to my sister. (It's difficult to talk to my sister)
  I *wish* you ***could*** come to the party. (You can't come)

c Work with a partner. In what situations might someone say these things?

1. I shouldn't have said that.
2. I wish I hadn't seen them.
3. I should have gone.
4. If only people wouldn't do that!
5. I wish you could see me now.

Interaction 9 DVD

Negotiating and responding

a 3.36 Listen to the conversation between Kai and his sister Leila. What is the problem? How do they solve it?

b 3.36 Listen again. Which phrases does Kai use to negotiate and which does Leila use to respond? Write *K* (Kai) or *L* (Leila).

1. I was just wondering if …
2. I wouldn't ask, but …
3. You always do this, it's not fair!
4. What's in it for me?
5. If you do this, I'll ..., I promise!
6. I'll do it, but just this once.
7. Cheers! I owe you one.
8. OK, but this is the last time!

c 3.37 Turn to page 124. Listen to the sentences and repeat them. Practise using the correct stress, weak forms and intrusion of /w/ and /j/ sounds.

d Work with a partner.
Student A: Turn to page 127.
Student B: Turn to page 130.

Portfolio 9 Asking for and giving advice

a Read Elene's letter on the webzine problem page and choose the best title for it. What advice would you give to Elene?

- She's so unreliable!
- She's so jealous!
- She's so disrespectful!

Yourzine!

http://interactive.cambridge.org

Yourzine! Ask Andy

interviews | true stories | fashion | music | movies

Are you having a hard time at school? Does your little brother or sister wind you up? Do your parents never see your point of view? Write and ask Andy for advice.

Your problem:

Dear Andy

My sister really gets on my nerves! She's always going into my room and taking my things without asking. I really wish she wouldn't. My room should be private! I've asked my parents to put a lock on my door, but they said no. They can be really stubborn sometimes! When I try talking to my sister she ignores me so I lose my temper and then we have a huge argument and she usually storms off. My parents say we're as bad as each other and should stop winding each other up. I wish they'd see my point of view. What should I do?

Elene (17)

Andy's advice:

Dear Elene

The first thing you ought to do is talk calmly to your parents on your own about the situation. You could suggest that they talk to your sister if you can't keep your cool when you talk to her. However, it sounds as though it's time you and your sister were a bit more respectful of each other and tried harder to keep the peace. She shouldn't have taken your things without permission, but you shouldn't lose your temper every time you talk to her. When she makes you feel angry, try counting to ten in your head or leave the room calmly.

Andy

b Read Andy's advice. Is his advice similar to yours?

c Read Elene and Andy's letters again. Who uses the following language in their letters? Copy and complete the table with the language in the correct column.

He/She is always + -ing
It's time you + past simple
What should I do?
I understand your problem.
I wish he/she would ...
Try + -ing
You should / ought to / could ...
You shouldn't have + past participle

Explaining the problem	Giving advice

d Write a letter to Andy to ask for advice about a problem you're having. You can invent the problem. Make sure you:

- explain the problem
- ask for advice

e Work with a partner. Swap letters with your partner and give him/her some advice. Make sure you:

- give advice to help to solve the problem
- use phrases to show you understand the problem

f Read your partner's letter of advice. Does he/she give you good advice for your problem? Why? / Why not?

Get it right!

***Advice* doesn't have a plural form and cannot be used with *a* or *an*.**

✓ *Andy's advice was very useful.*

✗ *Andy's ~~advices were~~ very useful.*

The Anthem

1 Song

a Work with a partner. Is it important for young people to make their own decisions? Why? / Why not? Should they make decisions for themselves, or should their friends, parents or teachers help them decide?

b 3.38 Listen to the beginning of the song and put the lines in the correct order.

At my high school it felt more to me

But every day it all just feels the same

It's a good life, that's what I'm told

It's a new day, but it all feels old

Like a jail cell, a penitentiary

My time spent there it only made me see

c 3.39 Listen and complete the chorus with the words in the box. There are two extra words.

anthem	do	don't	ever	hear
things	wanna	you	just	like

I don't ever wanna be [1] … you
I don't wanna [2] … the things you do
I'm never gonna [3] … the words you say
And I don't ever wanna, I don't [4] … wanna
be [5] … ,
Don't wanna be [6] … like you.
What I'm saying is, this is the [7] …
Throw all your hands up
You, don't [8] … be you.

d 3.40 Match the two parts of the sentences. Then listen to the next part of the song and check.

1 'Go to college
2 'Get a real job'
3 But I could never
4 I'm gonna get by and
5 Out of step while they
6 I'm just a minor threat

A all get in line.
B just do my time.
C or university'
D live the way they want.
E so pay no mind.
F That's what they said to me.

e 3.41 Listen to the whole song and then answer the questions.

1 What does the singer say his school is like? Why?
2 Who is the singer talking to when he says 'Do you really wanna be like them?'
3 Does the singer want to go to college or university? Why? / Why not?
4 Who would you like to be like? Why?
5 Do you think it's good to copy other people sometimes? Why? / Why not?

2 Sound check

a 3.42 To remember the lyrics to songs, first learn the words that are stressed. Say the stressed words from the chorus as you hear them.

I … wanna be … you
I … do … things … do
… never … hear … words … say
I … wanna, I … wanna … you …
Wanna … just … you

b Can you remember the unstressed words on each line? Work with a partner and try to remember the missing words in Exercise 2a.

c 3.43 Listen and say as many of the lyrics in the chorus as you can.

Calypso

Reggaeton

3 Musical notes

GOOD CHARLOTTE

Good Charlotte is an American rock band that formed in 1996. The lead singer Joel Madden and his twin brother Benji, who plays guitar, work with different charities to help people around the world. They recorded the song *We are the world 25 for Haiti* to help the victims of the earthquake in Haiti in 2010. Over 80 artists took part including Pink, Kanye West and Nick Jonas.

Salsa

Reggae

a 3.44 Haiti is in the Caribbean. Listen to the different types of music from the Caribbean and write three adjectives to describe each of them.

1 calypso **2** reggaeton **3** salsa **4** reggae

b What types of traditional and modern music come from your country? What kind of instruments are used to make the music? What is your favourite music from your country?

10 Creating a buzz

Reporting verbs
Participle clauses
Vocabulary: Advertising;
Phrasal verbs with *come*
Interaction 10: Giving a presentation

1 Vocabulary Advertising

a 3.45 Match the words with the definitions. Then listen and check.

1 advertising agency **2** brand **3** launch
4 logo **5** marketing campaign
6 pop-up **7** slogan **8** target customers

A a short phrase to advertise a product
B an advert which appears in a new window on a website page
C a business which helps people advertise products
D a group of people for whom a product is intended
E a design or symbol used to advertise a product
F a type of product made by a particular company
G planned activities or events to sell a particular product
H to start a campaign or put a product on the market

b 3.46 Listen and write the words from Exercise 1a.

1 … **2** … **3** … **4** … **5** … **6** …

c Work with a partner. Ask and answer questions.

1. Do you always buy the same brands? Why? / Why not?
2. What's your favourite product logo? Why do you like it?
3. Can you remember any good advertising slogans? Why are they good?

d Do you know any more *advertising* vocabulary? Write them in your Workbook (page 123 Exercise 1).

2 Speak

a Look at the statements and for each one, give yourself a mark from 1, completely agree, to 5, strongly disagree. Compare your opinions with a partner.

TV adverts should be banned during children's TV programmes.

Advertising on TV is boring and does not affect me.

People often buy a product because of its brand name.

Advertising is a creative art form.

b Work in a group. Discuss the statements together. Give reasons for your opinions. Then report on what your group thinks to the class.

Most of us think that advertising is creative, but one of us disagrees.

Culture Vulture

Did you know that animals and surreal humour are very popular in British adverts? For example, many people loved a man in a gorilla suit playing the drums to advertise chocolate. What kind of adverts are popular in your country? What are your favourite adverts?

3 Read and listen

a Look at the headings to different sections in the text. Can you guess what they mean?

1 Publicity stunts **2** Buzz agents **3** Negative buzz **4** Catch the cool kids **5** Online buzz

b Read the text quickly. Match the headings (1–5) with the paragraphs (A–E). Were your guesses correct?

How to create buzz

Something is happening in the world of advertising. Companies are increasingly turning to new forms of marketing and finding them much more successful than traditional advertising on TV or in print.

A flash mob in a train station.

A
Imagine this scenario. A good friend of yours is raving about a new film and recommends going to see it. You do, but later she explains that she had promised to talk positively about the film in return for free tickets. How would you feel? This is an example of *buzz*, or talking positively about a brand to increase sales. In the US over 280,000 teenagers (75% of them girls) help the biggest buzz agency. They recommend products to their friends and family without mentioning that they are working for anybody.

B
Bloggers can also make money on the internet by suggesting that people buy certain clothes or listen to certain music. Online buzz takes many forms. Before the release of *The Blair Witch Project*, a lot of fake sites were set up to give the impression that the film had a huge number of fans. Although the fans didn't exist, the online buzz convinced millions to see the film.

C
Advertisers are now also copying flash mobs. These were originally groups of people who agreed to do strange things in public places for fun, such as 4,000 people dancing silently to their MP3 players at a train station. A mobile phone company made a flash mob-style advert in another London station, using 400 dancers dressed in ordinary clothes. The viral video gained a lot of publicity for the company.

D
In Chicago, 'cool' schoolkids were invited to try out a new games console by market researchers. After accepting, the kids then received 10 free consoles to distribute to their friends. The campaign managed to distribute games to cool kids in 900 of Chicago's 1,400 schools. These 'free gifts' were really advertising: many children asked their parents to buy them the consoles because they wanted to copy their friends.

E
However, buzz can backfire. A big electronics company hired actors to walk around US cities pretending to be tourists, who then talked to people about how wonderful their camera phone was. When the company announced that it had carried out a successful undercover marketing campaign, many people were furious. After that, many companies have either avoided undercover marketing, or not admitted doing it.

It looks as if buzz is here to stay, at least until the next big thing. But there are quite a lot of questions about undercover marketing which have yet to be discussed. Is buzz persuading us to buy things in an honest way, or is it tricking us?

Which is right? Don't look at the text!
She recommends ***go/to go/going*** *to see the new film.*

c 3.47 Read the text again and listen. Answer the questions.

1 What is *buzz*?
2 What is one example of 'online buzz'?
3 What was the original purpose of flash mobs?
4 How did market researchers in Chicago promote a new games console?
5 How did one company promote their new camera phone?
6 Do companies talk about using undercover marketing nowadays?

d Work with a partner. Ask and answer the questions.

1 How would you feel if a friend tried to sell you something without telling you they were a buzz agent? Why?
2 Do you think buzz advertising exploits people?
3 Have you ever seen a flash mob or another kind of publicity stunt? Tell your partner about it.

4 Grammar

Reporting verbs

a Look at the examples and match them with the structures.

*She **recommends going** to see it.*
*She **had promised to talk** positively about the film.*
*Is buzz **persuading us to buy** things?*
*Bloggers can also make money on the internet by **suggesting that** people buy certain clothes …*

A verb + infinitive
B verb + *-ing*
C verb + *that* clause
D verb + object (person) + infinitive

Grammar reference: page 140

Check it out!

- Some reporting verbs can take two forms:
  You promised **to help** / **that you would help** me.
  We agreed **to try** the idea / **that** the idea **might work**.
  He admitted **feeling** / **that he felt** jealous.
  I recommend **seeing** / **that you see** the film.

b Find the verbs in the text in Exercise 3 and match them with the structures (A–D) in Exercise 4a.

1 mention
2 suggest
3 convince
4 agree
5 invite
6 admit

c Choose the correct verb forms.

1 He promised *to try* / *trying* the new gadget.
2 I didn't really want it, but she persuaded me *to buy* / *buying* it.
3 Let's offer *to be* / *being* buzz agents for the company.
4 They admitted *to think* / *thinking* up the terrible new slogan.
5 She complained *that the campaign was* / *the campaign to be* boring.
6 They warned *that I shouldn't go* / *me not to go* to that agency.

d Complete the sentences for you. Then compare with a partner.

1 Last year I invited …
2 If you like exciting films, I suggest …
3 Yesterday our teacher announced …
4 For a good read, I recommend …
5 I would never admit …

Get it right!

We usually use *the* before *internet*
✓ *People should have more privacy on the internet.*
✗ *People should have more privacy ~~on internet~~.*

5 Listen

a Look at the statements and decide if they are true or false.

1 When you are surfing the internet, you are anonymous.
2 Teenagers think a lot about whether they need things before buying them.
3 Many internet sites are free because they are paid for by advertising.

b 4.2 Listen to the presentation. What does Lucy say about the statements in Exercise 5a?

c 4.2 Listen again. Are the sentences *right* (✓) or *wrong* (✗)? Correct the wrong sentences.

1 In Japan there are billboards that will shout your name at you.
2 Facial recognition technology can tell your gender and how old you are.
3 It's possible that everything you do online is being followed by someone.
4 Advertisers usually know our names.
5 Teenagers are more easily influenced by advertisers than adults.
6 Advertising online is tightly regulated.

d Work with a partner. Ask and answer the questions.

1 Do you like receiving personalised adverts? Why? / Why not?
2 Do you think people should have more privacy on the internet?
3 Should there be more control over advertising on the internet?

6 Grammar

Participle clauses

a Look at the examples and choose the correct words to complete the rules.

Walking along, he passes lots of advertising billboards.
While searching for information, very often we are being recorded.
Having installed special tools in our computers without our knowledge, they follow nearly everything we do.
*It can be creepy when ads especially **meant** for us come up on our screens.*
*Not knowing this, someone **chatting** or **writing** an email online gives them even more information.*

- Present participles **always** / **often** end in *-ing*.
- Past participles **always** / **often** end in *-ed*.
- Past participles on their own always have **an active** / **a passive** meaning.
- Perfect participles, formed by *having* + past participle, refer to a time **before** / **after** the main action.
- Participle clauses at the beginning of a sentence refer to the **subject** / **object** of the main clause.

Grammar reference: page 138

b Choose the correct words.

1 While *surfing* / *surfed* the internet, I found a lot of information for my project.
2 *Looking* / *Looked* out of the window, they saw the storm move towards them.
3 What do you think of the actors *chosen* / *choosing* for the film?
4 *Having forgotten* / *Forgetting* her password, she wasn't able to log on.
5 After *having* / *had* a shower, Zac went out.
6 They had a final meeting, and *doing* / *having done* that, launched the campaign.

c Complete the sentences with the verb in the correct form.

1 By … (carry out) a buzz campaign, they managed to sell to a different market.
2 … (be) quite private, Mark doesn't post many photos on his social network page.
3 We weren't very happy with the advert … (send) by the agency.
4 After … (hear) Adele's latest album, Jess really wanted to see her in concert.
5 Before … (have) lunch, we ran round the park five times.
6 Not … (drive) before, he nearly hit someone … (cross) the road.

d Complete the sentences so that they are true for you.

1 Not being very … , I never …
2 Having been on holiday to … before, this year I'd like to go to …
3 While having breakfast, I usually …
4 Having left school last Friday afternoon, I …

7 Vocabulary

Phrasal verbs with *come*

a 4.3 Look at the examples and match the phrasal verbs with *come* with the definitions. Then listen and check.

1 Have you ever **come across** an ad that seems aimed just at you?
2 They've **come up with** a brilliant idea called tracking.
3 I'll **come back** to privacy later.
4 It can be creepy when personalised pop-up ads **come up** on our screens.
5 That was long before the internet **came along**.
6 My aunt **came over** last night. It was really nice to see her.
7 A film about social networking has just **come out**.
8 You've lost all your documents! How did that **come about**?

A to return to a place or an idea
B to happen
C to become available for people to buy or see
D to suggest or think of a new idea or plan
E to appear unexpectedly
F to find by chance
G to arrive
H to pay a casual visit to someone

b Rewrite the sentences, using a phrasal verb with *come* in the correct form.

1 I've just *thought of* a great idea for an advert.
2 Their new album *will be published* in the spring.
3 He said he was going to *return* to the house before he went out tonight.
4 My mother *found* these old photos when she was tidying up.
5 I waited ages for a bus, then three *arrived* at once!
6 My computer has crashed. I don't know how that *happened*.

Get it right!

After **is followed by the –ing form of the verb.**
✓ *After accepting, the kids received 10 free consoles.*
✗ *After ~~accept~~, the kids received 10 free consoles.*

Check it out!

- Some phrasal verbs are separable, and some are inseparable.
  Take something off *(separable)*:
  He **took** his coat **off**.
  He **took off** his coat.
  Come across something *(inseparable)*:
  I **came across** a funny ad. NOT
  ~~I **came** a funny ad **across**~~.

c Do you know any more phrasal verbs with *come*? Write them in your Workbook (page 123 Exercise 3).

d Work with a partner. Ask and answer the questions.

1 Has anyone interesting come over to your house to visit in the last week?
2 Have you come across any cool sites while surfing the internet?
3 Are you waiting for any albums or films to come out at the moment? If so, what?
4 Have you come up with any good ideas or plans recently?

8 Pronunciation DVD

Pitch in signalling words

a 4.4 When we speak, we use a higher pitch before we talk about new or important information. Listen to these signalling words.

OK, today I'd like to talk about …
Now, let's move on to …

b 4.5 Listen to the beginning of a presentation and write the signalling words.

> Right, everybody sit down, please. I'll just let everybody get settled. OK, I'll start. Well, firstly, I'd like to talk about how adverts are made. First a client comes along with a product they want to sell. Then the sales team talks to them about how much money they want to spend, and so on. After that, the creative team get involved. They are the people who come up with ideas for the advertising campaign. Next, they …

c 4.5 Listen again and read the text out loud.

d Practise the talk with a partner. Are your partner's signalling words clear?

Interaction 10 DVD

Giving a presentation

a 4.6 Listen to the beginning of a presentation about viral videos. Complete the titles of the videos Sarah and Frank talk about.

1 … baby.
2 The … of dance.
3 … rain.

b 4.6 Listen again and complete the sentences. Sometimes more than one word is necessary.

1 Today we'd … about viral videos.
2 First we're going to … how they started.
3 … next we'll … to talk about different types of video.
4 Then … we'd like to explain why they are important in modern advertising.
5 Anyway, as I … , viral videos really took off later.
6 Now I'll pass you … Frank, who is going to talk about …
7 Yes, … Sarah said, a meme is …

c 4.7 Turn to page 124. Listen to the sentences and repeat them. Practise using rising intonation on the signalling words and when you have more to say, and falling intonation when you have finished one part of your talk.

d Work with a partner.
Turn to page 131.

Portfolio 10 A product review

a What type of information would you expect to find in a product review? Choose from the items below.

a description of how the product looks
the manufacturer's claims for the product
personal experiences and opinions
a comparison with another product
how effective the product is
a recommendation

b Read the product review for a website for teenagers. Which information from Exercise a is in the review?

http://interactive.cambridge.org

VIVOBAREFOOT

MENS LADIES KIDS BAREFOOT REVIEWS INFO

PRODUCT REVIEW: VIVOBAREFOOT SHOES

VIVOBAREFOOT is a new kind of shoe based on the idea that being barefoot is very healthy. The shoes are designed so you feel as if you are not wearing anything on your feet, but you are actually protected by the extremely thin, but very strong soles. The manufacturers claim that the shoes make you stand correctly and strengthen the muscles in your feet. They also say that, because you can feel the ground through the shoes, the 200,000 nerves which end in your feet are all stimulated as you walk.

I like the trendy, grey and yellow trainers I bought, but some of the other models on the website look old-fashioned. At first I was a bit nervous about going outside and feeling the ground under my feet, but the soles do seem to be very strong and my feet have been protected. Having worn my trainers for a week now, I'm not sure whether my feet are stronger, whether I am standing straighter, or whether all my 200,000 nerve-endings have been stimulated, but the shoes are certainly very comfortable. Another good point is that the anti-bacterial lining inside is effective. My feet are less smelly than they usually are! To sum up, although the shoes are rather expensive, I would recommend buying them. Your feet will thank you for them.

Rate the product:

Looks:
OK / Good / Great

Practical:
Yes / No

Manufacturer's claims:
1 2 3 4 5 6 7 8 9 10

Price:
Good value / Reasonable / Expensive

Would you recommend?
Yes / No

c Read the product review again and write one example of:

1 the passive
2 a descriptive adjective
3 positive and negative comment
4 a personal experience
5 a recommendation of the product

d You are going to write a review of a product in one of the categories in the box.

a computer / computer accessory   a mobile phone / accessory   an item of clothing
a camera   a video game   a beauty product (e.g. hairdryer)

Make sure you include:

- the information which is included in the review in Exercise b
- passive forms where appropriate
- descriptive adjectives

e Work with a partner. Read your partner's review. Have they used passive tenses? Are there personal opinions and is there a clear recommendation in the review?

1

The first chocolate bar in the world was created in Bristol. Joseph Fry invented the delicious treat around the year 1720. Fry's also produced the first chocolate Easter egg in the UK in 1873. The company continues to produce chocolates and sweets to this day, although Fry's merged with the brand Cadbury in 1919.

2

Aardman has a deserved reputation as a world leader in model animation. Their award-winning work leads the field, producing a unique brand of independent film alongside work for broadcast and advertising spots. The studio has had seven Oscar nominations, and has won four.

In 1993 Aardman passed another milestone with the completion of Nick Park's Oscar-winning *The Wrong Trousers*. Acclaimed world-wide and winner of over thirty awards, *The Wrong Trousers* has become one of the most successful animated films ever made.

Chicken Run was Aardman's first full-length feature film to be funded by DreamWorks. Directed by both Peter Lord and Nick Park, it was released in June 2000 in the US and UK to excellent reviews and outstanding box office receipts. *Chicken Run* grossed over $220m at the worldwide box office.

From Peter and David's tabletop beginnings, Aardman has grown into a major, world class studio. Their work continues to be innovative, entertaining, brilliantly characterised and full of charm, reflecting the talent, energy and personal commitment of all the people who comprise the Aardman team.

3

BRISTOL: UK'S BEST MUSIC CITY?

According to a new study from royalties body PRS, Bristol is the UK's most musical place, with the biggest number of musicians among the population. It's well-known for giving birth to the trip-hop scene in the 1990s, spawning acts like Massive Attack, Portishead and Tricky. Despite Bristol's links through history with the slave trade, its multicultural population has really influenced the sounds of the Bristol music scene.

4

Famous people from Bristol

J.K. Rowling

Author J.K. Rowling was born and brought up in Chipping Sodbury, just outside Bristol. It is claimed that she invented her famous character Harry Potter after meeting a young boy named Ian Potter in the village where she grew up.

Banksy

Banksy is a controversial graffiti artist local to Bristol who is famous throughout the world for his street art. Some of his pieces have sold for hundreds of thousands of pounds, with Hollywood A-listers and celebrities being some of the top collectors of his work.

5

the ballad of Banksy

His name now is familiar to one and all
The graffiti artist who left his mark on the wall,
When he first started out he wasn't well-known
Yet kept his street art alive in Bristol ... alone.
Yes his artwork today is known worldwide!

6

The Bristol Belle was the first modern hot-air balloon in Western Europe and was developed and built in 1967.

The Bristol International Balloon Fiesta is held every summer in the city, and is Europe's biggest hot-air balloon event.

1 Culture UK: Bristol

a Look at the information about products and people from Bristol and answer the questions.

1 Which music scene started in Bristol in the 1990s?
2 Which two famous films were created by the Aardman studio?
3 Who gave money to the Aardman studio to create its first long film?
4 Why was 1873 an important year for the Fry family?
5 Which two chocolate companies joined together in 1919?
6 What can you see every summer in the skies of Bristol?
7 In which town near Bristol did a famous writer grow up?
8 In whose homes can you see examples of Banksy's art?
9 Where did Banksy first start to paint?

b Copy and complete the puzzle and find the mystery phrase.

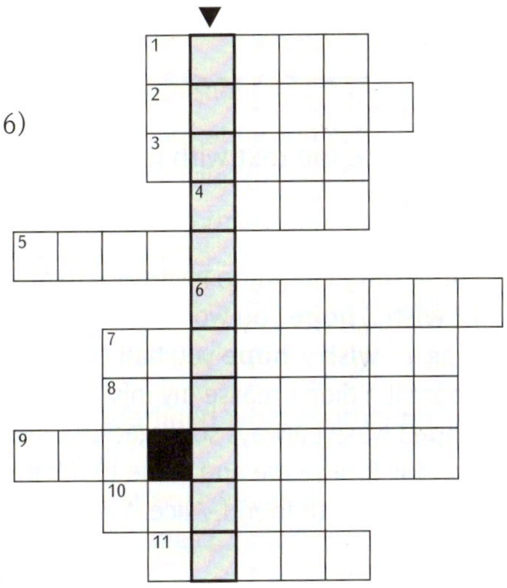

1 Something made of sugar. (text 1)
2 A very large balloon which can carry people is filled with this. (text 6)
3 A product made by a particular company. (text 1)
4 Something which joins or connects one thing to another. (text 3)
5 An official prize or money given for something done well. (text 2)
6 A type of film that is at least 90 minutes long. (text 2)
7 Writing or pictures painted on walls in public places. (text 5)
8 Something or someone people know well. (text 5)
9 A place where tickets are sold. (text 2)
10 The unit of money used in Britain. (text 4)
11 A famous prize given to actors or people who make films. (text 2)

c Work with a partner. Have you heard of any of the things/people from Bristol? Do you know anything else that was made or invented in the UK?

2 Your noticeboard

An advertisement for your town: 'Made in …'

a Work in a group. Make a list of products, things and people from your town or region that are world-famous. Use the internet to find out more information about them.

b Make a poster to advertise your town/region called 'Made in + *name of place*'.

Include information about the products and people and adverts, logos and pictures if possible.

Get it right!

advertisement

We spell *advertisement* with 'e' between 's' and 'm'.

✓ *Make an advertisement for your town.*
✗ ~~*advertisment*~~

11 Just the job

Modal verbs of deduction and possibility review
Question tag review
Vocabulary: Compound adjectives; Job collocations
Interaction 11: A job interview

1 Read and listen

a Work with a partner. Think of five things a private detective might do in a typical day at work. Read the text quickly and check your ideas.

A day in the life of a teen detective

Sitting in cafés or cars for hours, dressing up in school uniform, following people, filming with hidden cameras, researching people's digital footprints and writing top-secret reports are all part of Isla MacKinnon's job. Isla, aged 19, is a private detective, although one day she would like to be a world-famous actress. For now, going undercover gives her good practice at playing different roles.

Private detectives are hard-working and each day is full of surprises. [1] . Sometimes she works a 16-hour day and might not finish until after midnight, or she may find that an investigation is easy to complete and she can go home early. It all depends on the day, but Isla likes the job's unpredictable nature.

Isla's father is a policeman and initially he was worried about his daughter doing such a dangerous job. [2] . If Isla ever feels uncomfortable in a situation she puts her hair up, a signal to her team that they should come and help her. She has been in several situations that could have turned nasty but luckily she had the support of her colleagues.

You normally wouldn't suspect that a schoolgirl or a Goth was observing you, but Isla can easily dress up as these characters. [3] . That's why she is given jobs that nobody else at the detective agency could do. She sometimes has to check if a shop or bar is selling products to people who are underage. In other jobs, she knocks on the door of the person she's investigating and asks them some questions for an imaginary school survey. It doesn't get much easier than that!

A hidden camera and a voice recorder are part of Isla's equipment. Many cases involve following people who are cheating their employers by saying they are too ill to work, when in fact they are fine. [4] . However, she found out he was playing golf every day and dancing in nightclubs! Photos and videos of him doing these activities meant his employer could give him the sack.

Isla loves her job even though it's not very highly paid at a junior level. [5] . She must be very good at what she does as her boss is extremely happy with her work. In the past, it was seen as a job for older men in dark raincoats and sunglasses. The image of the private detective might have changed, but in a world where crime is the same as ever, there are now job opportunities in this field for people of all ages.

b Read the text again and complete it with sentences A–E.

A She's at an age where, with the right clothes, she can look much older or younger.
B Isla never knows exactly what her day's work will involve.
C She is proud to be part of a growing number of young private detectives in their late teens and early twenties.
D One man who Isla investigated wasn't going to work due to backache.
E However, he knows that she is always accompanied on risky missions.

c 4.12 Read the text again and listen. Check your answers to Exercise 1b.

d Work with a partner. Which qualities do you think are most important to be a good private detective? Choose your top three, then compare with another pair of students.

patience flexibility curiosity logic being secretive intelligence being respectful
being calm under pressure determination ambition physical fitness

2 Vocabulary

Compound adjectives

a 4.13 Match the words to make compound adjectives. Then listen and check.

1 badly **2** last **3** part **4** short
5 six **6** top

A paid **B** quality **C** minute **D** day
E sighted **F** time

b Complete the sentences with a compound adjective from Exercise 2a. Add a hyphen if necessary.

1 He loves his job, but it's really …
2 They decided to go on holiday on Friday and left on Saturday, it was a … decision.
3 She has to wear glasses to watch TV because she's …
4 That chocolate is the best that you can get, it's …
5 He only works on Mondays and Tuesdays so it's a … job.
6 He works a … week in the factory, he's only free on Sundays.

> **Check it out!**
>
> - Compound adjectives usually have a hyphen when they come before a noun.
>   She used to have a **part-time** job but her new job is **full time**.
>   We don't usually use a hyphen when the first word is an *-ly* adverb.
>   **highly paid**, **privately owned**

c Work in a group. How many of the following can you name in two minutes?

- English-speaking countries
- well-known actresses
- badly paid jobs
- top-quality brands
- money-saving ideas

> **Get it right!**
>
> **We use the infinitive without *to* after *must* and *might*.**
> ✓ *I must go shopping at the weekend.*
> ✗ *I must ~~to go~~ shopping at the weekend.*

3 Grammar

Modals of deduction and possibility review

a Look at the sentences and choose the correct word(s) to complete the rules.

> *Sometimes Isla **might not finish** until after midnight.*
> *She **may find** an investigation is easy to complete.*
> *Isla **must be** very good at what she does.*
> *The image of the private detective **might have changed**.*
> *She has been in several situations that **could have turned** nasty.*
>
> - We use *might*, *may* or *could* for deductions about the present or future when we're **sure** / **not sure** about something.
> - We use modal + *have* + past participle for possibilities in the **past** / **future**.
> - We use *must* when we are **sure** / **not sure** that something is true.
> - We use *can't* when we are **sure** / **not sure** that something is not true.

Grammar reference: page 139

b Work with a partner. Read the two sentences and discuss the differences in meaning.

1 I must go shopping at the weekend.
I might go shopping at the weekend.
2 She must have got the news already.
She may have got the news already.

c Rewrite the sentences using the modal verb in brackets.

1 Perhaps I'll go to the party on Saturday. (might)
2 I don't think he was Brazilian because he didn't speak Portuguese. (can't)
3 I'm possibly going to go away at the weekend but I'm not sure yet. (may)
4 He is a really good driver so I'm sure he's had lots of practice. (must)
5 There's a possibility that you'll pass the exam if you study a bit more. (might)
6 That was the phone, but I don't think it was Jack – he's in a meeting. (can't)

d Work with a partner. Ask and answer the questions.

1 What might you do this weekend?
2 Do you think that knowing English may help you in the future?
3 What do you think you might do when you leave school?
4 Do you think you could have studied harder last year?

4 Speak

a Work with a partner. Look at the jobs and choose the one you would most/least like to do. Explain your reasons.

actor architect author business person chef
computer programmer doctor journalist lawyer
professional footballer rubbish collector scientist
shop assistant supermodel surgeon teacher translator vet

b Discuss all the jobs in Exercise 4a with your partner. Which one(s) …

1 … are very well paid?
2 … are badly paid but you think should be better paid?
3 … would your partner be best at? Why?
4 … would you hate to do? Why?
5 … are most and least valued by society?
6 … are usually part-time jobs?
7 … usually involve weekend or night work?

c Work with a new partner. Compare your answers to Exercise 4b.

Get it right!

We use *a* or *an* when we talk about people's jobs.

✓ *Isla's father is a policeman.*
✗ *Isla's father ~~is policeman~~.*

5 Vocabulary

Job collocations

a 4.14 Match the two parts of the sentences. Then listen and check.

1 The company has just invited me to **have**
2 Most nurses and factory workers **work**
3 He is hoping to **be**
4 She's unemployed now; she **was**
5 There are fifty-two **members**
6 All the teachers stopped working and **went on**
7 He has **applied for**
8 You must **write your**

A **a job** as a chef, but hasn't had an interview yet.
B **an interview** on Wednesday at 10 o'clock.
C **of staff** in the marketing department.
D **CV** and send it to companies when you are looking for a job.
E **shifts**, as their place of work is open all the time.
F **strike** to protest against longer working hours.
G **promoted** to a better position in the company soon.
H **fired** for always arriving late to work.

b Complete the sentences with collocations from Exercise 5a. Use the correct form of the verb.

1 People who … at night get used to sleeping during the day.
2 How many … are there working at the sports centre?
3 He … for arriving late every day and now he's looking for a new job.
4 He's … for a job at the cinema, but doesn't know yet if he's got it.
5 It's important to … carefully as it's a document which employers often ask to see.
6 The bus drivers … to protest against low pay and I couldn't get to school.

c 4.15 Listen to the dialogues and write a short sentence to describe each situation.

1 … 2 … 3 … 4 …

d Work with a partner. Think of three good reasons for …

1 … getting promoted.
2 … getting fired.
3 … going on strike.
4 … trying to make a living from a hobby.

6 Listen

a 4.16 Complete the jobs with a word from each box. Then listen and check.

chocolate computer games water park music festival	tester (x2) taster blogger

1

2

3

4

b 4.16 Listen again. Are the sentences *right* (✓) or *wrong* (✗)? Correct the wrong sentences.

1. Bren thinks that Gillie would love being a music festival blogger.
2. Their mum thinks it would be great to be able to make a living from a hobby.
3. Gillie would like to eat chocolate every day.
4. Gillie thinks that the job of water park tester might be more difficult than it appears.
5. Bren thinks computer games testers might not earn very much.
6. Bren and Gillie's mum doesn't like working as a nurse.

c Work with a partner. Ask and answer the questions.

1. Which jobs in exercise 6a do you think would be the best? Why?
2. When do you think is a good age to decide what job you want to do?
3. Do you think it will be easy for you to get a good job that you enjoy in the future? Why? / Why not?

7 Grammar

Question tag review

a Look at the examples and choose the correct words to complete the rules.

You like your job, ***don't you?***
You could do that, ***couldn't you?***
You've decided what you want to do, ***haven't you?***
It wouldn't be like going to work though, ***would it?***
It isn't very realistic, ***is it?***

- We repeat the auxiliary verb or the **modal** / **main** verb in question tags (unless *be* is the main verb).
- We use **do** / **have** if there is no auxiliary or modal verb as the main verb.
- We usually use a **positive** / **negative** question tag after a positive statement and a **positive** / **negative** question tag after a negative statement.
- We use question tags mainly in informal **spoken** / **written** English to check information or invite agreement.

Grammar reference: page 139

b Put a question tag at the end of each sentence.

1. She isn't a doctor, …?
2. They work a six-day week, …?
3. You won't get the job if you don't apply for it, …?
4. When people really love their jobs you can tell, …?
5. It depends on your qualifications, …?
6. He downloaded the application form, …?

c Complete the sentences.

1. … the best worker in the company, is she?
2. … love to be a vet, wouldn't you?
3. … pass the exam, won't he?
4. … on a training course last week, wasn't he?

d Work with a partner. Write a dialogue about jobs and work. Include as many question tags as you can, then practise reading it aloud.

A: *You want to be a doctor, don't you?*
B: *Yes, I do. But it's difficult to get on the course, isn't it?*

Check it out!

- Remember these irregular question tags:
  Imperatives: use *will*, *can* or *would*
  Close the window, **will** you?
  Take my bag, **would** you? Help me, **can** you?
  Let's: use *shall*
  Let's go, **shall** we?

8 Pronunciation DVD Intonation in question tags

a 4.17 The intonation in question tags is important, as it changes the meaning of the question. Listen to the pronunciation of the sentences and match them to the meanings.

1 You were promoted last year, weren't you?
2 You were promoted last year, weren't you?

A She's checking that the information is true.
B She's asking for agreement, and is quite sure the information is true.

b 4.18 Listen to the sentences. Decide and write if the speaker is 'checking information' or 'asking for agreement'.

1 … 2 … 3 … 4 … 5 … 6 …

c 4.19 Listen and check your answers.

d Work with a partner. Take turns reading the sentences in Exercise 8b. Guess if your partner is checking information or asking for agreement.

Interaction 11 DVD

A job interview

a 4.20 Listen to the job interview. Does Cathy want a full-time or part-time position?

b 4.20 Listen again. Look at the questions and write the ones you hear.

1 Could you tell me about your work experience?
2 Could you tell me why you've applied for the job?
3 What do you do in your free time?
4 What hours could you work?
5 What languages do you speak?
6 Would I have to wear a uniform?
7 How much would I get paid?
8 What hours would I work?
9 Would you give me any training?
10 When will you let me know if I've got the job?

c 4.21 Turn to page 125. Listen to the questions and repeat them. Practise stressing key words.

d Work with a partner.
Student A: Turn to page 128.
Student B: Turn to page 130.

Culture Vulture

Did you know that teenagers in the UK who have part-time jobs are not allowed to work during school hours, and can only work for two hours on a school day?
Are under-18s allowed to work on a school day in your country? Do you think young people should be allowed to work as much as they like?

Portfolio 11 A job application

a A friend wants to apply for a job which she saw advertised on your school website. She has made some notes on the advert and written a letter of application. Read the advert and the application. Do you think she would get the job? Why? / Why not?

After-school group leaders needed!

We're looking for young people to work at our after-school club. We need people on Mondays and Wednesdays from 4–6pm. — *I could only work on Wednesdays.*

Ideally applicants should:

- Have some experience of being with children aged 4–8. — *I babysit for my cousin Alex twice a month. He's five.*
- Be interested in sports and activities. What could you offer our club? *Arts and crafts, cooking?*
- Speak some foreign languages. — *Can speak French quite well and know a few songs and games. Also speak a bit of Spanish.*

If you are interested in the job please send an email to the group organiser, Mrs. Davies at:
afterschoolclubsuk@parentsupport.co.uk

To: afterschoolclubsuk@parentsupport.co.uk
From: bethoneil@smilemail.com
Subject: Application for after-school group leader job

Dear Mrs. Davies

1 I am writing to apply for the job of after-school group leader at your club, which I saw advertised on the school website. Please find attached a copy of my CV.

2 I have a lot of experience of being with young children as I regularly babysit for my five-year-old cousin. I am quite good at art, particularly at crafts and making things, and I love cooking. I speak French quite well and I understand a little bit of Spanish. I can sing simple songs and play games in French.

3 It might be useful to tell you that at the moment I would only be available to work on Wednesdays, as on Mondays I play volleyball for a local club. Finally, how many children are usually in a group? Are they well behaved?

4 I look forward to hearing from you soon.

Yours sincerely,

Beth O'Neil.

Which is right? Don't look at the text!
*I look forward to **hear/hearing** from you soon.*

b Read the letter again. Match the paragraphs with the functions.

A Give more information and ask any questions. 3
B Finish your letter with a formal phrase. 4
C Explain why you are writing. 1
D Give information about your application 2

c You have seen this advert for a part-time summer job. Use the notes below and write a letter of application for the position. Make sure you:

- use a suitable beginning
- organise your email into clear paragraphs
- give relevant information about each point
- end your email appropriately

Are you interested in journalism, design or computers?

We're looking for four students to write and send the school's monthly e-newsletter and we will pay you to do it!

We're looking for students who can:

- Find out what's happening at our school. — *3 I'm in the football team and have friends in other teams and clubs.*
- Write clear articles. — *1 I write a blog on computer games which is becoming popular.*
- Design the newsletter. — *2 I helped my brother design the webpage for his music blog.*
- Create a mail list database. — *3 I have no idea how to do this, but I would like to find out! Training available?*

Think you may be the perfect candidate? If so, send an email to the headmistress, Ms. Hodson, explaining why you think you'd be good at the job.
headmistress@greenleavesschool.co.uk

d Work with a partner. Swap your letters. Do you think they have a good chance of getting the job? Why? / Why not?

The Best Job in the World?

THE BEST JOB IN THE WORLD.

Islands of the Great Barrier Reef, Queensland, Australia.

Position Vacant: Island Caretaker
Salary: AU $150,000 6-month contract

Responsibilities: • Feed the fish • Collect the mail • Explore and report back

Applications close: 22 February
Interviews: 4 May
Announcement made: 8 May
Work begins: 1 July

ANYONE CAN APPLY
www.islandreefjob.com

1 If you saw this job advert, would you apply? Well, 34,000 people from 200 different countries did! The job was advertised by Tourism Queensland, as part of an award-winning publicity campaign which aimed to increase the number of visitors to Australia. To get the job of island caretaker in the Great Barrier Reef, applicants had to make a one-minute video to persuade Tourism Queensland that they would be the best person for the role. 16 finalists were taken to the island for the final part of the selection process, which involved a formal interview, an English test, health checks and some fun activities which were designed to show their real personalities.

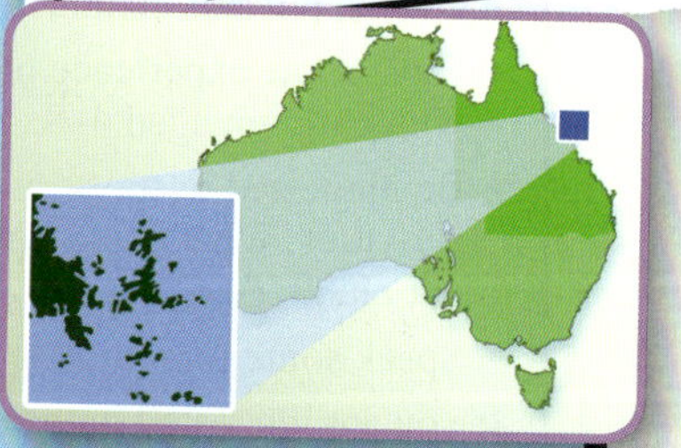

The Winner

2 Despite the extremely tough competition, Ben Southall, a charity worker from the UK, got the job. Ben lived on Hamilton Island, in the Whitsundays in the Great Barrier Reef. He was given a beautiful house to live in and he was allowed to bring his girlfriend too! In fact, he believes that it was his girlfriend who really had the best job in the world; all the fun but none of the work involved in maintaining a blog of life on the island! He spent his days doing water sports, exploring and checking out the hotels and restaurants. In the evenings, he would blog about his day and post photos and videos to show the world how much fun can be had on the islands. You can still read Ben's blog at: http://islandreefjob.com.au/island-caretaker-blog/

Quick Facts

3 **The Great Barrier Reef ...**

- is the world's largest tropical reef system
- covers an area of 348,000 square kilometres
- is made up of 900 individual coral reefs and 900 islands and coral cays
- is home to more than 1,500 species of marine fish, 500 species of seaweed and 15 species of sea snakes which can kill humans!
- is the only living organism that can be seen from space

5 From Best Job to Best Career in the World

When Ben finished his six-month job of island caretaker, Tourism Queensland were keen to give him another one. He now works as a Tourism Ambassador and travels the planet to tell people more about the Great Barrier Reef and has given TV interviews about his experiences as island caretaker in many countries.

4 What to do on the islands of the Great Barrier Reef

Try a new water sport: choose from jet-skiing, kayaking, sailing and lots more.

Snorkelling and diving: with the most spectacular underwater gardens and coral in the world, you'd be crazy not to take a look!

Meet the turtles: if you visit when it's turtle nesting season, you can see baby turtles racing into the water at night.

1 Culture World: The Great Barrier Reef

a Before you read the article, choose the tasks in the box which you usually have to do when you apply for a job.

have an interview	give a presentation
make a video	write a letter
do the job for a day	present a report
write a CV	write a blog

b Read the magazine page quickly. What did Ben have to do to get the best job in the world?

c Read the article again. Are the sentences *right* (✓) or *wrong* (✗)?

1 All the applicants for the job were from Australia. ✗ different countries
2 Tourism Queensland won awards for their publicity campaign. ✓
3 Ben had to write a blog about his experiences living on Hamilton Island. ✓
4 There are dangerous creatures living on the Great Barrier Reef. ✓
5 You can't see the Great Barrier Reef from space. ✗
6 When Ben finished his job as island caretaker, he returned to the UK. ✗

d Find the word(s) in the article that mean …

1 someone who is employed to take care of a large building or similar place. (para 1) caretaker
2 to look after or care for something (para 2)
3 a line of rocks, sand or coral which can just be seen beneath the surface of the sea (para 3)
4 a time of year when animals make nests and reproduce (para 4)
5 an important official who represents a country or organisation (para 5)

e Work with a partner. Ask and answer the questions.

1 If you had seen the advert in the newspaper, would you have applied? If so, do you think you would have had a chance of getting the job? Why? / Why not?
2 Do you think the publicity campaign launched by Tourism Queensland would work for your area / in your country? Why? / Why not?

2 Your project

Job advertisement: The best job in my country

a Work in a group. Make a list of some of the best jobs that people could do in your country.

b Imagine you are going to plan a publicity campaign to help promote tourism in your country. You are going to prepare an advert for the best job in your country. As well as the advert itself you should consider:

- what the job involves
- what qualities the applicants should have
- how people will find out about the job
- what the applicants have to do to get the job
- how you will select the successful applicant

c Make the advert for your job. It could be a written advert for a newspaper or a video advert to go online. Include the information from Exercise 2b.

The Best Job in My Country

We are looking for a self motivated individual to join our Skydiving team in Seville, Spain. The purpose of this role is to take wonderful photographs of skydivers – of our team of instructors when they practice, and of our customers – in that exceptional environment. The photographer will also need to capture the beautiful landscape around Seville, as seen from the sky!

Key tasks will include:
- **assisting the skydiving instructors in the plane**
- **taking fun photographs of skydivers and of Seville while skydiving**
- **selecting pictures and putting them up on the club's website**

A genuine interest in photography and in skydiving (including a desire to jump off a plane!) is needed. Training will be given.

Send your application to us as soon as possible.

There will be an interview and a 20-minute task.

Application deadline: 22 April
Interviews: 27 April
Job starts: 5 May

12 Changing times

Reported speech review
Relative clauses
Vocabulary: Expressions with *time*; Loan words in English
Interaction 12: Keeping a conversation going

1 Listen

a 4.22 Look at the pictures. Which of the things have been popular in your country? Who were they popular with? Listen to the interview and choose the pictures that are mentioned.

1

Lava lamp

2

Hula hoops

3
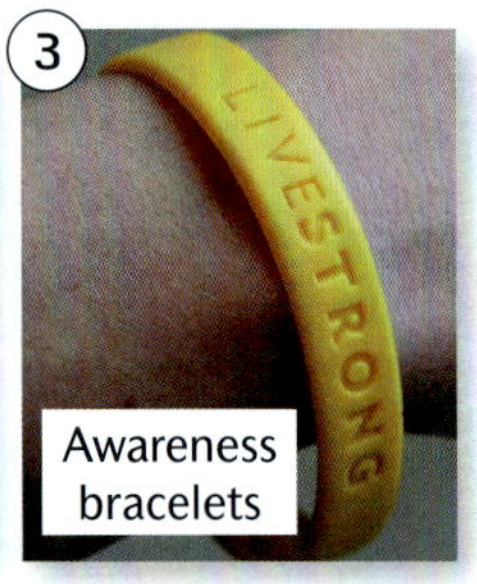

Awareness bracelets

4

Ugg boots

5

Pokémon

6

Silly Bandz

b 4.22 Listen again and choose the correct answer: A, B or C.

1 A fad …
A is followed by many people. **B** is usually unpopular.
C lasts forever.

2 *Silly Bandz* were successful because they were …
A colourful. **B** useful. **C** inexpensive.

3 Which famous person wore *Silly Bandz*?
A Thierry Henry **B** Sarah Jessica Parker
C Ronaldinho

4 Awareness bracelets are popular because …
A people like the colours.
B famous people wear them.
C people can support a cause.

5 Teenagers often follow fads because they want to …
A be different. **B** feel part of a group.
C spend all their money.

6 The *Pokémon* brand …
A will disappear in the future.
B has developed various products.
C was only successful for a short time.

2 Vocabulary

Expressions with *time*

a 4.23 Match the phrases in **bold** with the definitions. Then listen and check.

1. **From time to time** a new fad comes along.
2. Everyone wants to wear the same thing **at the same time**.
3. **Most of the time** people who take part in fads want to belong to a group.
4. Fads usually only last **for a short time**.
5. One of the biggest fads **of all time** has to be Pokémon.
6. New fads appear **all the time**.

A again and again / constantly **B** ever
C usually **D** not very long **E** sometimes
F together

b Choose the correct expression.

1. You can't watch Pokémon on TV and play the video game *at the same time / of all time*, that's impossible!
2. The Rubik's Cube is the best-selling puzzle game *at the same time / of all time*.
3. My sister wears her favourite jacket *all the time / from time to time*. She never takes it off!
4. Some critics said that social networking sites would only last *from time to time / for a short time*, but they were wrong.
5. We speak English *most of the time / all the time* in English class, but *of all time / from time to time* the teacher lets us speak Italian.

c Write three true and three false sentences about yourself using the expressions in Exercise 2a. Work with a partner. Read your partner's sentences and decide which are true and which are false.

A: *I go mountain biking with my friends from time to time.*
B: *False.*
A: *Yes, I go mountain biking with my friends all the time!*

3 Grammar

Reported speech review

a Look at the examples and complete the direct speech. Then choose the correct words to complete the rules.

→ *I **asked her what** a fad **was**.*
'What … a fad?'

*I **asked** Jenny **why** awareness bracelets **had been** so popular.*
'Why … awareness bracelets … so popular?'

*She **said that** the biggest fad ever **was** Pokémon.*
'The biggest fad ever … Pokémon.'

*I **asked whether** another big fad **would** come along soon.*
'… another big fad come along soon?'

- If the verb is in the present in direct speech, it usually changes to a **present** / **past** tense in reported speech.
- If the verb is in the past simple or present perfect in direct speech, it usually changes to the **present** / **past perfect** in reported speech.
- In reported questions we use the same word order as a **statement** / **question**.
- In reported *yes/no* questions we use *if* or **whether** / **a question word**.
- If we use **the present tense** / ***will*** in direct speech, it normally changes to *would* in reported speech.

Grammar reference: page 139

Check it out!

- If a situation described by someone remains the same when we report it, we don't need to change the tense.
'I **love** wearing Crocs,' said Megan.
Megan said that she **loves**/**loved** wearing Crocs.

Get it right!

We do not use *to* after *ask*.
✓ *I asked her what a fad was.*
✗ *I asked ~~to~~ her what a fad was.*

b Rewrite the sentences in reported speech.

1 'Most fads haven't lasted for a long time,' said Jenny.
2 'Lance Armstrong won the Tour de France seven times in a row between 1999 and 2005,' Jenny explained.
3 'Did Lance Armstrong start a fad?' asked Karl.
4 'The word *wiki* means *quick*, explained Alana.
5 'Why are you arguing so much with your brother?' asked Mia's dad.
6 'Has the internet influenced advertising?' Alice wanted to know.

c Work in a group. Ask and answer questions about fads. Write down each other's answers.

1 What fads have you followed in the past?
2 What fads have been popular in our country?
3 Are you following any fads at the moment?

d Report the questions and answers back to the class in reported speech.

→ *We asked Olga what fads she had followed and she told us that she used to wear Silly Bandz all the time.*

4 Speak

a Work with a partner to exchange information about two popular fads. First, write the questions you need to ask your partner to complete your fact file. Student B: Turn to page 125.

The Rubik's cube was invented by the Hungarian design professor, Ernö … (name) in … (year). In the early 1980s the Rubik's cube became the most popular puzzle in the world and over … (number) of the toys have been sold. People hold competitions to solve the cube as quickly as possible. In … (year) the world record for solving the classic 3x3 cube was … (time).

The Tamagotchi is a digital pet.
A Tamagotchi was sold for the first time in Japan in 1996.
Over 70 million Tamagotchis have been sold.
The player should look after the Tamagotchi pet all the time, or it will die.
A film was made in 2007 called *Tamagotchi: The Movie*.

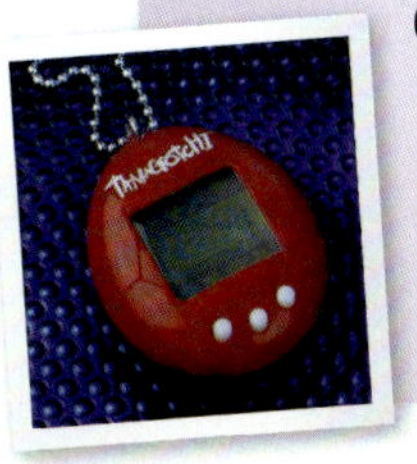

b Ask and answer questions with your partner to complete the fact files.

c Compare your fact files with your partner. Do you each have the correct information?

5 Read and listen

a What do you know about English around the world? Work with a partner and do the quiz. Read the text quickly and check your answers.

Culture Vulture

Did you know that the most widely spoken languages in the UK after English are *Punjabi*, *Bengali* and *Saraiki*, from India and Pakistan? Which other languages are spoken in your country? Which are spoken in your family?

Which English do you speak?

No one is sure exactly how many people speak English around the world. Experts estimate that there are around 400 million native speakers in countries like the UK, the USA and Australia and 600 million people in places where it is an official second language, such as India, Singapore and Kenya. In addition, hundreds of millions of people speak English as a foreign language. Altogether, there are at least 1.5 billion speakers of English around the globe, and speakers whose mother tongue is not English far outnumber native speakers.

People who already speak one language perfectly may think it is unfair to have to learn another, but in the twenty-first century the common language used to share information about technology, science, medicine and education by everyone around the globe is English. However, there are so many varieties that some people may not know which one to learn. A standard form like British or American English? Or what about a more distinct variety like *Hinglish*? Hinglish, which is a mixture of Hindi and English, is spoken in India by 350 million people. In the USA, where *Spanglish* speakers switch between English and Spanish all the time, you will often hear phrases like 'I'm going to hanguear at the mol', which means 'I'm going to hang out at the shopping mall'.

English is spreading into other languages too. In Polish you might hear the words *jogging* or *market* from time to time in a conversation whereas in Italian people may talk about *fashion* and the *weekend*. In France, where they are trying to stop English words (or anglicisms) coming into French, it is illegal to use an English word in an official document if a French word exists. However, languages that come into contact with one another naturally exchange words, and English has borrowed words such as *ballerina* from Italian and *yoghurt* from Turkish. Loan words are often preferable to English translations of the foreign words.

There are more words in English than any other language on the planet. With so many words, so many varieties and so many speakers, it is not surprising that English is the global language of the twenty-first century. However, it is spreading and changing so rapidly that nobody really knows what the future holds. What English will you be speaking in 20 years' time?

Quiz

1 How many people speak English around the world?
2 In which countries is English the first language?
3 Hinglish is a mixture of ... and English.
4 Which language does the word *yoghurt* originate from?

b 4.24 Read the text again and listen. Then answer the questions.

1 What do the numbers in the text refer to?
400 million 350 million 20
2 Which countries mentioned in the text use English as an official second language?
3 Which two standard forms of English are mentioned?
4 Which varieties of English in the text are a mixture of English and another language?
5 Where are English words being rejected and how?
6 What are loan words?

c Work in a group. Do you agree or disagree with the statements? Why?

1 English is the best choice for a common language in the twenty-first century.
2 It is best to learn a language when you are a child.
3 Some languages are more important than others.
4 Loan words are very useful in a language.

6 Grammar

Relative clause review

a Look at the examples and choose the correct word(s).

Defining relative clauses

Languages ***that*** *come into contact with one another naturally exchange words.*

People ***who*** *already speak one language perfectly may think it is unfair to have to learn another.*

Speakers ***whose*** *mother tongue is not English far outnumber native speakers.*

Non-defining relative clauses

Hinglish, *which is a mixture of Hindi and English, is spoken by 350 million people.*

In France, ***where*** *they are trying to stop English words (or anglicisms) coming into French, it is illegal to use an English word in an official document.*

- We use *who* for **people** / **things** and *which* for **people** / **things** in relative clauses.
- We use *where* for **places** / **possession** and *whose* for **places** / **possession** in relative clauses.
- Defining relative clauses contain **essential** / **extra** information and non-defining relative clauses contain **essential** / **extra** information.
- We can also use *that* for people and things in **defining** / **non-defining** clauses.
- We always use commas and a relative pronoun (but never *that*) in **defining** / **non-defining** clauses.

Grammar reference: page 140

b Join the two sentences using a defining relative clause.

1 That girl is speaking Spanish. She is my sister.
The girl who …

2 He speaks English. He speaks Chinese.
The languages that …

3 The passengers are waiting on the platform. Their train is delayed.
The passengers whose …

4 We stayed in a hotel on holiday. The hotel was very modern.
The hotel where …

5 English is spoken on TV. The English is standard English.
The English which …

c Join the two sentences using a non-defining relative clause.

1 My Spanish teacher comes from Mexico. He's funny.
My Spanish teacher, …

2 Anglicisms are words borrowed from English. Anglicisms are becoming more common in other languages.
Anglicisms, …

3 The biggest group of students are Indian. Their mother tongue is Hindi.
The biggest group of students, …

4 In Singapore, English is spoken by 71% of people. Standard English is preferred to Singlish in formal communication.
In Singapore, Standard English, …

d Complete the sentences so they are true for you.

1 The language that I like best …
2 At the weekend I go to places where …
3 I get on well with people who …

7 Vocabulary

Loan words in English

a 4.25 Match the words to the languages they come from. Then listen and check.

Spanish: 3 fiesta, …

1 ballet **2** champagne **3** fiesta **4** karaoke
5 ketchup **6** kiosk **7** mosquito **8** piano
9 spaghetti **10** sushi **11** kung fu **12** yoghurt

Chinese French Italian
Japanese Spanish Turkish

b Which of the words in Exercise 7a do you use in your language?

c 4.26 Listen to the definitions of six loan words from Exercise 7a and write them down.

1 … **2** … **3** … **4** … **5** … **6** …

d Do you know any more loan words in English? Write them in your Workbook (page 125, Exercise 4).

8 Pronunciation DVD

Pronouncing loan words in English

a 4.27 The pronunciation of loan words in English is often different to the pronunciation in the original language. Listen to the words. First you will hear the pronunciation in English, then the original language.

piano karaoke kung fu

b 4.28 Copy the table and listen to the pronunciation of the words in English and the original language. Which pronunciation do you hear first? Tick (✓) the correct column.

	Pronunciation in English	Original pronunciation
1 fiesta		
2 kiosk		
3 mosquito		
4 spaghetti		
5 champagne		
6 yoghurt		
7 sushi		
8 ballet		

c 4.29 Listen and repeat the pronunciation in English of the words in Exercise 8b.

d In pairs write mini-dialogues using as many loan words as possible. Then read them to the class with the pronunciation of the loan words in English.

Interaction 12 DVD

Keeping a conversation going

a 4.30 Listen to two conversations between students on an English course. Which conversation is better? Why?

b 4.31 Listen again to the second conversation and write *A* (Alain) or *Y* (Yoko) for each phrase.

1 How's it going?
2 So, what's new?
3 What about you?
4 I know what you mean.
5 I know what I was going to ask you.
6 By the way, I wanted to ask you something.
7 Let me think ...
8 That's good to know.

c 4.32 Turn to page 125. Listen to the sentences and repeat them. Practise saying the short phrases with the correct rhythm.

d Work with a partner.

Student A: Turn to page 128.
Student B: Turn to page 130.

Portfolio 12

Correcting your own mistakes

a Hasan regularly visits an English learning website to help improve his English. Read the website message and Hasan's reply. Then answer the questions.

1 Why is English important in Hasan's country?
2 What does Hasan want to do in the future?

"This week *English Zone* is checking out what you think about learning English. Tell us why you're learning English and how you plan to use it in the future. We also want to know how important English is where you live. We can't wait to hear what you have to say."

http://interactive.cambridge.org

Hello everyone!

Posted 9th June at 4.30pm

I've been visiting *English Zone* since a few weeks ago and I love it. There are always lots of interesting things to read and I like talk to people from other countries in English online. Sometimes for me it's more easy to write in English than talk because I don't have to ask anyone to speak more slow! You ask whether is English important in my country. Let me tell you about it. I live in Ankara, in Turkey, where you need very good English to get into university or to get a good job, so most young people have to learn English. I want go to university to study medicine and after that I'd like to get a work as a doctor, so I need English. The problem is that I've been learning it for a long time, but I still make mistakes every time. I think it's important speak English with people from other countries, not just with people from Turkey. It's easy to understand people from your country, but much difficulter to understand people who first language is different. I also like chatting to people from different places to find out how their countries are like.

Hasan

Comment | Like | Share

Which is right? Don't look at the text!
I've been learning it for a long time, but I still ***make/do*** *mistakes.*

b Read the message again and correct the highlighted mistakes in Hasan's email.

c It is important to check and correct mistakes in your own writing. Look back through all your Portfolios. Do you often make the same mistake? What type of mistakes do you often make with ...

- grammar?
- vocabulary?
- word order?
- spelling?
- punctuation?

d Write a message about yourself for *English Zone*. Make sure:

- you include the information from the website message in your own message.
- it is interesting to read.
- you check and correct mistakes with grammar, vocabulary, word order, spelling and punctuation.

e Swap your message with a partner. Has he/she included all the information in the website message? Write a comment about his/her message.

ILLEGAL COPY
4.33
RUBY! I WOULDN'T HAVE EXPECTED TO SEE YOU HERE.
DAN?
WHAT'S HAPPENED TO YOUR FOREHEAD?
I HAD AN ACCIDENT.
WHAT?! WHEN?
ABOUT THREE WEEKS AGO. SOMEONE WAS CHASING ME AND I CRASHED MY CAR. I'VE BEEN IN HOSPITAL EVER SINCE!
BUT I'VE SEEN YOU ON THE NEWS EVERY DAY FOR THE LAST THREE WEEKS. YOU'RE ON TV ALL THE TIME!
I'M GOING TO YOUR PRESS CONFERENCE LATER.
THAT WASN'T ME.
BUT THAT'S IMPOSSIBLE. IT COULDN'T HAVE BEEN ANYONE ELSE.
I HAVE NO IDEA WHAT'S GOING ON, DAN. IT'S REALLY WEIRD. BUT I REALLY NEED YOUR HELP.
LATER THAT DAY.
SO ARE THERE ANY MORE QUESTIONS? DAN.
I'VE GOT A QUESTION FOR RUBY. WHY HAVE YOU CANCELLED YOUR PLANS TO RECORD AN ALBUM?
I'VE DECIDED TO CONCENTRATE ON MY ACTING AT THE MOMENT.
REALLY? BUT YOU SAID LAST MONTH YOU WERE GOING TO RECORD A NEW ALBUM. MAYBE IT'S BECAUSE YOU CAN'T SING.
DON'T BE RIDICULOUS, DAN. EVERYONE KNOWS RUBY CAN SING.

WELL, SING US A SONG THEN. IF YOU SANG A SONG, EVERYONE WOULD KNOW YOU COULD REALLY SING.
ER ... NO ... I'VE GOT A ... A SORE THROAT!
COME ON, RUBY, SING US A SONG.
YES, SING US 'SECRETS INSIDE'.
I, I, I ...
THAT'S IT, DAN. I'VE HAD ENOUGH OF THIS.
I'LL GET YOU FIRED IN THE MORNING.
... I CAN'T.
BUT I CAN.
YOU THINK YOU KNOW ME BUT BABY YOU'LL SEE, YOU'VE GOT SO MANY THINGS TO LEARN ABOUT ME.
RUBY?!
WHAT ARE YOU DOING HERE? I THOUGHT—
YOU HAD GOT RID OF ME? IF ONLY YOU HAD THOUGHT THINGS THROUGH, KAREN. I'M THE REAL RUBY RED!
AND I'M CALLING THE POLICE!
A WEEK LATER.
SO KAREN'S CONFESSED TO EVERYTHING.
YES, SANDRA WAS A SECRETARY AT THE FILM COMPANY WHEN I HAD THE ACCIDENT.
KAREN DIDN'T WANT TO DELAY THE PREMIERE AND LOSE MONEY. SO SHE USED SANDRA INSTEAD OF ME.
DID THEY GIVE HER PLASTIC SURGERY?
THAT'S THE STRANGEST THING. SHE DIDN'T NEED IT. SHE LOOKED JUST LIKE ME. A LITTLE MAKE-UP, SOME NICE CLOTHES—
BUT SHE COULDN'T SING.
SO WHAT ARE YOU GOING TO DO NOW?
I'M GOING TO LOOK FOR A NEW MANAGER AND RECORD MY ALBUM.
AND WHAT ABOUT CARL?
HE WAS MORE INTERESTED IN HIS CAREER THAN HE WAS IN ME. YOU KNOW, I'D RATHER BE WITH SOMEONE THAT KNOWS WHO I REALLY AM.

Get it right! 11 and 12

Common errors

1 job or work?

Make sure you know the differences between these two nouns.

Use *job* to talk about the regular work you do to earn money

✓ *I think that Ben has the best* ***job*** *in the world.*

✗ *I think that Ben has the best ~~work~~ in the world.*

Use *work* to talk about activities that you do when you do your job.

✓ *Thank you for all your hard* ***work***.

✗ *Thank you for all your hard ~~job~~.*

Remember that *work* is an uncountable noun. Don't say ~~a work~~ or ~~some works~~.

Complete the sentences with the correct word.

1 I have applied for a … in a bookshop.
2 I am looking for part-time … to do in the summer holidays.
3 Let's go for a coffee after we finish … .
4 There are lots of … for young people in London.
5 Every day, when I leave …, I go to the gym.

2 Relative pronouns

Use pronouns correctly in relative clauses.

Do not repeat the subject of the main clause in the relative clause.

✓ *I get on well with people* ***who are funny***.

✗ *I get on well with people who ~~they~~ are funny.*

Circle five incorrect pronouns in these relative clauses.

1 I went for something that it might help me.
2 There is no problem that it does not have a solution.
3 My sister, who I love very much, is getting married in June.
4 I'm going to visit my cousin who he lives in Wales.
5 The shop is in central London, which it is great!
6 Zoos protect animals that they might not survive in the wild.

3 Reporting questions

Use the correct words and word order in reported questions.

When we report a question, we change the word order to the form of a statement.

✓ *I asked her* ***what a fad was***.

✗ *I asked her ~~what is a fad~~.*

For a *yes / no* question, we use *if* or *whether*.

✓ *You asked me* ***whether*** *I had any plans before starting college.*

✗ *You asked me ~~that~~ I had any plans before starting college.*

a Read the text and correct the five mistakes.

My friend, Jim, asked me what was I doing in the summer. I told him I wasn't sure and asked him why did he want to know. I couldn't believe it when he asked me could I go to Scotland with him to visit his cousins! I asked my parents that I could go. They asked me if would I text them every day, and I said 'yes, of course!' So now, I'm going to Scotland this summer!

b 4.34 Listen and check your answers.

4 Say it right!

Tricky endings

a 4.35 Some words have endings that are difficult to pronounce. Listen to the example words and repeat paying attention to the letters in bold.

anglic**ism** mess**age** fam**ous** puzz**le**

b 4.36 Copy and complete the words with the correct ending; *-ism*, *-age*, *-ous* or *-le*. Then listen, check and repeat.

danger__ gigg__ im__ jeal__ journal__ langu__ organ__ peop__ seri__ tour__ turt__ vill__

c Work with a partner. Say the beginning of words in Exercise b and your partner closes their book and says the whole word.

Review 11 and 12

1 Grammar

a Choose the correct words.

1 Phoebe *may / can't* apply for the job. She hasn't decided yet.
2 She *may / can't* earn very much. She only works for a few hours a week.
3 It *might / must* be better to send your CV by email. That way it can't get lost.
4 Alex's studying medicine at university. He *must want / must have wanted* to be a doctor.

b Complete the sentences with question tags.

1 You work as a teacher, …?
2 They're never on time, …?
3 He hasn't been fired, …?
4 She's not going to apply for the job, …?
5 Let's go and get a drink, …?

c Write the underlined parts of the conversation in reported speech.

Lara: Hi Kika, how's it going?
Kika: Oh hi, Lara. I'm fine. How about you?
Lara: Yeah, great. [1]<u>I've finally finished all my exams</u>!
Kika: That's good. Me too. [2]<u>Are you going on holiday soon</u>?
Lara: Yeah, [3]<u>next week. I'm going to the beach</u>. Hey, [4]<u>are you going to Dec's party on Saturday</u>?
Kika: [5]<u>I don't know yet.</u>
Lara: Well, Naomi and I are definitely going. [6]<u>Do you want to come with us?</u>
Kika: Yes, that would be great!

1 Lara said that …
2 Kika asked Lara …
3 Lara told Kika that …
4 Lara asked Kika …
5 Kika said that …
6 Lara asked Kika …

d Complete the relative clauses with *who, which, where, whose* or *that* and put in the commas in the non-defining clauses.

1 The cyclist … won the Tour de France this year is Spanish.
2 The languages I study at school … I have been learning since I was 11 are French and Italian.
4 The Bollywood actress Aishwarya Rai … mother tongue is Tulu can speak several languages.
5 The language … we speak at home is Polish.

2 Vocabulary

a Match the two parts of the sentences.

1 Even though the job is badly
2 After the success of his latest novel, he's now a world
3 I can't tell you! It's top
4 Annie's always working. She often works 12
5 Eddie wants a part
6 Harry's team are going to present some energy
7 The company offered me a three
8 Professional footballers are among the most highly

A -famous author.
B -hour days.
C -month contract.
D -paid people in the world.
E paid, I love what I do.
F -saving ideas to the rest of the staff.
G -secret information.
H -time job to earn some money for his holiday.

b Complete the sentences with the job collocations.

interview CV fired a job
promoted shifts strike

1 The train drivers are going on … next week. They want better pay.
2 Firefighters have to work … either during the day or at night.
3 Can you help me write my … ? I've got to send it tomorrow.
4 She's so happy. She's been … to assistant manager.
5 Last week I had an … , but I didn't get the job.
6 Over 50 people have been … from the same company. It's terrible news.
7 I think you should apply for … at the animal sanctuary.

c Replace the underlined words with an expression with *time*.

1 <u>Usually</u> I get to school at 8 o'clock.
2 Last summer we watched that film <u>again and again</u>.
3 If you all talk <u>together</u>, I can't hear anybody.
4 <u>Sometimes</u> he follows the latest fashions.
5 I think that *Halo* is the best video game <u>ever</u>.
6 I have only been learning French <u>not long</u>, so I can't say very much.

Skills 4 Real
UNITS 1–4

1 Speaking

a A *screenager* is a teenager who spends a lot of time in front of a screen. Put the screen activities in order from the ones you do most to least. Add more if you need to.

Playing games	Watching videos
Using email / messenger	Watching television
Social networking	Texting
Looking for information	Other …

b Work with a partner. Discuss the order of your lists. Are they similar? Why? / Why not?

2 Reading

a Read the introduction to the questionnaire. Do you agree that social networking sites can become addictive? Why? / Why not?

Are You Addicted to Social Networking Sites?

Social networking sites are great resources for staying in touch with friends, but they should never become a substitute for real interaction with others. Unfortunately checking in on social networking sites can sometimes become an addiction for some people.

To help you determine if you use social networking sites appropriately, answer yes or no to each question below, then total your answers and check your results.

Questionnaire

1. Are you a member of multiple social networking sites?
2. Do you visit your social networking sites with no goal or specific purpose in mind?
3. Are you ever surprised by how much time you spend on a social networking site?
4. Have you ever said no to an activity with your family or friends because of social networking sites?
5. Have you ever ignored a responsibility like homework or chores because of social networking sites?
6. Do you ever stay up late or get up early to spend time on social networking sites?
7. Have you ever hidden your time on social networking sites from family or friends?
8. Do you prefer to interact with people on social networking sites rather than face to face?
9. Do you have more friends on your social networking sites than you do in real life?
10. Do you become frustrated or angry when a social networking site is unavailable?

RESULTS

YES 1–3 questions
You don't have a problem with social networking sites and probably use them to extend your relationships with friends and family. You recognise that keeping up with these sites is less important than strengthening the relationships that exist outside the internet.

YES 4–7 questions
You may be addicted to social networking. For the next week write down every time you visit a site and how long you spend on it. At the end of the week, total up the time. You might be surprised by the results and need to cut down!

YES 8–10 questions
Your use of social networking sites might be getting in the way of your real life and you may be using them as a substitute for going out and making real friends. Try to spend more time on activities away from the computer. Join a club or take up a new hobby and study somewhere without an internet connection.

b Work in a small group. Read the questionnaire individually, then read and compare your results with each other.

c Match the words or phrases from the text with the meanings.

1 substitute	**A** domestic tasks that are often boring or unpleasant
2 determine	**B** feeling annoyed or less confident
3 chores	**C** something that is used instead of something else
4 strengthen	**D** discover the facts or truth about something
5 frustrated	**E** make something stronger or more effective

d Work with a partner. Ask and answer the questions.

1 Do you like doing surveys and questionnaires like this one? Why? / Why not?
2 How accurate do you think the results of this type of survey are?

3 Listening

a 4.37 Listen to three people talking about social networking sites. Match the opinions with the speakers.

1 I use social networking sites most days.
2 I speak to people less because of social networking sites.
3 I don't like social networking sites.

b 4.37 Listen again.
Take notes on the speakers' answers.
What questions does the interviewer ask?

c Work with a partner. Compare your notes and ask and answer the questions in Exercise 3b together.

4 Writing

a Some social networking sites, like Twitter, limit the number of characters you can use in a message, or tweet, to 140 characters. Read the tweets below. Who is giving advice? Who wants to arrange a meeting?

@myfriend I think you should give up sn sites for a while. Take time out and enjoy the fresh air.

@greatgirl Yes – thanks for the tweet. I'm much better today. Only logged on twice! Want to meet up later?

b Work in a small group. Write a short message, making sure you don't use more than 140 characters. Your message could be to share any of the following:

- The results from the survey you've just done.
- Some advice to a friend who's addicted to social networking sites.
- Your plans for after the class.
- How you're feeling today.
- A useful piece of information.
- The last film you saw or book you read.

c Take turns to show your message to the group. Write a short message as a response to your group's messages.

Skills 4 Real
UNITS 5–8

1 Speaking

a Work with a partner. Ask and answer the questions.
- Does your school / library / local arts or sports centre provide free activities?
- What activities can you do for free in these places?
- What activities or events would you like to be available for free?

b Compare your ideas with another pair. Who has more ideas?

2 Reading

a Read the free event leaflet below to see how many of your ideas from Exercise 1a were mentioned.

The Cherry Hill Public Library's Teen Department Presents

FREE EVENTS FOR TEENS–WINTER

Writer's Block

Meetings include: writing games and prompts, writing tips and strategies, sharing your work with other writers, and sharing and receiving constructive feedback!

Wednesdays: 6pm–7pm
Jan 12 & 26, Feb 9 & 23, Mar 9 & 23

LIMITED SPACE: REGISTRATION REQUIRED

Anime Days

Watch your favorite anime while you make your own candy sushi and perfect your origami skills (PG-13)

Wednesday: Jan 19
6pm–8pm
Saturday: Feb 26
2pm–4pm
Saturday: Mar 26
2pm–4pm

Multicultural Room

NO REGISTRATION REQUIRED

Dungeons and Dragons

Join local Dungeon Master Dan Zucharelli (from perpetualgeekmachine.net) and other area teens once a month to play the classic game. All skill levels welcome. (beginners too!)

Saturdays: 2.30pm–4.30pm
January 22, February 12, March 5

LIMITED SPACE: REGISTRATION REQUIRED

Stix: get your knit on!

Learn to knit while making a difference! Work on blankets and scarves to give to local charities. Community Service hours available. Crocheters welcome!

Please bring your own needles and yarn. For beginners we recommend 8 or 9 gauge needles and yarn.

Thursdays, Jan 6, Mar 31 5pm-6pm

NO REGISTRATION REQUIRED

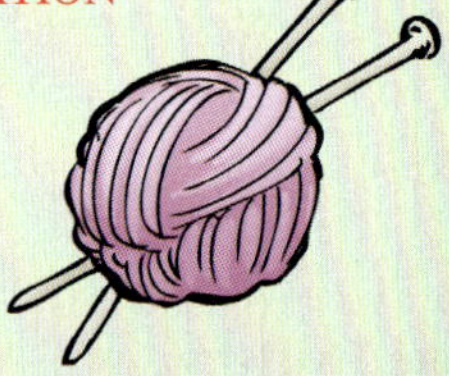

The Danger: Diabolique Comic Book Club

Addicted to comic books and graphic novels? Come and hang out, get cool freebies and find out what's coming out next!

Light refreshments served.

Thursdays: 6pm–7pm
Jan 6 & 20
Feb 3 & 17
Mar 3, 17 & 31

NO REGISTRATION REQUIRED

Teen Activity Board

Hang out with the other Cherry Hill Teens while earning Community Service hours. Help plan and run events for young children and other teens. Light snacks provided.

Middle School Meetings

Saturdays:
Jan 15, Feb 12 & Mar 12: 1pm–2pm
Wednesdays:
Jan 26, Feb 23 & Mar 23: 7pm–8pm

High School Meetings

Mondays: 5.30pm–6.30pm
Jan 10 & 24, Feb 7 & 28, Mar 7 & 21

National Teen Tech Week: March 6–12

March 6 CHPL celebrates National Teen Tech Week. Check out some of our regularly scheduled events with an added *tech twist*!

Acting up: Teen Improv!

Join us for some fun improvisation and acting! Play games and act silly!

Saturday, Jan 15 2pm–3.30pm
Wednesday, Feb 16 6.30pm–8pm
Saturday, Mar 12 2pm–3.30pm

LIMITED SPACE: REGISTRATION REQUIRED

b Read the leaflet again and find an activity for somebody who ...

1 likes improvising short theatrical sketches
2 would like to help a charity in their free time
3 wants to know about the latest graphic novels
4 enjoys preparing food
5 is good with young children
6 is keen on fantasy role-playing games

c Match the words or phrases from the text with the meanings.

1 feedback
2 origami
3 knit
4 freebies
5 refreshments
6 improv

A to make things with two long needles and wool
B small amounts of food and drink
C making something up as you perform it (short for improvisation)
D Japanese art of paper folding
E criticism (written or spoken)
F things you don't have to pay for

d Work with a partner. Ask and answer the questions.

1 Which of the activities in the library would you like to do? Why? / Why not?
2 Can you suggest any other activities which the library could hold?

3 Listening

a 4.38 Listen to three people talking about things they like doing for little or no money. Match the opinions with the speakers.

1 I like rollerblading and going swimming.
2 I like window shopping when I don't have any money.
3 I like hanging out with friends.

b 4.38 Listen again. Take notes on the speakers' answers. What questions does the interviewer ask?

c Work with a partner. Compare your notes and ask and answer the questions in Exercise 3b together.

4 Writing

a Work with a partner. You're going to write a leaflet for free activities in your local cultural centre / library. First decide on the activities. Use three of the ideas in the box or your own ideas.

learn to do a craft
improve your computer/sports skills
form a cinema club/discussion group
be a better performer
work with children / old people
join a creative/cookery/dressmaking workshop

b Write your leaflet. Make sure you:

- include a title for the leaflet
- explain what happens in the events
- say who the event is aimed at
- use imperatives, adjectives and questions to make the events sound interesting

c Swap your leaflet with another pair. Would you like to go to any of their events?

Skills 4 Real
UNITS 9–12

1 Speaking

a Work with a partner. How would you feel in each situation?

- Getting told off by a teacher in front of the whole class.
- Going on a really fast rollercoaster.
- Doing your end-of-year exams.
- Celebrating after your exams.
- Talking to a friend.
- Watching someone being unkind to an animal.
- Watching a horror film on your own.

2 Reading

a Read the text quickly. Choose the best description of the article.

1 Famous people who have been in trouble for getting angry.
2 The physiological changes in our bodies when we get angry.
3 The reasons why most people get angry.

Red Alert

Anger is a powerful emotion and it can have destructive results – for the angry person and those around them. Deborah Black takes a deep breath and counts to ten ...

Anger triggers your body's 'fight or flight' response – just as fear, excitement and anxiety do. When you start to get angry, your brain triggers the release of a range of hormones that affect every part of your body. The adrenal glands flood your body with stress hormones, such as adrenaline and cortisol. The brain shifts blood away from your gut, where it is less needed, and towards your muscles, to get you ready for action. It also directs blood to your brain, to sharpen and focus your mind. Your heart rate, blood pressure and respiration increase, your body temperature rises and your skin perspires. You are on red alert!

The effect of all this hormonal activity is a rapid heartbeat, breathlessness (as your lungs struggle to take in more oxygen), high blood pressure and a raised body temperature. Don't worry though, it's only the Incredible Hulk who turns green and bursts out of his clothes when he's angry.

HEALTH PROBLEMS

If you get angry a lot, the flood of stress chemicals that go with regular, unmanaged anger can eventually harm your body. Some of the health problems linked to unmanaged anger include headaches, digestion problems, insomnia, increased anxiety, depression, high blood pressure, skin problems like eczema, strokes and heart attacks. Best to get it under control, then.

Some people have little control over their anger and their temper can isolate them from family and friends. Some angry people have low self-esteem, and use their anger as a way to feel powerful. Other people think anger is a 'bad' emotion and try to bottle it up. This often turns into depression and anxiety. They get rid of their bottled-up rage by exploding at friends or family.

HELPFUL WAYS TO DEAL WITH ANGER

- If you feel out of control, walk away from the situation until you cool down.
- Recognise and accept angry feelings as normal and part of life.
- Try to pinpoint the exact reasons why you feel angry. Once you have identified the problem, try to think of different ways to remedy the situation.
- Do something physical – go for a run or play sport.

LONG-TERM ANGER MANAGEMENT

- Keep a diary of your outbursts, to see if you can understand how and why you get mad.
- Learn some relaxation techniques, such as meditation or yoga.
- Take regular exercise. It can improve your mood and reduce stress levels. Exertion boosts production of feel-good chemicals in your body, including endorphins.
- See a counsellor or psychologist if you still feel angry about events that occurred in your past.

b Read the text again and answer the questions.

1 Which emotions can cause your body to want to fight or run away?
2 Which stress hormones affect your body when you feel angry?
3 What happens to your body when you get angry?
4 Why is it not good for your body to feel angry regularly?
5 Why do some people who don't feel good about themselves, get angry?
6 How can physical exercise help people who feel angry?

c Choose the correct meaning of the words from the text: A, B or C.

1 triggers	**A** stops	**B** starts	**C** reduces
2 gut	**A** muscles	**B** brain	**C** stomach
3 circumstances	**A** conditions	**B** films	**C** clothes
4 eczema	**A** a sad feeling	**B** a heart problem	**C** red, dry skin
5 rages	**A** happiness	**B** uncontrollable anger	**C** controlled sadness

d Work in a group. Look at the advice given in the text to help deal with anger and for long-term anger management. Which ideas do you think are the best? Why?

3 Listening

a 4.39 Listen to three people talking about things that make them feel angry. Match the opinions with the speakers.

1 I take a few deep breaths and lie down when I'm angry.
2 If I'm angry, I relax by going out in the evening with friends.
3 I get frustrated when people let me down.

b 4.39 Listen again. Take notes on the speakers' answers. What two questions does the interviewer ask?

c Work with a partner. Compare your notes and ask and answer the questions in Exercise 3b together.

4 Writing

a Work in a group. Choose a negative emotion and make a list of situations that can make you feel that way. Then prepare a list of helpful ways of dealing with the emotion.

Helpful ways of dealing with ...

- **anxiety** (e.g. before exams)
- **embarrassment** (e.g. having to talk in front of people)
- **fear** (e.g. of spiders or of going to the dentist)

b Make a leaflet with your ideas to give to students in your school to help them. Make sure you include:

- positive ideas to help with the problem
- a range of ideas to suit different personalities
- language of giving advice (look at Unit 9 for ideas)
- ideas to help people now and in the long term

Unit 4 Interactive Art: Lights, camera, action!

1 Camera shots

a Read about different camera shots and match them with the pictures.

Camera shots

In a good film, the camera operator uses a range of different camera **shots**. The more variety of shots in the film, the more interesting it is for us to watch. The same **scene** can be shot from totally different **angles** and with each angle we feel a different emotion. Here are a few examples.

A

Close-up ...

In a close-up, the character is very near the camera and the actor's face fills the entire screen. We don't usually see the background, but we see lots of detail, for example a character's emotions. Close-ups are used with main characters so that they look more important than the other characters.

Long shot ...

In a long shot, we can see the whole object or body of the actor and the background because we need to know the character's situation, but we don't need lots of close detail. In an extreme long shot the camera can be as far away as 300m. It shows action on a big scale, for example in disaster movies like *Titanic*.

D

B

High-angle shot ...

In a high-angle shot, the camera is physically higher than the actor or subject of the shot. The character looks small or weak because we are looking down on him or her.

E

Low-angle shot ...

Low-angle shots are taken when the camera is lower than the actor or subject of the shot so we are looking up at them. The character looks big and powerful.

C

Dutch shot ...

In a Dutch shot, the camera isn't horizontal, it's at an angle. This creates tension and excitement, for example in horror films or thrillers.

Did you know?

the word 'cinema' comes from the Greek word *kinema* which means 'movement'.

b Read the text again. Complete the notes with the names of the camera shots in your notebook.

1 ________	This makes a character look unimportant or is used in situations when he or she is scared.
2 ________	This shows exciting or frightening action when the director wants the audience to feel the tension.
3 ________	This shows details such as a character's feelings.
4 ________	This shows the actor in his or her location.
5 ________	This makes a character look important or strong, for example when he or she is in control.

2 Camera movement

a 4.40 Listen to the information about camera movement and match the diagrams to the types of movement.

zooming panning tilting tracking steadicam

1 The camera moves from left to right.

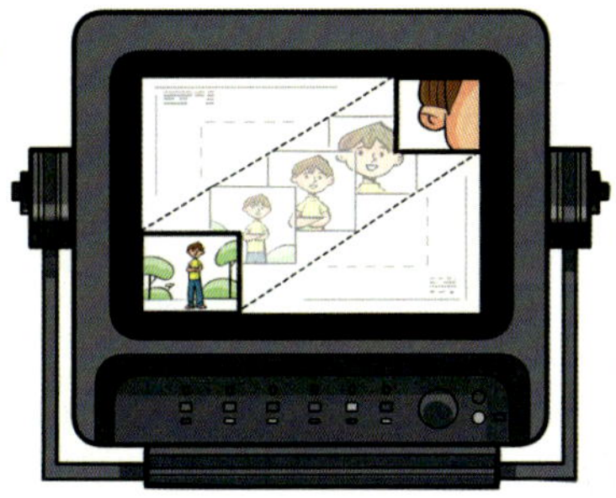

3 The camera lens moves backwards and forwards.

2 The camera moves with the actor.

4 The camera follows the actor.

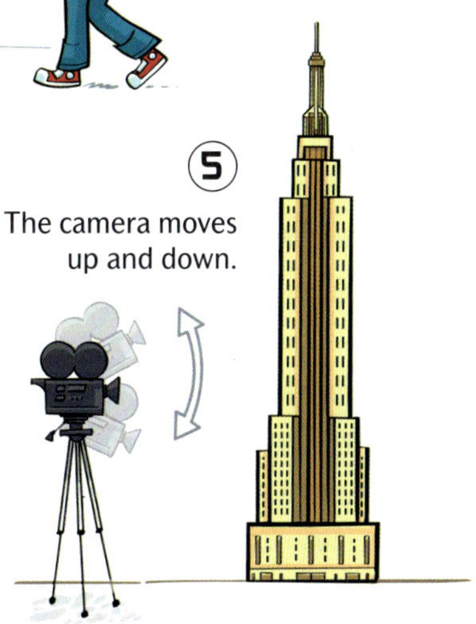

5 The camera moves up and down.

b 4.40 Read the sentences and listen again. Then write *Z* (zooming), *P* (panning), *Ti* (tilting), *Tr* (tracking) or *S* (steadicam) in your notebook.

This technique:

1 is used to make the image bigger or smaller. ___
2 is used to film a room or place before we meet a main character. ___
3 is used to film a building from bottom to top. ___
4 is used to follow the action. ___ ___
5 uses a tripod. ___ ___ ___
6 is a modern technique. ___ ___
7 requires the camera operator to stand. ___ ___ ___
8 requires the camera operator to move. ___ ___

mini-dictionary

range (n) = variety
shoot (v) (past participle = shot) = to film
entire (adj) = complete or whole
background (n) = things at the back of a view or film scene.

3 Final task

Work in a group. Choose a film clip or advert and analyse the different camera shots and movements in the clip. Present your findings to the class. Show the clip and explain why each type of shot or movement is used.

Unit 8 Interactive Maths: Representing frequency

1 Frequency tables and pie charts

a 4.41 We can represent data in frequency tables and pie charts. Look at the information below then listen to a teacher talking and complete the missing information (1–9).

We asked 60 students about their favourite free-time activities. Here are the results in a **frequency table** and a **pie chart**.

Favourite activity	Frequency
doing sport	16
listening to music	12
chatting to friends	14
using the computer	10
reading	8
Total	60

Pie chart: Favourite free-time activities

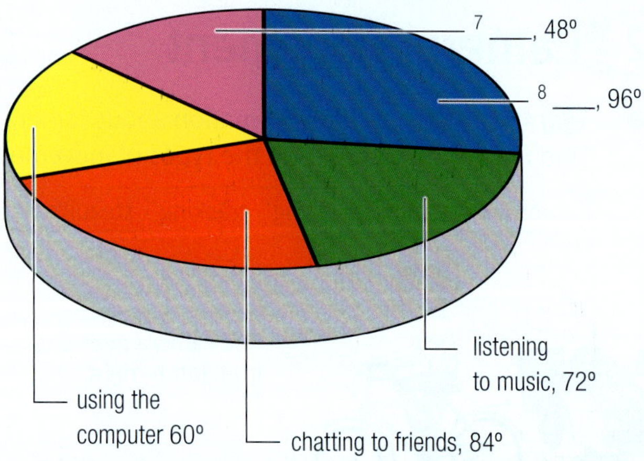

Each sector in this pie chart represents 1 ____.

This pie chart represents a total of 2 ____ **people**.

There are 3 ____º in a circle.

We divide **360** by 4 ____ and get 5 ____ so one person is represented by **6º**.

The **angle** for each activity = *number of people for the activity (frequency) x* 6 ____.

Check your calculations!

If we add all the degrees together we get 360º

48+96+60+72+84 = 360º.

b Use the data below to draw a pie chart about part-time jobs.

Part-time job	Frequency
babysitting	10
teaching	16
working in a café	24
working in a restaurant	53
working in a shop	37
other	20
no part-time job	20
Total	180

Did you know?

...a pie chart is called a pie chart because it looks like a pie which has been cut into pieces? A pie is a typical British dish.

2 Compound bar charts

a We can represent data with **bar charts** too. Look at the data in the table and how it is represented in a compound bar chart. Answer the questions.

Money spent	Frequency	
	girls	boys
clothes and accesories	4	3
computer games	2	3
music	3	3
magazines and books	2	1
sport	3	3
other	1	1
Total	?	?

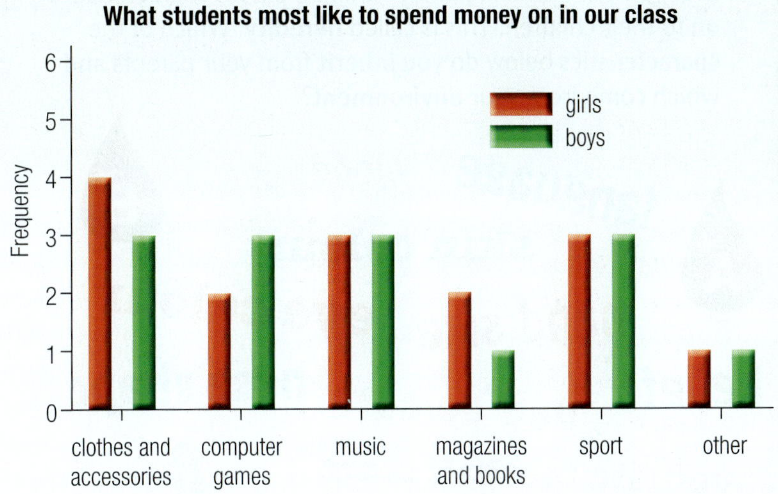

1 How many girls are there? And boys?
2 What do most girls like to spend their money on? And boys?
3 How many students spend their money on sport?

b The table shows the number of students in three different schools that got A grades last term. Represent the information as a compound bar chart.

Subject	Frequency		
	school X	school Y	school Z
Maths	7	11	9
English	10	6	12
History	8	4	5
Biology	5	9	4

3 Final task

Do a survey in your class about what students most like to spend their money on. Make a frequency table to show the data of the results. Then make a pie chart and a bar chart to represent the data.

Unit 12 Interactive Science: Genetic inheritance

1 Heredity or environment?

Every parent (human, plant or animal) passes characteristics on to their children. This is called **heredity**. Which of the characteristics below do you **inherit** from your parents and which come from your **environment**?

language blood type

skin colour

hand size eye colour

beliefs hair colour nose shape

favourite football team

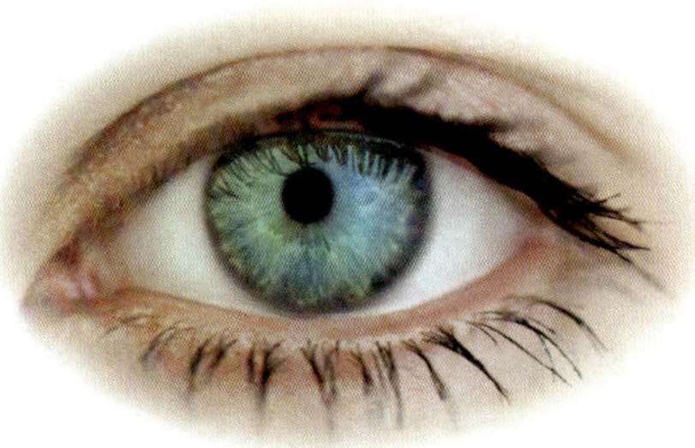

2 Genes and alleles

a Work with a partner and see how many questions you can answer in the quiz.

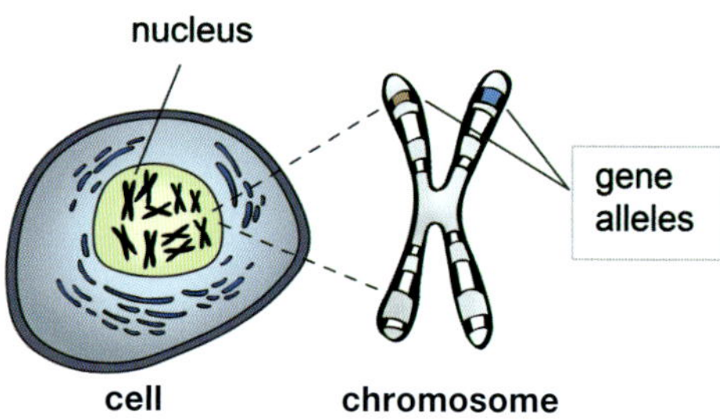

1 How many **chromosomes** do humans have in each cell?
   a 2. **b** 23. **c** 46.
2 How many **genes** are in each chromosome?
   a 23. **b** 1,000s. **c** None.
3 Which **characteristics** are passed on in chromosomes?
   a Language. **b** Many, including eye colour and blood type.
   c Eye colour only.
4 What are **alleles**?
   a Different forms of the same gene. **b** Types of chromosomes. **c** Eyes.
5 How many alleles do we have for **eye colour**?
   a 4. **b** 2. **c** 23.
6 What colour are your eyes if you have two alleles for blue eyes?
   a Brown. **b** Blue or brown. **c** Blue.
7 Which eye colour is **dominant**?
   a Brown. **b** Blue. **c** Green.
8 Which eye colour is **recessive**?
   a Brown. **b** Blue. **c** Green.
9 If the mother and father have brown eyes, what colour eyes can their children have?
   a Brown only. **b** Blue only. **c** Brown or blue.

b 4.42 Now listen and check your answers to the quiz.

3 Eye colour

a Look at the diagram and read the text about eye colour. What colour eyes can the child have?

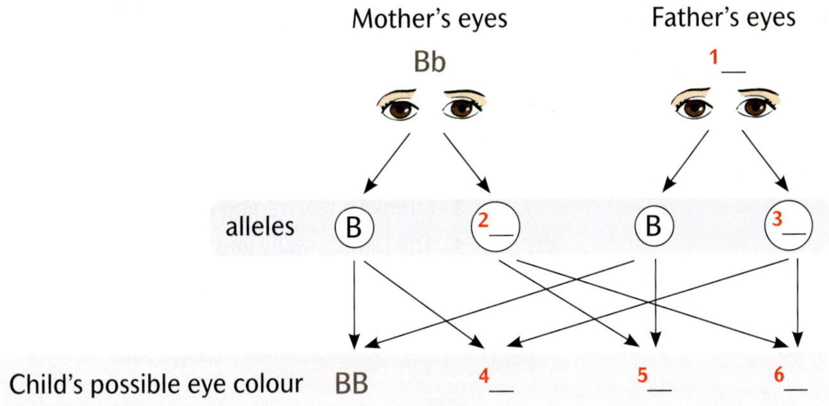

Key
B = dominant allele for brown eyes
b = recessive allele for blue eyes

How is it possible for parents with brown eyes to have children with blue eyes?

Each person has two genes, or alleles, for eye colour which can be brown or blue. We can refer to the brown, **dominant** allele as B and the blue, **recessive** allele as b.

Let's imagine that the mother and father in the diagram above have brown eyes of the type Bb. This means that they both have one brown allele B and one blue allele b and because the brown allele is dominant, their eyes are brown. Both the father and the mother can pass on a brown allele B or a blue allele b to their child. The child takes one allele from the mother and one allele from the father, so there are four possible combinations:

- Combination 1 is B from the mother and B from the father, which gives BB, so the child has brown eyes.
- Combination 2 is B from the mother and b from the father, which gives Bb, so the child has brown eyes.
- Combination 3 is b from the mother and B from the father, which gives Bb, so the child has brown eyes.
- Combination 4 is b from the mother and b from the father, which gives bb, so the child has blue eyes.

b Read the text again. Then copy and complete the diagram in Exercise 3a.

c Complete the final sentence from the text.

So, the probability of a child with brown eyes is ..., and the probability of a child with blue eyes is ....

Did you know?

In Estonia 99% of people have blue eyes?

4 Final task

Work with a partner. Work out the possible eye colour of a child when the mother has brown eyes and the father has blue eyes. Draw diagrams to illustrate the possible options and calculate the possibility of them having a child with blue eyes and a child with brown eyes. Remember, brown eyes can be BB or Bb so you will need to draw two diagrams.

Interaction: Pronunciation practice

Interaction 1 page 8

C 1.11 Listen to the sentences and repeat them. Practise sounding enthusiastic.

1 It's so nice to meet you too.
2 We've got so much in common.
3 They're really cool!
4 Wow! These are fantastic!
5 She won't believe we're actually together in a café.

Interaction 2 page 16

C 1.26 Listen to the sentences and repeat them. Practise showing regret or disappointment.

1 Well, the thing is, I can't make it today.
2 I've got a bit of a problem.
3 I've still got loads of work to do.
4 I'm really sorry.
5 OK, never mind.

Interaction 3 page 26

C 1.38 Listen to the sentences and repeat them. Practise using the weak forms in red.

1 It must be very difficult.
2 Things will get better you'll see.
3 Being homesick can be awful.
4 You mustn't let it get you down.
5 You'll feel better soon, when you've settled in a bit.

Interaction 4 page 34

C 2.11 Listen to the sentences and repeat them. Emphasise the key words.

1 Hang on a sec!
2 Carry on…
3 No way!
4 If you let me get a word in, I'll tell you!
5 Let me finish, will you?

Interaction 5 page 44

C 2.25 Listen to the sentences and repeat them. Practise challenging other people's ideas and expressing strong opinions.

1 You're not serious, are you?
2 Do you really mean that?
3 I can't believe what I'm hearing!
4 Don't be ridiculous. That's no excuse.
5 Don't change the subject.
6 That's totally different!

Interaction 6 page 52

C 2.41 Listen to the sentences and repeat them. Practise being persuasive.

1 You're brilliant at art.
2 You'd be great on TV.
3 I think I'd feel nervous.
4 The letter's really important.
5 You're so much better at writing than me.

Interaction 7 page 62

C 3.11 Listen to the sentences and repeat them. Practise using the correct stress.

1 They both seem to be of teenagers' bedrooms.
2 It's messy, whereas the other bedroom is very tidy.
3 It appears to have been designed by a professional.
4 Although this room is much tidier than the other one, I prefer the messy room.

Interaction 8 page 70

C 3.23 Listen to the sentences and repeat them. Practise using linking.

1 How much_is_it?
2 Can you afford_it?
3 You_owe me seven
4 There's ten pounds_off.
5 What_a rip-off!

Interaction 9 page 80

C 3.37 Listen to the sentences and repeat them. Practise using the correct stress and weak forms in red.

1 I was just wondering if …
2 Well, you should have done it before.
3 I won't see her for a month after today.
4 What's in it for me?
5 I'll do your washing up for the rest of the week.

Interaction 10 page 88

C 4.7 Listen to the sentences and repeat them. Practise using rising and falling intonation.

1 Today we'd like to talk about viral videos.
2 First we're going to look at how they started.
3 Then finally we'd like to explain why they are important in modern advertising.
4 Anyway, as I was saying, viral videos really took off later.

Interaction 11 page 98

c 4.21 Listen to the questions and repeat them. Practise stressing key words.

1 What hours could you work?
2 Have you got any questions for me?
3 How much would I get paid?
4 Would you give me any training?
5 When will you let me know if I've got the job?

Interaction 12 page 106

c 4.32 Listen to the sentences and repeat them. Practise using the correct rhythm.

1 How's it going?
2 So, what's new?
3 What about you?
4 I know what you mean.
5 That's good to know.

Speaking activities

Unit 2, page 14

Student B: Complete the questions with the correct form of the verbs.

1 Which sports or hobbies that you do are the most fun … (do)? Why?
2 Which sport or hobby would you never choose … (learn)? Why?
3 Who do you enjoy … (work) with in class? Why?
4 Which new sport or hobby are you most interested in … (try)? Why?

Unit 4, page 32

Student B: Put the words into the correct order to make questions.

1 kite-surfing / try / Would you ever ?
2 incredibly fast / Would you ever / down / skate / a hill ?
3 watch / Would you ever / horror film / alone / an extremely scary ?
4 spider / touch / Would you ever / extremely hairy / an ?
5 in front of / give / school / Would you ever / the whole / a presentation ?
6 incredibly / Would you ever / old house / sleep alone / an / in ?

Unit 8, page 67

Student B: You are Mark Boyle. Re-read the article in Exercise 1a and try and imagine that you really are Mark. You can make up any information you don't know the real answer to! Use the ideas below to help you.

- Friends and family – reactions?
- Daily routine
- Good/bad things about new life
- Future plans
- Things you miss
- Entertainment

Unit 12, page 103

Student B: Write the questions you need to ask your partner to complete your fact file.

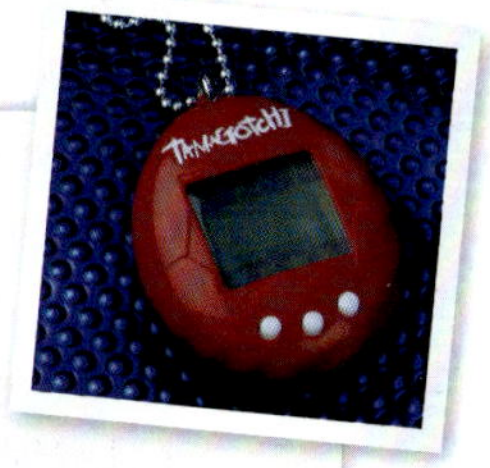

The Tamagotchi is a … .
A Tamagotchi was sold for the first time in … (place) in … (year).
Over … million Tamagotchis have been sold.
The player should look after … all the time. If not, it will die.
A film was made in … (year) called *Tamagotchi: The Movie*

The Rubik's cube was invented by the Hungarian design professor, Ernö Rubik in 1974.
In the early 1980s the Rubik's cube became the most popular puzzle in the world and over 350 million toys have been sold.
People hold competitions to solve the cube as quickly as possible.
In 2009 the world record for solving the classic 3x3 cube was 7.08 seconds.

Interaction: Student A

Interaction 1 page 8

d Imagine you and your partner are online friends who met on a fan page of a social network site because you both share the same hobby (both decide the hobby). You meet in real life and have a conversation. Use the Interaction language and the facts below to help you.

- Student B looks very different from his/her profile picture (you decide why).
- You must ask Student B about an online friend that you think they might know. He's called Will and has a profile picture of a skateboard.
- You are good online friends with a girl called Bao who has an excellent blog.

Interaction 2 page 16

d Look at the information and act out the conversations with your partner. Use the Interaction language to help you.

Conversation 1: You have arranged to go to the cinema with a friend tonight for his/her birthday, but another friend has asked you to go to a party instead. You really want to go to the party (you decide why). Talk to your friend and make an excuse.

Conversation 2: You are a Maths teacher and you have noticed that one of your students who is usually good at Maths has done very badly in an exam. You want to know why. Talk to the student, find out his/her excuse and decide on a solution.

Interaction 3 page 26

d Look at the information and act out the conversations with your partner. Use the Interaction language to help you.

You are staying at a summer camp and doing a sports course. You really miss your friends and family and you don't think you're doing very well on the course. Everything is so different here, you can't get used to it. You want to go home! You are talking on the phone to Student B. Explain the situation and tell him/her how you feel.

Now Student B is going to phone you to tell you about a problem. Listen and sympathise with him/her. Try and make him/her feel better.

Interaction 4 page 34

d Look at the information and act out the conversations with your partner. Use the Interaction language to help you.

Conversation 1: Tell Student B about a film you've seen recently (you decide which one). Give as much detail as possible and don't let your partner interrupt too much.

Conversation 2: Student B is going to tell you about a day out at a theme park. Interrupt to show lots of interest in what he/she says. Try to:

- ask if he/she is talking about the same place you went to last year
- ask if he/she would recommend going again
- tell him/her about a similar place you know
- think of other questions to ask

Interaction 5 page 44

d Read the statements below and choose one that you feel strongly about. Think about the reasons why you agree/disagree with the statement.

> Wearing clothes made of animal fur or skin is cruel.
> Dogs should be banned from city centres.
> It doesn't matter if some animals become extinct.
> Young people spend too much time online.
> Students should be paid to attend school.

Tell Student B which statement you've chosen and the reasons why you agree/disagree with it. Student B is going to disagree with what you say. Support your ideas and use the Interaction language to help you.

Now Student B is going to tell you about their statement. Disagree with what they say and use the Interaction language to support your ideas.

Interaction 6 page 52

d With Student B and Student C, you are going to plan a fund-raising campaign. First decide what or who you would like to raise money for, then think of five jobs to do to raise the money. In your groups, decide who will do which job. Persuade the others to let you do the job(s) you want to do, and persuade them to do the jobs you don't want to do. You don't have much time at the moment, so you'd like to do just one job. Use the Interaction language to help you.

- You don't like using computers very much.
- You are good at Art and you love writing letters.
- Student B has a terrible singing voice. Don't let him/her sing.
- Persuade Student C to make a video for the internet.

Interaction 8 page 70

d Look at the information and act out the conversations with your partner. Use the Interaction language to help you.

Conversation 1: You are shopping with Student B. They ask to borrow some money from you. You decide to lend them part of the money (you decide how much), but you can't afford to lend them the whole amount.

Conversation 2: You need to buy a birthday present for a special friend and have found the perfect present at a bargain price. You don't have enough money to buy what you want (you decide on what the present is, and who it is for) so ask Student B to lend you some.

Interaction 9 page 80

d Look at the information and act out the conversations with your partner. Use the Interaction language to help you.

Conversation 1: Your parents have asked you to babysit for your ten-year-old brother this evening while they go out. However, you've arranged to meet your friends at the sports ground. Your older brother/sister is at home and isn't going out. Negotiate with him/her to do the babysitting. You could offer to do his/her jobs around the house. You both have to take turns to walk the dog and take the rubbish out every day.

Conversation 2: You're staying in and have invited some friends round to play computer games. Your brother/sister wants to go out and wants you to clean the kitchen for him/her, but you don't want to! He/She wants to negotiate with you. Remember, you could ask him/her to do some of the other jobs you have to do around the house in return for helping him/her. Both of you have to take turns to do the washing and cook dinner twice a week.

Interaction 11 page 98

d Look at the information and act out the interviews with your partner. Use the Interaction language to help you.

Interview 1: You are the manager of a sports shop and you are going to interview Student B for a part-time job. You are looking for somebody to work on Saturdays from 9am to 6pm. You want somebody who loves sports and has some experience of working with the general public. Use the Interaction language to help you.

Interview 2: Now Student B is going to interview you for a part-time job in a fast-food restaurant. You used to work in an expensive restaurant as a waiter but you weren't very good and you were fired. You really want to get the job to earn some money to buy a laptop! Try your best to get the job. Use the Interaction language to help you.

Interaction 12 page 106

d Look at the information and act out the conversations with your partner. Use the Interaction language to help you.

Conversation 1: You have just started English classes at an English school in London. Introduce yourself to Student B and find out information about:

- things to do at the weekend
- where you can buy good food
- places to go out in the evenings
- anything else

Keep the conversation going for as long as possible!

Conversation 2: You have been learning English at an English school in New York for three weeks. Introduce yourself to Student B and answer his/her questions about:

- things to do in the evenings
- where you can buy clothes and shoes
- places to do sport
- anything else

Keep the conversation going for as long as possible!

Interaction: Student B

Interaction 1 page 8

d Imagine you and your partner are online friends who met on a fan page of a social network site because you both share the same hobby (both decide the hobby). You meet in real life and have a conversation. Use the Interaction language and the facts below to help you.

- Student A looks exactly like his/her profile picture.
- You use a profile picture of yourself which was taken at a special party last year.
- You have an online friend called Will and his profile picture is a photo of himself.
- One of your favourite bloggers at the moment is a girl called Bao, and you want to know if Student A knows her.

Interaction 2 page 16

d Look at the information and act out the conversations with your partner. Use the Interaction language to help you.

Conversation 1: You are going to the cinema with a friend tonight. You're really excited because it's your birthday and you've been wanting to see this film for ages (you decide which film). Your friend looks a bit worried. Talk to him/her and find out what the problem is.

Conversation 2: You were supposed to study for your Maths exam last night but you couldn't (you decide why). You couldn't answer any of the questions in the exam, but you do understand the subject. You would like to do the exam again if possible. Talk to your teacher and make your excuse.

Interaction 3 page 26

d Look at the information and act out the conversations with your partner. Use the Interaction language to help you.

Student A is going to phone you to tell you about a problem. Listen and sympathise with him/her. Try and make him/her feel better.

Now phone Student A and tell him/her your problem. Your grandfather is ill and your mother has taken you with her to stay in his house while she looks after him. Unfortunately your grandfather isn't getting better and your mother says you'll have to start the new school term in your grandfather's town. You miss your friends and don't want to start school somewhere else! Explain the situation to Student A and tell him/her how you feel.

Interaction 4 page 34

d Look at the information and act out the conversations with your partner. Use the Interaction language to help you.

Conversation 1: Student A is going to tell you about a film they've seen. Interrupt to show lots of interest in what he/she says. Try to:

- ask what other films the main actors have been in
- ask if he/she would recommend watching it
- tell him/her about another film you've seen
- think of other questions to ask

Conversation 2: Tell Student A about a day you spent at a theme park (or another place of your choice). Give as much detail as possible and don't let your partner interrupt too much.

Interaction 5 page 44

d Read the statements below and choose one that you feel strongly about. Think about the reasons why you agree/disagree with the statement.

> Wearing clothes made of animal fur or skin is cruel.
> Dogs should be banned from city centres.
> It doesn't matter if some animals become extinct.
> Young people spend too much time online.
> Students should be paid to attend school.

Student A is going to tell you about a statement they have chosen. Disagree with what they say and use the Interaction language to support your ideas.

Now tell Student A about a different statement you've chosen and the reasons why you agree/disagree with it. Student A is going to disagree with what you say. Support your ideas and use the Interaction language to help you.

Interaction 6 page 52

d With Student A and Student C, you are going to plan a fund-raising campaign. First decide what or who you would like to raise money for, then think of five jobs to do to raise the money. In your groups, decide who will do which job. Persuade the others to let you do the job(s) you want to do, and persuade them to do the jobs you don't want to do. You don't have much time at the moment, so you'd like to do just one job. Use the Interaction language to help you.

- You like organising social events.
- You are good at writing songs and playing the guitar.
- You've seen a video that Student C made and it was terrible.
- Student A would be good at writing blogs.

Interaction 8 page 70

d Look at the information and act out the conversations with your partner. Use the Interaction language to help you.

Conversation 1: You are shopping with Student A and you have found something (you decide what it is) that you have been looking for, for a long time. It's a lot more expensive than you had hoped, but ask Student A to lend you some money to buy it.

Conversation 2: You don't have any extra money this week, and you think what Student A wants to buy is a rip-off. In fact, you've just seen something (you decide what it is) that you've wanted for a long time and it has a 25% discount! You really, really want it but you are a bit short of money, so ask Student A to lend you some until next week when you'll pay him/her back.

Interaction 9 page 80

d Look at the information and act out the conversations with your partner. Use the Interaction language to help you.

Conversation 1: You're staying in tonight to watch a horror film with a friend. Your younger brother/sister wants to go out but your parents have asked him/her to babysit for your baby brother. Even though you're at home, you don't want to babysit. Your brother/sister wants to negotiate with you. Remember, you could ask him/her to do some of your jobs around the house in return for helping with the babysitting! Both of you have to take turns to walk the dog and take the rubbish out every day.

Conversation 2: Your mum/dad has asked you to clean the kitchen. You've arranged to go to the cinema with a friend and have to leave in half an hour. Your brother/sister is at home and isn't going out. Negotiate with him/her to clean the kitchen so you can go out. Remember, you could offer to do some of his/her other jobs around the house in return for helping you. At home you both have to take turns to do the washing and cook dinner twice a week.

Interaction 11 page 98

d Look at the information and act out the interviews with your partner. Use the Interaction language to help you.

Interview 1: Student A is going to interview you for a part-time job in a sports shop. You're not a big sports fan but you saw the job advertised in a newspaper and you have got an interview. You want to buy a motorbike so you need to earn some money! Try your best to get the job. Use the Interaction language to help you.

Interview 2: Now you are going to interview Student A for a part-time job in a fast-food restaurant. You are the manager and are looking for part-time workers. The pay and the conditions are terrible so most workers don't stay for very long. Use the Interaction language to help you.

Interaction 12 page 106

d Look at the information and act out the conversations with your partner. Use the Interaction language to help you.

Conversation 1: You have been learning English at an English school in London for one month. Introduce yourself to Student A and answer his/her questions about:

- things to do at the weekend
- where to buy good food
- places to go out in the evening
- anything else

Keep the conversation going for as long as possible!

Conversation 2: You have just started English classes at an English school in New York. Introduce yourself to Student A and find out information about:

- things to do in the evenings
- where you can buy clothes and shoes
- places to do sport
- anything else

Keep the conversation going for as long as possible!

Interaction: Student C; Units 7 and 10

Interaction 6 page 52

d With Student A and Student B, you are going to plan a fund-raising campaign. First decide what or who you would like to raise money for, then think of five jobs to do to raise the money. In your groups, decide who will do which job. Persuade the others to let you do the job(s) you want to do, and persuade them to do the jobs you don't want to do. You don't have much time at the moment, so you'd like to do just one job. Use the Interaction language to help you.

- You are very sporty.
- You like making videos.
- Student A isn't very good at drawing.
- Persuade Student B to organise a disco or another event.

Interaction 7 page 62

d Compare the two pictures with your partner. Find at least four differences and two similarities between them. Use the Interaction language to help you.

Interaction 10 page 88

d You are going to give a presentation together about an advert on TV that you both like. Plan the talk together using the ideas in the box. Use signalling words and the Interaction language to help you.

the music the photography the actors
the message the connection with the product
or the company why you like the advert

e Work with another pair. Give your talk and listen to theirs. Do they use the Interaction language correctly? Is the talk clear?

Grammar reference

1 Simple and continuous tense review

Present simple	Present continuous
Jane usually **sits** at the back of the bus. He **doesn't work** on Sundays. **Do** you often **go** to the cinema?	Jane **is sitting** in the garden at the moment. He **isn't working** today. Hi, Rosa. Where **are** you **going**?
Past simple	**Past continuous**
We **walked** into the room and **sat** down. He **didn't work** hard enough last term. **Did** you **go** to the gym yesterday?	At 1:00 yesterday we **were sitting** in the café. I couldn't call you because my phone **wasn't working**. I saw you in Park Street. **Were** you **going** to the gym?

- We use the present simple for permanent situations and regular or repeated actions in the present. We also use it to describe events in a book or film.
- We use the present continuous for actions that are in progress now. We also use it for future arrangements.
- We use the past simple for completed actions in the past. It is often used with past time expressions (*last month*, *two weeks ago*, etc.).
- We use the past continuous for actions that were in progress over a period of time in the past. It often describes what was happening at a certain time.
- We can use the past simple and past continuous together. The past continuous action is longer and started earlier. It was already in progress when the past simple action happened.
  *They **were having** dinner when I **arrived**.* *He **got** the injury while he **was playing** football.*
- We don't normally use the continuous form for these verbs:
  like love hate prefer want need know believe understand agree belong own mean

★ For more notes on future arrangements, see page 133.

★ For a list of irregular verbs, see page 143.

2 Perfect tense review

Present perfect simple	Present perfect continuous
I'**ve stayed** in this hotel before. They **haven't won** any matches yet. **Has** she **finished** her homework?	I'**ve been staying** here since last Friday. They **haven't been playing** well lately. **Has** she **been doing** her homework every day?

- The present perfect tenses always make a connection between the past and the present.
- We use the present perfect simple to talk about actions at some time in the past up to now.
  *Jill **has rung** me three times today.* (= from the start of the day up to now)
  ***Have** you ever **been** to Brazil?* (= at any time in your life up to now?)
- We use the present perfect simple for past actions that directly affect the present. They are often recent actions.
  *Someone **has stolen** my wallet!* (It isn't here now!) ***Has** he **arrived** yet?* (Is he here now?)
- We use the present perfect simple with *for* and *since* for actions that started in the past and are still happening now.
  *I'**ve known** Ali for five years.* (I still know him now.) *We'**ve been** here since 10:30.* (We're still here now.)
- We use the present perfect continuous for actions that have been in progress over a period of time up to now. The action may have finished recently or it may still be happening now.
  *Eva **has been talking** on the phone for over an hour.* *How long **have** you **been waiting** here?*

★ For irregular past participles, see page 143.

3 Perfect tense review

Past perfect simple	Past perfect continuous
The match **had started** when we got there. I knew she **hadn't heard** what I'd said. He got home at 1:00 a.m. Where **had** he **been**?	They'**d (had) been playing** for ten minutes. She **hadn't been listening**. What **had** he **been doing**?

- The past perfect simple is used when we are already talking about a time in the past. We use it to describe a completed action that happened before that time.
  *By the time she got to the cinema, the film **had** already **begun**.*
  *We were amazed by Steve's voice. We **hadn't heard** him sing before.*

★ For irregular past participles, see page 143.

- The form *had* + past participle is the same for all subjects.
- We use the past perfect continuous for an action that was in progress over a period of time before a later event happened. We are showing that the earlier action continued for some time.
  *I wasn't surprised when he lost his job. I**'d been expecting** it for a long time.*
  *Ella left Berlin last year. She**'d been living** there since 2008.*
  *He **hadn't been driving** for long when he got his driving licence.*
  *A: Tom and Anna broke up two weeks ago. B: How long **had** they **been going** out together?*
- The form *had* + *been* + past participle is the same for all subjects.

4 *used to, be used to* and *get used to*

used to + infinitive

*My sister **used to love** the Jonas Brothers when she was younger.*
*I **didn't use to watch** documentaries, but I find them interesting now.*
*What **did** people **use to wear** in the 1950s?*

> ✱ Don't confuse *used to* + infinitive with the verb *use*.
> *I **used to have** a slower computer.*
> *I **used** my computer to design this poster.*

- We use *used to / didn't use to* + infinitive for actions that happened normally or frequently in the past, but don't happen now.
- The form is the same for all subjects.

be used to and *get used to*

*Polar bears **are used to** a cold climate.*
*He hadn't travelled outside the UK before, so he **wasn't used to** driv**ing** on the right.*
*The noise might annoy you at first, but you'll soon **get used to** it.*
*The conditions in the factory were terrible. I couldn't **get used to** work**ing** there.*

- We use *be/get used to* to talk about someone's familiarity with a situation that seemed strange earlier.
- *Be used to something* means 'to <u>be</u> familiar and comfortable with something'.
- *Get used to something* means 'to <u>become</u> familiar and comfortable with something'. It is often used with *can* or *could*.
- *Be used to* and *get used to* are followed by a noun/pronoun or by the *-ing* form of a verb.

5 *will, going to* and present continuous

- We use *will* + infinitive to make predictions about the future. The verbs *think*, *suppose*, *believe*, *hope*, *expect* and adverbs like *maybe*, *perhaps*, *probably* are often used with *will* predictions.
  *I think you**'ll enjoy** this film.* *It probably **won't rain** on Saturday.* *Where **will** we **be** in ten years' time?*
- We also use *will* for decisions made at the time of speaking. The decision may be an offer or a promise.
  *I **won't go** out now. It's too cold outside.* *Let's meet at the café. **I'll buy** you a coffee.*
- We use *going to* + infinitive for future plans and intentions.
  *Eva **is going to buy** a car.* *I**'m going to work** harder next term.* *What **are** you **going to wear** tomorrow?*
- We also use *going to* for predictions based on present evidence. It seems as though the future outcome has been decided already.
  *The temperature is rising. It**'s going to be** hot tomorrow.*
  *It's already five to eight. We **aren't going to get** there on time.*

> ✱ *Will* and *going to* predictions are similar and often both forms are correct.

- We use the present continuous to talk about future arrangements, often for the near future.
  *I**'m meeting** Marta at 6:30.* *The trains **aren't running** tomorrow.* *What time **is** the race **starting**?*
- Arrangements with the present continuous are often similar to plans with *going to* and both forms may be correct. However, for an intention with no definite arrangement, we can't use the present continuous.
  *I**'m meeting** / **going to meet** her at 6:30.* *I**'m going to work** harder.* (**not** ~~*I'm working*~~)

6 Future continuous

- We use the future continuous for actions that will be in progress at a time in the future.
  *At 8:00 the ferry **will be crossing** the English Channel.* *This time tomorrow I**'ll be doing** my Science exam.*
  *What **will** you **be doing** at midnight on New Year's Eve?*
- We also use the future continuous for things that we expect to happen or intend to do. Used like this, it has almost the same meaning as the present continuous for arrangements or *going to* for intentions.

*My friends **will be arriving** soon.*	(= *My friends **are arriving** soon.*)
*I **won't be staying** up late tonight.*	(= *I**'m not going to stay** up late tonight.*)
*What time **will** you **be leaving**?*	(= *What time **are** you **going to leave**?*)

7 Future perfect and future perfect continuous

Future perfect simple	Future perfect continuous
He's leaving Paris on Sunday. He **will have spent** three days there.	He **will have been staying** there for three days.
At the end of May I still won't have my licence. I **won't have had** my driving test by then.	I **won't have been driving** for long enough.

- The future perfect tenses describe a future action in relation to a later time in the future.
- We use the future perfect simple to show that an action will be completed before a later time in the future.
  *In a couple of minutes' time we **will have downloaded** all the tracks on this album.*
  ***Will** she **have completed** her work by tomorrow?*
- We use the future perfect continuous to show that an action will be in progress up to a later time in the future. Often the action will still be happening at that later time.
  *At the end of November, they **will have been living** here for eight years.*

8 Infinitive and *-ing* review

Verb + verb

- With verbs for likes/dislikes, a following verb is usually in the *-ing* form.
  *Do you **like sailing**? She **hates being** late. I **enjoyed talking** to him.*
- Other verbs followed by verb + *-ing* include:
  admit avoid deny imagine keep miss practise recommend suggest
  *Why do you **keep arguing** with me? I **practise diving** at the pool.*
- Some verbs are followed by *to* + infinitive. Examples include:
  agree arrange choose decide expect forget hope learn
  need offer plan prepare pretend promise seem want
  *We **arranged to meet** at 3:30. I've **decided not to go** out tonight.*
- The verbs *start*, *prefer* and *continue* can be followed by either form.
  *He's **started writing / to write** his essay.*
  *The band **continued playing / to play** until midnight.*

★ It is possible to use *like*, *love* and *hate* with *to* + infinitive.
*He **likes to get** up early.*
*I **love to hear** people laugh.*
Would like/love/hate is always used with *to* + infinitive.
***I'd like to go** swimming tomorrow.*

★ Verbs can also be followed by *to* + infinitive when the meaning is 'in order to do something'.
*We ran **to catch** the bus.*
*She's working **to earn** money.*

Preposition + verb

- With prepositions, a following verb is always in the *-ing* form.
  *Liam is good **at painting**. I'm not very keen **on listening** to jazz. Have you ever thought **of doing** karate?*

be + adjective + verb

- After the verb *be*, some adjectives can be followed by *to* + infinitive. Examples include:
  amazed dangerous determined difficult easy hard lucky (im)possible ready safe surprised
  *She was **surprised to see** us. Are you nearly **ready to leave**? It isn't **difficult to use** a webcam.*

remember, *stop* and *try* with *-ing* and the infinitive

- The verbs *remember*, *stop* and *try* can be followed by either form, but the meaning changes.

*I **remember locking** the door.*	(= I locked the door earlier and I can remember it now.)
*I **remembered to lock** the door.*	(= I remembered that I had to lock the door and then I did it.)
*You should **try playing** chess.*	(= you should try it as an experiment.)
*You should **try to play** chess.*	(= you should make an effort to do it.)
*They **stopped talking** to us.*	(= they no longer talked to us.)
*They **stopped to talk** to us.*	(= they stopped something else in order to talk to us.)

9 *as*, *like* and *such as*

- We use *as* + noun to talk about someone's job or role, or the way something is used.
  *My sister works **as** a journalist. He knows a lot, but he's not very good **as** a teacher.*
  *She is regarded **as** one of our best writers. You can use your phone **as** a camera.*
- We use *as* + a full clause (with a subject and verb) to talk about actions that happen in a similar way. When speaking informally, we may use *like* instead of *as*.
  *I added some garlic, **as** you suggested. We were hanging out at the surf club **like** we usually do on Saturdays.*
- We use *like* + a noun/pronoun or a verb with *-ing* to mean 'similar to'.
  *Lucy looks **like** her mother. I admire people **like** you. Walking in Death Valley was **like** being on the moon.*
- We use *like* or *such as* + noun for giving examples.
  *She enjoys team sports **like / such as** basketball.*
  *They grow vegetables, **like / such as** peas and beans.*

10 Adverbs

- Adverbs are often formed from an adjective with an *-ly* ending.
  *quick > quick**ly***   *safe > safe**ly***   *professional > professional**ly***
  *happ**y** > happi**ly***   *bus**y** > busi**ly***
  *suit**able** > suitab**ly***   *incred**ible** > incredib**ly***
  *bas**ic** > basical**ly***   *automat**ic** > automatical**ly***   (**but** *publ**ic** > public**ly***)

> ✱ However, frequency adverbs usually go before the verb.
> *We **often/usually** have lunch here.*

- Some adverbs are irregular. The adverb form of *good* is *well*. The adverbs *fast*, *early*, *late* and *hard* have the same form as the adjective.
- Adverbs usually describe a verb, but they may also describe an adjective or another adverb.
  *The car was travelling **slowly**.   This is a **deliciously** sweet dessert.   They performed **extremely** well.*
- When the verb has an object, the most common word order is verb + object + adverb.
  *She speaks English **fluently**.   I want to finish my homework **quickly**.*
- The adverbs *absolutely*, *completely*, *totally* and *entirely* usually go before a verb or an adjective.
  *I **totally** agree with you.   They were **absolutely** exhausted.*
- Other emphatic adverbs, e.g. *really*, *extremely*, *incredibly*, usually go before an adjective or adverb.
  *It's going to be **really** cold tomorrow.   She works **incredibly** hard.*
- The following adverbs often go at the beginning of a sentence: *suddenly*, *finally*, *eventually*, *luckily*, *(un)fortunately*, *personally*.
  ***Suddenly** the door opened.   **Personally**, I thought the book was too long.*
- The comparative form is usually *more* + adverb. However, for irregular adverbs, the comparative has the same form as the comparative adjective.
  *Could you speak **more slowly**, please?   He dresses **more fashionably** than his friends.*
  *You need to try **harder**.   Trains go **faster** than buses.   I can swim a lot **better** than I used to.*

11 Making comparisons

- We use a comparative adjective or adverb + *than* to compare things. To show a small difference between them we can add *a bit*, *a little* or *slightly*. To show a large difference we can add *far*, *much*, *a lot* or *a great deal*.
  *Your hair is **a bit longer than** mine.   This printer works **much more reliably than** my old one.*
- We repeat comparatives with *and* to show that a certain quality keeps increasing over time.
  *This film is becoming **stranger and stranger** / **more and more confusing**.*
  *The team played **better and better** / **more and more confidently** as the match went on.*
- We use *the* + comparative … *the* + comparative to show that one situation depends on another.
  ***The faster** you run, **the more quickly** your heart beats.*
  ***The better** the design is, **the more attractive** your website will be.*

  With comparative adjectives, we can sometimes leave out the verb *be*.
  The better the design, the more attractive your website (will be).
- We use *as* + adjective/adverb + *as* to talk about things being alike or equal in some way.
  *Jess is **as tall as** her brother.   The weather isn't **as bad as** it was last week.*
  *I can't sing **as well as** you.   Please come **as quickly as** you can.*

12 Expressing contrast

- We use *although / even though / though* and *in spite of / despite* to make a contrast.
- *Although*, *even though* and *though* are followed by a full clause (with a subject and verb). The words have the same meaning, but we don't normally use *though* at the beginning of a sentence.
  *We're good friends, **although / even though / though** we often disagree.*
  ***Although / Even though** they scored three goals, they didn't win the match.*
- *In spite of* and *despite* are followed by a noun/pronoun or the *-ing* form of a verb.
  *We're good friends, **in spite of / despite** our disagreements.*
  ***In spite of / Despite** scoring three goals, they didn't win the match.*
- If we want to use a full clause after *in spite of / despite*, we add *the fact that*.
  *We're good friends, **in spite of / despite the fact that** we often disagree.*

13 Reflexive pronouns and *each other*

- Reflexive pronouns and *each other* come after a verb. They can be the direct or indirect object of the verb or they can follow a preposition.
- We use a reflexive pronoun when the person/thing we are referring to is also the subject of the verb.

Singular	I > **myself** you > **yourself** he > **himself** she > **herself** it > **itself**
Plural	we > **ourselves** you > **yourselves** they > **themselves**

> ✱ We can also use reflexive pronouns for emphasis.
> *Did you make this cake **yourself**?*

*Angela hurt **herself** when she fell.* *We've bought **ourselves** a new TV.* *He walked home by **himself**.*

- We use *each other* for a mutual action, when each person in a pair or group does something to the other(s). The subject is always plural.
  *We've known **each other** for ages.* *They gave **each other** presents.* *People should be kind to **each other**.*

14 Expressions of purpose, reason and result

Purpose	Reason	Result
for + noun or *-ing* *to / in order to / so as to* + infinitive *so that* + subject + verb	*because* + subject + verb *because of / due to / as a result of* + noun or *-ing*	*so* + subject + verb *therefore* + subject + verb

- We use *for*, *to / in order to / so as to* and *so that* to talk about someone's aim or goal when taking an action. *So that* is often followed by a verb with *can/could* or *will/would*.
  *I went to the shop **for** some bread.* *You can use this application **for** editing your photos.*
  *Dolphins come to the surface **in order to** breathe.* *I locked the cupboard **so as to** keep my things safe.*
  *We went to the cinema early **so that** we could get good seats.*
- We use *because (of)*, *due to* and *as a result of* to talk about what caused an action to happen.
  *We had to drive slowly **because** it was foggy.* *They've closed the airport **because of** the fog.*
  *Delays are expected **due to** an accident on the M1.* *The engine stopped **as a result of** overheating.*
- We use *so* or *therefore* to talk about the result of an action.
  *She's had her hair cut very short, **so** she looks quite different now.*
  *Global temperatures are rising. **Therefore** sea levels will also rise.*

15 Passive review

Present simple passive							
It	**'s (is)**	**made**	of plastic.	It	**isn't**	**made**	of plastic.
They	**'re (are)**	**written**	in English.	They	**aren't**	**written**	in English.
Is	it	**made**	of plastic?	Yes, it **is**.		No, it **isn't**.	
Are	they	**written**	in English?	Yes, they **are**.		No, they **aren't**.	

- In a passive sentence the subject doesn't do the action. It is the 'receiver' of the action, which is done by something/someone else.

Active	Passive
They produce this cheese in France.	*This cheese **is produced** in France.*
Someone stole two paintings last night.	*Two paintings **were stolen** last night.*

- We often use the passive when we don't know who/what does the action, or when it isn't important to identify them. If we want to say who/what does the action, we use *by*.
  *The building was designed **by** Gaudí.* *Damage is often caused **by** storms.*
- We form passives with the verb *be* + past participle.
- Most tenses have a passive form. To make a present simple verb passive, we use the present simple form of *be*; for the past simple passive, we use the past simple form of *be*, and so on.

Past simple:	*When **was** that album **recorded**?*
Present continuous:	*Plans **are being made** for a new concert hall.*
Past continuous:	*We couldn't go along West Street because the road **was being repaired**.*
Present perfect:	*Lots of books **have been written** on this subject.*
Past perfect:	*By Monday morning, all the tickets **had been sold**.*

- We can also use modal verbs + *be* + past participle.
  *My new desk **will be delivered** next week.*
  *More details **can be found** on our website.*
  *Computers **must be switched** off while the plane is landing.*
  *The dish **should be cooked** for about an hour.*

16 *have/get* something done

*My parents are going to **have** the house **painted**.*
*Have you **had** your television **repaired** yet?*
*I want to **get** my hair **dyed** black.*
*They **got** an extra room **built** on their house.*

- We use *have/get* + object + past participle when we arrange for someone else to do a service for us.
- If we want to identify the person doing the service, we use *by*.
  *They had/got their wedding photos taken **by** a professional photographer.*

17 Conditionals

First conditional

***If** I **see** Carla, I**'ll tell** her to call you.*
***If** it **doesn't rain**, we**'ll play** tennis this afternoon.*
*Dave **will come** round later **if** he **has** time.*
*What **will** you **do if** you **can't** get a job?*

- We use the first conditional to talk about possible situations in the future. The action depends on a condition that is possible but not certain.
- Instead of *if* + *not*, we can use *unless*.
- In the result clause, we can use *might* or *may* instead of *will* if we are more uncertain about the result.
  *Dave **might/may** come round later if he has time.*

***If** it **doesn't rain**,* ***Unless** it **rains**,*	*we'll play tennis this afternoon.*

Second conditional

***If** I **won** lots of money, I**'d travel** round the world.*
***If** the air **didn't contain** oxygen, we **wouldn't be** able to survive.*
*More people **would buy** these products **if** they **weren't** so expensive.*
*Where **would** you **live if** you **could** choose any place in the world?*

- We use the second conditional when we are imagining an unreal situation now or in the future. The action depends on a condition that is unlikely or impossible.
- When the verb in the *if* clause is *be*, we sometimes use *I/he/she/it* ***were*** instead of *was*. This is usual when the subject is *I*. With *he/she/it* this form is less commonly used.
  *If I **were** you, I'd see a doctor.* (**not** ~~*was*~~)
  *We'd have lunch in the garden if it **wasn't / weren't** so windy.*
- In the result clause, we can use *might* instead of *would* if we are more uncertain about the result. We can use *could* to mean 'would be able to'.
  *More people **might** buy these products if they weren't so expensive.*
  *If the air didn't contain oxygen, we **couldn't** survive.*

Third conditional

*If Lisa **had needed** help, she **would have called** us.* (But she didn't need help, so she didn't call.)
***If** they **hadn't** invited us, we **wouldn't have come**.* (But they did invite us, so we came.)
*I **wouldn't have failed** the test **if** I**'d studied** for it.* (But I didn't study for it, so I failed.)
*What **would** you **have done if** we **hadn't been** here?*

- We use the third conditional when we are imagining a situation in the past that did not happen in reality. The action depends on a condition that is impossible because the past can't be changed.
- In the result clause, we can use *might have* or *may have* instead of *would have* if we are more uncertain about the result. We can use *could have* to mean 'would have been able to'.
  *If we hadn't played so badly, we **might/may** have won.*
  *If Lisa had needed help, she **could have** called us.*

18 *should, ought to, had better* and *it's time*

- We use *should* or *ought to* + infinitive to give advice or to say what we believe is right or appropriate.
  *You **should try** to finish your essay before you go out.*
  *People **shouldn't care** so much about money.*
  *It's a good film. You **ought to go** and see it.*
  *We **ought to be** able to trust our politicians.*
- The usual negative form is *shouldn't*. *Ought not to* is also correct, but it isn't commonly used.
- We use *had better* + infinitive to give advice, often as a warning. We mean that if the action isn't taken, a negative result is likely to follow.
  *It's getting late. I**'d better go** now.*
  *You**'d better get** up at 6:30 if you want to catch the early train.*
  *We**'d better not leave** our bags here. They might get stolen.*
- The negative form is *had better not*.
- We use *It's time* + past simple when we want to criticise someone's present behaviour.
  ***It's time** she **cleaned** up her room. It looks awful!*
  ***It's time** he **learned** how to cook.*
- There is no negative form for this structure.
  ***It's time** you **stopped** wasting money.* (**not** ~~*It isn't time you wasted*~~ or ~~*It's time you didn't waste*~~)

19 Expressing wishes and regrets

wish and *if only*

- We use *wish* and *if only* when we want something to be true, even though it is unlikely or impossible. *If only* is similar to *I wish*, but stronger.
- We use *wish / if only* + past simple when we want a present situation to be different but can't change it.
  *I wish we **lived** in New York.* (But the reality is that we don't live there.)
  *If only the tickets **didn't cost** so much!* (But they do cost a lot.)
- We use *wish / if only* + *would* + infinitive when we would like something/someone else to take action now or in the future. We have no power to make this happen.
  *If only Leo **would change** his mind!* (It's possible but unlikely that he will do this.)
  *I wish my sisters **wouldn't argue** all the time.* (They could stop doing this, but they probably won't.)
- We use *wish / if only* + past perfect to express regret about an action or situation in the past.
  *I wish I**'d brought** a jumper with me.* (But I didn't bring one and the past can't be changed.)
  *If only it **hadn't been** so cold!* (But it was cold.)

should have

- We use *should have* + past participle to express regret or to criticise someone's behaviour in the past.
  *There aren't any seats left. We **should have got** here earlier.*
  *I didn't know about Renata's illness. You **should have told** me.*
  *Sorry – I **shouldn't have said** that. It was a stupid thing to say.*
  *She **shouldn't have embarrassed** Ben in front of his friends.*

20 Participle clauses

- Present participles are the *-ing* form of the verb.
- Past participles usually have the same form as the past simple.
- Perfect participles are formed by *having* + past participle.

* For irregular past participles, see page 143.

Connecting two actions

- A clause starting with a present participle often describes something happening at the same time as the main action or just before it.
  ***Walking to school**, we often see Kate on her way to work.*
  *He came inside, **carrying the baby in his arms**.*
  ***Grabbing my bag**, I ran out into the street.*
- We can also use a present participle with some conjunctions (e.g. *while*, *before*, *after*) and prepositions (e.g. *by*, *without*, *instead of*).
  ***While driving back from London**, she ran out of petrol.*
  ***After working hard all week**, we were glad to relax at the weekend.*
  *They searched for an hour **without finding anything**.*

> * We can also start a clause with a past participle. Here the meaning is passive.
> ***Served with cream**, this cake makes a delicious dessert.*
> ***Written in 1998**, the novel was an instant best-seller.*

- A clause starting with a perfect participle describes something happening before the main action.
  ***Having spent all her money**, Jane couldn't afford to eat out.*
  ***Having crossed the bridge**, you should take the first street on the right.*
  *He's watching television now, **having finished his homework**.*
- In this type of sentence the participle clause and the main clause must have the same subject.
  ***Looking** at Sofia, ~~she was~~ upset.*
  ***Looking** at Sofia, **I could see** she was upset.*
  ***Having seen** the film before, ~~it wasn't~~ so exciting this time.*
  ***Having seen** the film before, **we didn't find** it so exciting this time.*

Acting as a relative clause

- A clause with a present or past participle can also be used instead of a relative clause to give information about a noun.
- The present participle is active and is used for continuous actions.
  *Can you hear that bird **singing outside**?* (= which is singing)
  *I noticed two men **coming out of the building**.* (= who were coming)
  *The girl **talking to David** is my cousin Sara.* (= who is talking)
- The past participle is passive.
  *Tickets **bought online** cost €45.* (= which are bought)
  *Our next-door neighbour is a man **called Mr Johnson**.* (= who is called)
  *The Eiffel Tower, **built in 1889**, is a symbol of France.* (= which was built)

* For relative clauses, see page 140.

21 Modals of deduction and possibility review

Not sure					
I He We	**might** **may** **could**	**be** in the team. **arrive** soon. **have seen** this film.	I He We	**might not** **may not**	**be** in the team. **arrive** soon. **have seen** this film.
Sure					
She You They	**must**	**be** Spanish. **arrive** soon. **have seen** this film.	She You They	**can't** **couldn't**	**be** Spanish. **have seen** this film.

- We use modal verbs + infinitive to talk about possibilities in the present or future.
- We use *might*, *may* or *could* when we think something is possibly true, but we aren't sure. For the negative we use *might not* or *may not* (but not *could not*).
  A: Who's that girl? B: I don't know. She ***might/may/could be*** *Matthew's sister.*
  I'll try to see you before you leave, but I ***might/may not get*** *there in time.* (**not** ~~could not get~~)
- We use *must* when we feel sure that something is true. We use *can't* or *couldn't*, usually followed by the verb *be*, when we feel sure that something is not true.
  They left the gym half an hour ago, so they ***must get*** *home soon.*
  He ***can't/couldn't be*** *in Madrid. He told me he was going to Switzerland.* (**not** ~~He mustn't be~~)
- We use the same modal verbs + *have* + past participle to talk about possibilities in the past.
  I'm a bit worried – I ***might have forgotten*** *to lock the back door before I left.*
  It's probably too early to ring Simon. He ***may not have woken*** *up yet.*
  Clare was sitting right in front of us. You ***must have seen*** *her!*
  I'm sure their story was true. They ***can't/couldn't have made*** *it up.*

22 Question tag review

Positive statement	Question tag	Negative statement	Question tag
I'**m** in the team,	**aren't** I?	I'**m not** a great singer,	**am** I?
He **was** surprised,	**wasn't** he?	She **wasn't** unhappy,	**was** she?
You'**re** working,	**aren't** you?	You **aren't** listening,	**are** you?
She'**s** gone home,	**hasn't** she?	He **hasn't** left,	**has** he?
It'**ll** be fun,	**won't** it?	It **won't** rain,	**will** it?
They **can** fly,	**can't** they?	They **can't** see us,	**can** they?
I **should** leave,	**shouldn't** I?	I **shouldn't** be here,	**should** I?
She wears glasses,	**doesn't** she?	He **doesn't** drive,	**does** he?
You went out,	**didn't** you?	You **didn't** see me,	**did** you?

- We add a question tag to a statement to check information or to invite agreement.
- If the main verb is positive, the question tag is negative. If it is negative, the question tag is positive.
- When the main verb is *be*, we repeat the verb *be* in the question tag.
- For other verb forms, we repeat the auxiliary or modal in the question tag. For a present or past simple positive verb, where there is no auxiliary or modal, we use *don't/doesn't* or *didn't*.
- We can add a question tag to an imperative to make a request. We use *will*, *would* or *can* + *you*.
  Put *this bowl on the table,* ***will you?*** *Take out the rubbish,* ***would you?*** *Give me a hand,* ***can you?***

23 Reported speech review

Direct speech	Reported speech	
'I **want** to have an ice cream.' 'The TV **isn't working**.' 'My results **have improved**.' 'Someone **stole** my wallet.' 'The exhibition **will** be interesting.' 'I **can't** remember my password.'	Tom said (that) Tom told me (that)	he **wanted** to have an ice cream. the TV **wasn't working**. his results **had improved**. someone had **stolen** his wallet. the exhibition **would** be interesting. he **couldn't** remember his password.
'When **are** they **arriving**?' 'Who **did** you **speak** to?' '**Are** you **learning** English?' '**Has** Alice **called**?'	Julia asked (me)	when they **were arriving**. who I **had spoken** to. **if/whether** I **was learning** English. **if/whether** Alice **had called**.
'**Stop** complaining!' '**Don't take** photos in the gallery.'	He told me	**to stop** complaining. **not to take** photos in the gallery.

- When we report a statement or a question, we usually change the tense. The verb usually moves 'one step back' into the past: present > past, past > past perfect, *will* > *would*, *can* > *could*.
- However, when reporting something that remains true, we don't need to change the tense.
  'I like living in Prague.' *She said she* ***likes/liked*** *living in Prague.*
  'Toledo is a city in Spain.' *He told me Toledo* ***is/was*** *a city in Spain.*
  'Napoleon died in 1821.' *She said that Napoleon* ***died/had died*** *in 1821.*
- When we report a question, we change the word order to the form of a statement. For an information question, we repeat the question word. For a *yes/no* question, we use *if* or *whether*.
- For a command, the reporting verb is usually *tell*. The form is *tell* someone (*not*) *to* + infinitive.
- Pronouns and possessive adjectives may need to change in reported speech.
  *'**I** rang **you** on **your** mobile.'* *Annie told me **she** had rung **me** on **my** mobile.*

24 Reporting verbs

- Most reporting verbs are followed by *that* + a full clause in reported speech.
  He mentioned / explained / complained / announced / reported / replied ***that*** *the concert had been delayed.*
- The verbs *admit*, *deny*, *recommend* and *suggest* can also be followed by a verb with *-ing*.
  She admitted / denied ***taking / that she had taken*** *the money.*
  They recommended / suggested ***trying / that we try*** *their new product.*
- The verbs *agree*, *offer*, *promise* and *refuse* are followed by *to* + infinitive.
  I agreed / offered / promised / refused ***to lend*** *him the money.*

★ For other verbs followed by *-ing* or the infinitive, see page 134.

- These verbs are followed by *to* + object (person) + infinitive: *advise*, *ask*, *convince*, *encourage*, *invite*, *order*, *persuade*, *tell*, *warn*. Some of these can also be followed by object + *that* clause.
  She advised / asked / encouraged / invited / ordered ***us to tell*** *the truth.*
  He convinced / persuaded / told / warned ***them to stop / them that they should stop*** *smoking.*
- For verbs with the infinitive, notice the difference between these negative forms.
  I didn't promise to come. (= I didn't make this promise.) *I promised not to come.* (= I said, 'I won't come.')
  She won't persuade him to buy it. (= She won't manage to persuade him.)
  She'll persuade him not to buy it. (= He won't buy it because of her persuasion.)

25 Relative clause review

Defining relative clauses

I know lots of people ***who/that come from Scotland****.*
Jack is someone ***whose jokes always make me laugh****.*
The bus ***that/which goes along King Street*** *will take you to the station.*
The shop ***where Lara works*** *isn't open on Sundays.*

- A relative clause refers to someone or something earlier in the sentence.
- A defining relative clause gives essential information – we need it to identify the person/thing we are talking about.
- We normally use *who* for people, but we can also use *that*.
  It was Tony ***who/that*** *persuaded me to enter the competition.*
- We use *whose* for people when we want to talk about something that belongs to them. *Whose* is a possessive form which we use instead of *his*, *her* or *their*. It is always followed by a noun.
  We've never met the woman ***whose*** *flat is above ours.*
- We use *that* or *which* for things.
  These are the gloves ***that/which*** *I bought for Mum's birthday.*
- We use *where* for places. It means 'in which', 'at which' or 'to which' and it is followed by a noun or pronoun.
  Málaga is the city ***where*** *Picasso was born.* (*where* = in which)
  Did they like the hotel ***where*** *they were staying?* (*where* = at which)
  The café ***where*** *we used to go has been sold.* (*where* = to which)
- In a defining relative clause, we can often leave out *who*, *which* or *that* when it is the object of the verb.
  She's someone we met at Sam's party. (= who/that we met)
  Did you get the postcard I sent you? (= that/which I sent you)

Non-defining relative clauses

At the market I bumped into Paula, ***who was on her way to the gym****.*
The woman at the bank, ***whose name I've forgotten now****, was very helpful.*
They're building a new theatre, ***which should be finished by the end of the year****.*
Bari, ***where Stefano grew up****, is in the south of Italy.*

- A non-defining relative clause is not essential but adds extra information. It is separated from the rest of the sentence by commas.
- The pronouns are mostly the same as in defining relative clauses. However, in non-defining clauses we don't use the pronoun *that*.
  I was staying with my aunt, ***who*** *lives in a village near Bristol.* (**not** *my aunt, ~~that~~ …*)
  The film, ***which*** *was directed by Tom Hooper, was released in 2011.* (**not** *The film, ~~that~~ …*)

Wordlist

(adj) = adjective (adv) = adverb (adv ph) = adverbial phrase
(n) = noun (npl) = plural noun (prep) = preposition
(pp) = past participle (v) = verb

Unit 1

Online communication

digital footprint (n) /ˌdɪdʒɪtəl ˈfʊtprɪnt/
defriend (v) /dɪˈfrend/
friend (v) /frend/
friend request (n) /ˈfrend rɪˌkwest/
go viral (v) /ˌɡəʊ ˈvaɪrəl/
link (n) /lɪŋk/
privacy settings (npl) /ˈprɪvəsi ˌsetɪŋz/
spam (n) /spæm/
tag a (photo) (v) /tæg ə/

Phrasal verbs with *up*

build up (v) /ˌbɪld ˈʌp/
charge up (v) /ˌtʃɑːdʒ ˈʌp/
come up (v) /ˌkʌm ˈʌp/
give up (v) /ˌɡɪv ˈʌp/
look something up (v) /ˌlʊk sʌmθɪŋ ˈʌp/
make something up (v) /ˌmeɪk sʌmθɪŋ ˈʌp/
set up (v) /ˌset ˈʌp/
turn something up (v) /ˌtɜːn sʌmθɪŋ ˈʌp/

Unit 2

Sports equipment

board (n) /bɔːd/
cricket bat (n) /ˈkrɪkɪt bæt/
goggles (npl) /ˈɡɒɡəlz/
golf club (n) /ˈɡɒlf klʌb/
helmet (n) /ˈhelmət/
hockey stick (n) /ˈhɒki stɪk/
net (n) /net/
oar (n) /ɔː/
pads (npl) /pædz/
racket (n) /ˈrækɪt/
skates (npl) /skeɪts/
stick (n) /stɪk/

Sports collocations

beat a team (v) /ˈbiːt ə ˌtiːm/
beat a time (v) /ˈbiːt ə ˌtaɪm/
break a record (v) /ˌbreɪk ə ˈrekɔːd/
break a rule (v) /ˌbreɪk ə ˈruːl/
competitive sports (npl) /kəmˈpetɪtɪv spɔːts/
contact sports (npl) /ˈkɒntækt spɔːts/
extreme sports (npl) /ɪkˈstriːm spɔːts/
hold a record (v) /ˌhəʊld ə ˈrekɔːd/
hold a sports event (v) /həʊld ə ˈspɔːts ɪˌvent/
individual sports (npl) /ˌɪndɪˈvɪdʒuəl spɔːts/
play at home (v) /ˌpleɪ ət ˈhəʊm/
play a game (v) /ˌpleɪ ə ˈɡeɪm/
score a goal (v) /ˌskɔːr ə ˈɡəʊl/
score a point (v) /ˌskɔːr ə ˈpɔɪnt/
sports centre (n) /ˈspɔːts ˌsentə/
sports event (n) /ˈspɔːts ɪˌvent/
sports fan (n) /ˈspɔːts ˌfæn/
sports kit (n) /ˈspɔːts ˌkɪt/
sports star (n) /ˈspɔːts ˌstɑː/
sports team (n) /ˈspɔːts ˌtiːm/
team sports (npl) /ˈtiːm ˌspɔːts/
win a match (v) /ˈwɪn ə ˌmætʃ/
win a game (v) /ˈwɪn ə ˌɡeɪm/
winter sports (npl) /ˌwɪntə ˈspɔːts/

Unit 3

Extended family

aunt (n) /ɑːnt/
cousin (n) /ˈkʌzən/
ex-husband (n) /ˌeksˈhʌzbənd/
ex-wife (n) /ˌeksˈwaɪf/
grandmother (n) /ˈɡrænˌmʌðə/
great-grandfather (n) /ˌɡreɪtˈɡrænˌfɑːðə/
great-grandmother (n) /ˌɡreɪtˈɡrænˌmʌðə/
half-sister (n) /ˈhɑːfˌsɪstə/
mother-in-law (n) /ˈmʌðərɪnˌlɔː/
second cousin (n) /ˌsekənd ˈkʌzən/
second wife (n) /ˌsekənd ˈwaɪf/
sister-in-law (n) /ˈsɪstərɪnˌlɔː/
son-in-law (n) /ˈsʌnɪnˌlɔː/
stepbrother (n) /ˈstepˌbrʌðə/
stepmother (n) /ˈstepˌmʌðə/
stepsister (n) /ˈstepˌsɪstə/
stepson (n) /ˈstepˌsʌn/

British/American vocabulary

autumn (B.) (n) /ˈɔːtəm/
biscuit (B.) (n) /ˈbɪskɪt/
candy (Am.) (n) /ˈkændi/
chips (B.) (n) /tʃɪps/
cookie (Am.) (n) /ˈkʊki/
fall (Am.) (n) /fɔːl/
French fries (Am.) (n) /ˌfrenʃ ˈfraɪz/
garbage (Am.) (n) /ˈɡɑːbɪdʒ/
garden (B.) (n) /ˈɡɑːdən/
gas (Am.) (n) /ɡæs/
holiday (B.) (n) /ˈhɒlədeɪ/
lorry (B.) (n) /ˈlɒri/
pants (Am.) (n) /pænts/
petrol (B.) (n) /ˈpetrəl/
rubbish (B.) (n) /ˈrʌbɪʃ/
sweets (B.) (n) /swiːts/
trousers (B.) (n) /ˈtraʊzəz/
truck (Am.) (n) /trʌk/
vacation (Am.) (n) /vəˈkeɪʃən/
yard (Am.) (n) /jɑːd/

Unit 4

Verbs of fear

beat fast (v) /ˌbiːt ˈfɑːst/
breathe quickly (v) /ˌbriːð ˈkwɪkli/
gasp (v) /ɡɑːsp/
giggle (v) /ˈɡɪɡəl/
scream (v) /skriːm/
shake (v) /ʃeɪk/
shiver (v) /ˈʃɪvə/
shout (v) /ʃaʊt/
stutter (v) /ˈstʌtə/
sweat (v) /swet/
whisper (v) /ˈwɪspə/

Expressions of fear

be on the edge of your seat /biː ɒn ðə ˌedʒ əv jɔː ˈsiːt/
frighten the life out of someone /ˌfraɪtən ðə ˈlaɪf aʊt əv sʌmwʌn/
have butterflies in your stomach /hæv ˈbʌtəflaɪz ɪn jɔː ˌstʌmək/
hold your breath /ˌhəʊld jɔː ˈbreθ/
jump out of your skin /ˌdʒʌmp aʊt əv jɔː ˈskɪn/
make your blood run cold /meɪk jɔː ˌblʌd rʌn ˈkəʊld/
shake like a leaf /ˌʃeɪk laɪk ə ˈliːf/
your heart misses a beat /jɔː hɑːt ˌmɪsɪz ə ˈbiːt/

Unit 5

The animal kingdom

cage (n) /keɪdʒ/
endangered (adj) /ɪnˈdeɪndʒəd/
habitat (n) /ˈhæbɪtæt/
hunt (v) /hʌnt/
rare (adj) /reə/
sanctuary (n) /ˈsæŋktʃʊəri/
species (n) /ˈspiːʃiːz/
survival (n) /səˈvaɪvəl/
tame (v) /teɪm/
wild (adj) /waɪld/

Physical habits

blink (v) /blɪŋk/
burp (v) /bɜːp/
chew (v) /tʃuː/
hiccup (v) /ˈhɪkʌp/
rub (v) /rʌb/
scratch (v) /skrætʃ/
sneeze (v) /sniːz/
yawn (v) /jɔːn/

Unit 6

Campaigning

campaign (n) /kæm'peɪn/
campaigner (n) /kæm'peɪnə/
charity (n) /'tʃærɪti/
flyer (n) /'flaɪə/
make a donation (v) /ˌmeɪk ə də'neɪʃən/
raise awareness (v) /ˌreɪz ə'weənəs/
raise money (v) /ˌreɪz 'mʌni/
support (n) /sə'pɔːt/
voluntary work (n) /'vɒləntri ˌwɜːk/

Phrasal verbs with *take*

take away (v) /ˌteɪk ə'weɪ/
take in (v) /ˌteɪk 'ɪn/
take it out on someone (v) /ˌteɪk ɪt 'aʊt ɒn sʌmwʌn/
take off (v) /ˌteɪk 'ɒf/
take someone up on something (v) /ˌteɪk sʌmwʌn 'ʌp ɒn sʌmθɪŋ/
take something down (v) /ˌteɪk sʌmθɪŋ 'daʊn/
take up (v) /ˌteɪk 'ʌp/

Unit 7

Describing clothes and materials

baggy (adj) /'bægi/
bluey-green (adj) /'bluːiˌgriːn/
checked (adj) /tʃekt/
flowery (adj) /'flaʊəri/
green-ish (adj) /'griːnɪʃ/
greeny-blue (adj) /'griːniˌbluː/
plain (adj) /pleɪn/
scruffy (adj) /'skrʌfi/
short-sleeved (adj) /ʃɔːt'sliːvd/
spotted (adj) /'spɒtɪd/
striped (adj) /straɪpt/
tight (adj) /taɪt/
trendy (adj) /'trendi/

Body idioms

a pain in the neck /ə ˌpeɪn ɪn ðə 'nek/
nosy (adj) /'nəʊzi/
big-headed (adj) /bɪg'hedɪd/
cost an arm and a leg /kɒst ən ˌɑːm ənd ə 'leg/
from head to foot /frɒm 'hed tə ˌfʊt/
put your foot in it /ˌpʊt jɔː 'fʊt ɪn ɪt/
pull someone's leg /ˌpʊl sʌmwʌnz 'leg/
set your heart on something /ˌset jɔː 'hɑːt ɒn sʌmθɪŋ/

Unit 8

Phrasal verbs and expressions with *give*

give away (v) /ˌgɪv ə'weɪ/
give back (v) /ˌgɪv 'bæk/
give in (v) /ˌgɪv 'ɪn/
give something your all (v) /ˌgɪv sʌmθɪŋ jɔːr 'ɔːl/
give something a go (v) /ˌgɪv sʌmθɪŋ ə 'gəʊ/
give someone a hand with something (v) /ˌgɪv sʌmwʌn ə 'hænd wɪð sʌmθɪŋ/
give out something to someone (v) /ˌgɪv 'aʊt sʌmθɪŋ tuː sʌmwʌn/
give your opinion on something (v) /ˌgɪv jɔː ə'pɪnjən ɒn sʌmθɪŋ/

Numbers and symbols

degree (n) /dɪ'griː/
divided by (pp) /dɪ'vaɪdɪd baɪ/
equals (v) /'iːkwəlz/
is (v) /ɪz/
kilogramme (n) /'kɪləgræm/
minus (adv) /'maɪnəs/
multiplied by (pp) /'mʌltɪplaɪd baɪ/
nil (n) /nɪl/
nought (n) /nɔːt/
oh (n) /əʊ/
percent (n) /pə'sent/
plus (adv) /plʌs/
point (n) /pɔɪnt/
times (prep / adv) /taɪmz/
zero (n) /'zɪərəʊ/

Unit 9

Adjectives of character

aggressive (adj) /ə'gresɪv/
cheerful (adj) /'tʃɪəfəl/
disrespectful /ˌdɪsrɪ'spektfəl/
enthusiastic (adj) /ɪnˌθjuːzi'æstɪk/
imaginative (adj) /ɪ'mædʒɪnətɪv/
impolite (adj) /ˌɪmpəl'aɪt/
irresponsible (adj) /ˌɪrɪ'spɒnsəbəl/
jealous (adj) /'dʒeləs/
rebellious (adj) /rɪ'beliəs/
reliable (adj) /rɪ'laɪəbəl/
smart (adj) /smɑːt/
spoilt (adj) /spɔɪlt/
stubborn (adj) /'stʌbən/
unimaginative (adj) /ˌʌnɪ'mædʒɪnətɪv/
unfriendly (adj) /ʌn'frendli/
unreliable (adj) /ˌʌnrɪ'laɪəbəl/

Expressions for arguments

get on your nerves (v) /ˌget ɒn jɔː 'nɜːvz/
keep the peace (v) /ˌkiːp ðə 'piːs/
keep your cool (v) /ˌkiːp jɔː 'kuːl/
lose it (v) /'luːz ɪt/
lose your temper (v) /ˌluːz jɔː 'tempə/
see someone else's point of view (v) /siː sʌmwʌn ˌelsɪz pɔɪnt əv 'vjuː/
storm out (v) /'stɔːm aʊt/
wind someone up (v) /ˌwɪnd sʌmwʌn 'ʌp/

Unit 10

Advertising

advertising agency (n) /'ædvətaɪzɪŋ ˌeɪdʒənsi/
brand (n) /brænd/
launch (v) /lɔːnʃ/
logo (n) /'ləʊgəʊ/
marketing campaign (n) /'mɑːkɪtɪŋ kæmˌpeɪn/
pop-up (n) /'pɒpʌp/
slogan (n) /'sləʊgən/
target customers (npl) /'tɑːgɪt ˌkʌstəməz/

Phrasal verbs with *come*

come about (v) /ˌkʌm ə'baʊt/
come across (v) /ˌkʌm ə'krɒs/
came along (v) /ˌkeɪm ə'lɒŋ/
come back (v) /ˌkʌm 'bæk/
come out (v) /ˌkʌm 'aʊt/
came over (v) /ˌkeɪm 'əʊvə/
come up with (v) /ˌkʌm 'ʌp wɪð/
come up (v) /ˌkʌm 'ʌp/

Unit 11

Compound adjectives

badly-paid (adj) /'bædli ˌpeɪd/
English-speaking (adj) /'ɪŋglɪʃˌspiːkɪŋ/
highly-paid (adj) /'haɪli ˌpeɪd/
last-minute (adj) /ˌlɑːst 'mɪnɪt/
money-saving (adj) /'mʌniˌseɪvɪŋ/
part-time (adj) /ˌpɑːt'taɪm/
privately-owned (adj) /'praɪvətli ˌəʊnd/
short-sighted (adj) /ʃɔːt'saɪtɪd/
six-day (adj) /'sɪksˌdeɪ/
top-quality (adj) /ˌtɒp 'kwɒləti/
well-known (adj) /ˌwel'nəʊn/

Job collocations

apply for a job (v) /ə'plaɪ fər ə ˌdʒɒb/
be promoted (v) /biː prə'məʊtɪd/
be fired (v) /biː 'faɪəd/
go on strike (v) /ˌgəʊ ɒn 'straɪk/
have an interview (v) /ˌhæv ən 'ɪntəvjuː/
members of staff (npl) /'membəz ɒv ˌstɑːf/
work shifts (v) /ˌwɜːk 'ʃɪfts/
write your CV (v) /ˌraɪt jɔː ˌsiː'viː/

Unit 12

Expressions with *time*

all the time (adv ph) /ˌɔːl ðə 'taɪm/
at the same time (adv ph) /æt ðə ˌseɪm 'taɪm/
for a short time (adv ph) /fɔːr ə ʃɔːt 'taɪm/
from time to time (adv ph) /frɒm ˌtaɪm tə 'taɪm/
most of the time (adv ph) /ˌməʊst əv ðə 'taɪm/
of all time (adv ph) /ɒv ˌɔːl 'taɪm/

Loan words in English

ballet (n) /'bæleɪ/
champagne (n) /ʃæm'peɪn/
fiesta (n) /fi'estə/
karaoke (n) /ˌkæri'əʊki/
ketchup (n) /'ketʃʌp/
kiosk (n) /'kiːɒsk/
kung fu (n) /ˌkʊŋ'fuː/
mosquito (n) /mɒs'kiːtəʊ/
piano (n) /pi'ænəʊ/
spaghetti (n) /spə'geti/
sushi (n) /'suːʃi/
yoghurt (n) /'jɒgət/

Irregular verbs

Verb	Past simple	Past participle
be	was/were	been
become	became	become
begin	began	begun
blow	blew	blown
break	broke	broken
bring	brought	brought
build	built	built
burn	burned/burnt	burned/burnt
buy	bought	bought
can	could	been able
catch	caught	caught
choose	chose	chosen
come	came	come
cost	cost	cost
cut	cut	cut
do	did	done
draw	drew	drawn
drink	drank	drunk
drive	drove	driven
eat	ate	eaten
fall	fell	fallen
feel	felt	felt
fight	fought	fought
find	found	found
fly	flew	flown
forget	forgot	forgotten
get	got	got
give	gave	given
go	went	gone/been
grow	grew	grown
have	had	had
hear	heard	heard
hit	hit	hit
hold	held	held
hurt	hurt	hurt
keep	kept	kept
know	knew	known
learn	learned/learnt	learned/learnt
leave	left	left
lend	lent	lent
let	let	let

Verb	Past simple	Past participle
lose	lost	lost
make	made	made
mean	meant	meant
meet	met	met
pay	paid	paid
put	put	put
read	read	read
ride	rode	ridden
ring	rang	rung
run	ran	run
say	said	said
see	saw	seen
sell	sold	sold
send	sent	sent
set	set	set
shake	shook	shaken
shoot	shot	shot
shut	shut	shut
sing	sang	sung
sit	sat	sat
sleep	slept	slept
speak	spoke	spoken
spell	spelled/spelt	spelled/spelt
spend	spent	spent
spin	span/spun	spun
stand	stood	stood
steal	stole	stolen
strike	struck	struck
swim	swam	swum
swing	swung	swung
take	took	taken
teach	taught	taught
tell	told	told
think	thought	thought
throw	threw	thrown
understand	understood	understood
wake	woke	woken
wear	wore	worn
win	won	won
write	wrote	written

Phonemic chart

Consonant sounds

Vowel sounds

Go to the Interactive website for more pronunciation practice!

http://interactive.cambridge.org